GW00995103

FROM HARDY TO FAULKNER

From Hardy to Faulkner

Wessex to Yoknapatawpha

John Rabbetts
Lecturer in English
Exeter College, Exeter

St. Martin's Press   New York

First published in the United States of America in 1989

Printed in Hong Kong

ISBN 0-312-02510-6

Library of Congress Cataloging-in-Publication Data
Rabbetts, John, 1949–
    From Hardy to Faulkner: Wessex to Yoknapatawpha.

    Bibliography: p.
    Includes index.
    1. Hardy, Thomas, 1840–1928—Criticism and interpretation.   2. Faulkner,
William, 1897–1962—Criticism and interpretation.   3. Wessex (England) in
literature.   4. Dorset (England) in literature.   5. Yoknapatawpha County
(Imaginary place)   6. Mississippi in literature.   7. Regionalism in
literature.   8. Setting (Literature).   9. Literature, Comparative—English and
American.   10. Literature, Comparative—American and English.   I. Title.

PR4754.R34   1989   820'.9'32   88–26358
ISBN 0-312-02510-6

To Ivy
and to the memory of Jack (1912–82)

Contents

Contents

Preface

The novels of Thomas Hardy and William Faulkner may not immediately appear to have much in common, other than a formidable accumulation of critical scholarship devoted to their respective achievements. What then is the purpose of this study? Its genesis was, quite simply, an unpremeditated consideration of the reasons why I had long found each writer's fiction so deeply fascinating. Rather unexpectedly, a list of common features began to emerge; and the impulse behind this book was a sudden conviction that the two separate bodies of novels, augmented by short stories, demonstrated an unconscious yet strangely intimate and engrossing relationship with one another, which invited a comparative analysis. The parallel had seldom been drawn before, and never at length.

Two common factors in particular seemed significant. One was the creation of fictional microcosms of remote regions: within these, Hardy and Faulkner could examine dilemmas which were both local and universal. Dorset and Mississippi seem very distinct (though I have argued that in some ways they are not) but the artistic frameworks of Wessex and Yoknapatawpha can be perceived as allied or closely compatible countries. Working as they both did in traditional rural communities exposed to traumatic social change, the two writers seemed to have drawn upon comparable sources of inspiration, adopted analogous fictional strategies, and evolved similar responses to the problems of their protagonists. My second starting-point was the perception of a common attitude of ambivalence, permeating both the form and content of their fiction: an authorial ambivalence towards the rival claims of past and present, tradition and modernity, nature and society, which confront the inhabitants of these regional microcosms. A very modern sense of confusion assails these protagonists, firmly linking the two writers' work, and this study has taken shape from my attempts to identify examples and trace common patterns of this phenomenon. One such moment which seems especially significant to me, and to which I frequently refer throughout the book as a paradigm of Hardy and Faulkner's true common subject, occurs in *Tess of the d'Urbervilles*, when Angel is first attracted to Tess:

> She was expressing in her own native phrases – assisted a little
> by her Sixth Standard training – feelings which might almost
> have been called those of the age – the ache of modernism. The
> perception arrested him less when he reflected that what are
> called advanced ideas are really in great part but the latest
> fashion in definition – a more accurate expression, by words in
> -*logy* and -*ism*, of sensations which men and women have
> vaguely grasped for centuries. (p. 163)

Hardy uses the phrase 'the ache of modernism' to connote a
perception of social and cultural dislocation – a feeling that the
world in which one lives is becoming increasingly unstable and
unknowable, one both universal (as Angel realises) and yet
peculiarly characteristic of traditional agricultural societies, such as
Dorset and Mississippi, as they became increasingly influenced by
modern, urban and commercial pressures. Ambivalent reactions to
this sense of disorientation not only inspire much of Hardy and
Faulkner's subject-matter, but also, crucially, influence the tone
and structure of their narratives, as I attempt to show. This book
was therefore written in the modest hope that the reader who
enjoys Hardy's novels may experience an uncanny shock of
recognition upon encountering Faulkner's work, or vice versa, and
that a comparative interpretation may shed some useful light upon
the nature of this affinity.

   Their fiction is rooted in a precise sense of time and place, even
before the concepts of Wessex and Yoknapatawpha were
formulated. In my endeavour to show how and why their art
seems to correspond, I therefore begin discussion of each man's
work by examining his relationship with his regional environment,
considering particular socio-historical contexts, and the writer's
equivocal attitudes to social change. The emphasis of both men's
interest in the historical process falls upon the prevalence of
tragedy, and my third chapter explores some of their most sombre
works. Possible antidotes to this tendency are discussed in the
fourth chapter, through a consideration of the relationship
between man and nature, and the role of more integrated,
enduring protagonists, who again share some significant characteristics. The final chapter attempts to draw together the strands of
my discourse by focussing upon a common feature stressed

throughout, namely the unity of form and content evinced by each writer's fictional work.

Any discussion of the novels of Hardy and Faulkner must lean heavily upon a wealth of previous literary scholarship. I hope that my obvious indebtedness to numerous critics is sufficiently acknowledged either in the text or the notes, but I should like to pay special tribute here to several books whose influence has been fundamental. Michael Millgate's *The Achievement of William Faulkner* (1966) and *Thomas Hardy: His Career as a Novelist* (1971) have proved an indispensable resource of critical insights; furthermore, both works pointed out the Hardy–Faulkner affinity long before I noticed it. Other invaluable sources include Michael Millgate's *Thomas Hardy: A Biography* (1982), John Bayley's *An Essay on Hardy* (1978), Ian Gregor's *The Great Web: The Form of Hardy's Major Fiction* (1974), Raymond Williams's *The Country and the City* (1973), Merryn Williams's *Thomas Hardy and Rural England* (1972), Douglas Brown's *Thomas Hardy* (1954), Joseph Blotner's *Faulkner: A Biography* (1974), Cleanth Brooks's *William Faulkner: The Yoknapatawpha Country* (1963), Richard Gray's *The Literature of Memory* (1977), Robert Penn Warren's essay on Faulkner in his *Selected Essays* (1985), and David Minter's *William Faulkner: His Life and Work* (1980). Other stimulating material was discovered in volumes of social and regional history; I can only hope that the literary relevance of my forays in this direction has been justified, and that in my efforts to synthesise ideas I have not prevented some original insights from emerging, nor obscured the clarity of previous scholars' researches, resulting as they have here in an unavoidably rich diet of quotations, notes and bibliography. I must also beg the reader's indulgence for making lavish quotations from the primary sources.

I am grateful to the Macmillan Press Ltd, for permission to quote extracts from Florence Emily Hardy's *The Life of Thomas Hardy, 1840–1928*, and to Random House Inc., New York, and Curtis Brown Ltd, London, on behalf of Random House Inc., for permission to quote extracts from *Absalom, Absalom!* and *Light in August* by William Faulkner.

Finally, I am conscious of a deep personal debt to the many friends and colleagues who have helped me during this book's

lengthy gestation. I should particularly like to thank Martin
Boston, Joanna Burt, Caroline Butler, Herbie Butterfield, Bob
Casanta, Ted and Maggie Hopkin, Alan McLean, Keith Neville,
Mary and Eddie Neville, David and Carol Piper, and Christina
Wahle, for their generous encouragement at different times over a
long period. I owe especial gratitude to Margaret Harris and Anne
Constable, who produced the typescripts cheerfully and efficiently
from labyrinthine manuscripts; to Richard Gray, a friend and
teacher whose advice has always been unfailingly valuable; to my
parents, for their support over many years; and to my colleagues
and students at Exeter College.

J. R.

List of Abbreviations and Editions Cited

The following abbreviations are used in the text and notes. The publication details in parentheses refer to the actual editions cited.

WORKS BY HARDY

ACM   *'A Changed Man', 'The Waiting Supper', and Other Tales* (London: Macmillan, 1927)

CL   *The Collected Letters of Thomas Hardy*, ed. R. L. Purdy and M. Millgate (Oxford: Clarendon Press, 1978–)

CP   *The Collected Poems of Thomas Hardy*, ed. James Gibson (London: Macmillan, 1976)

TDL   *The Dorsetshire Labourer*, in *Longman's Magazine*, vol. 2 (July 1883), in *Thomas Hardy: Stories and Poems*, ed. D. J. Morrison (London: Dent, 1970)

    The Dynasts (London: Macmillan, 1921)

DR   *Desperate Remedies* (London: Macmillan, New Wessex Edition, 1975)

FFTMC   *Far from the Madding Crowd* (London: Macmillan, New Wessex Edition, 1974)

AGOND   *A Group of Noble Dames* (London: Heron Books, 1970)

THOE   *The Hand of Ethelberta* (London: Macmillan, New Wessex Edition, 1975)

    An Indiscretion in the Life of an Heiress (London: Macmillan, 1976)

Jude   *Jude the Obscure* (London: Macmillan, New Wessex Edition, 1974)

AL   *A Laodicean* (London: Macmillan, New Wessex Edition, 1975)

LLI   *Life's Little Ironies* (London: Macmillan, 1937)

Life   *The Life of Thomas Hardy, 1840–1928*, ed. Florence
               Emily Hardy (London: Macmillan, 1972); originally
               published as *The Early Life of Thomas Hardy, 1840–91*
               (London: Macmillan, 1928) and *The Later Years of
               Thomas Hardy, 1892–1928* (London: Macmillan, 1930);
               these memoirs were written by Hardy, composed in
               the third person, and published after his death under
               his wife's name.

TMOC   *The Mayor of Casterbridge* (London: Macmillan, New
               Wessex Edition, 1974)

               Old Mrs Chundle and Other Stories (London: Macmillan,
               1977)

APOBE   *A Pair of Blue Eyes* (London: Macmillan, New Wessex
               Edition, 1975)

TROTN   *The Return of the Native* (London: Macmillan, New
               Wessex Edition, 1974)

Tess   *Tess of the d'Urbervilles* (London: Macmillan, New
               Wessex Edition, 1974)

               Thomas Hardy's Personal Writings, ed. H. Orel (Law-
               rence, Kan.: University of Kansas Press, 1966)

TTM   *The Trumpet-Major* (London: Macmillan, New Wessex
               Edition, 1974)

TOAT   *Two on a Tower* (London: Macmillan, New Wessex
               Edition, 1975)

UTGT   *Under the Greenwood Tree* (London: Macmillan, New
               Wessex Edition, 1974)

TWB   *The Well-Beloved* (London: Macmillan, New Wessex
               Edition, 1975)

WT   *Wessex Tales* (London: Macmillan, New Wessex Edi-
               tion, 1974)

TW   *The Woodlanders* (London: Macmillan, New Wessex
               Edition, 1974)

WORKS BY FAULKNER

AA   *Absalom, Absalom!* (London: Chatto & Windus, 1964)

AILD   *As I Lay Dying* (Harmondsworth, Middx: Penguin, 1963)

    Big Woods (New York: Random House, 1955)

DM   *Doctor Martino, and Other Stories* (London: Chatto & Windus, 1934)

    Early Prose and Poetry, ed. Carvel Collins (Boston, Mass.: Little, Brown, 1962)

    Essays, Speeches, and Public Letters, ed. James B. Meriwether (London: Chatto & Windus, 1966); contains essay 'Mississippi', referred to in text by abbreviation *Miss.*

AF   *A Fable* (London: Chatto & Windus, 1955)

    The Faulkner–Cowley File: Letters and Memories, 1944–1962, ed. Malcolm Cowley (New York: Viking Press, 1966)

    Faulkner at Nagano, ed. R. A. Jelliffe (Tokyo: Kenkyusha, 1956)

    Faulkner in the University: Class Conferences at the University of Virginia, 1957–1958, ed. F. L. Gwynn and J. L. Blotner (Charlottesville, Va: University of Virginia Press, 1959)

    Faulkner at West Point, ed. J. L. Fant and R. Ashley (New York: Random House, 1964)

    Flags in the Dust, ed. Douglas Day (New York: Random House, 1973)

GDM   *Go Down, Moses* (Harmondsworth, Middx: Penguin, 1960)

TH   *The Hamlet* (London: Chatto & Windus, 1957)

    'An Introduction to *The Sound and the Fury*', in *Mississippi Quarterly*, vol. 26 (Summer 1973); and in *Southern Review*, vol. 8 (Autumn 1972)

IITD	*Intruder in the Dust* (Harmondsworth, Middx: Penguin, 1960)
KG	*Knight's Gambit* (London: Chatto & Windus, 1969)
LIA	*Light in August* (Harmondsworth, Middx: Penguin, 1960)
	Lion in the Garden: Interviews with William Faulkner, 1926–1962, ed. James B. Meriwether and Michael Millgate (New York: Random House, 1968)
TM	*The Mansion* (London: Reprint Society, 1962)
	Mosquitoes (London: Chatto & Windus, 1955)
	New Orleans Sketches, ed. Carvel Collins (London: Sidgwick & Jackson, 1959)
	Pylon (London: Chatto & Windus, 1967)
TR	*The Reivers* (Harmondsworth, Middx: Penguin, 1970)
RFAN	*Requiem for a Nun* (Harmondsworth, Middx: Penguin, 1960)
	Sanctuary (Harmondsworth, Middx: Penguin, 1953)
	Sartoris (London: Chatto & Windus, 1964)
SP	*Soldier's Pay* (Harmondsworth, Middx: Penguin, 1970)
TSATF	*The Sound and the Fury* (Harmondsworth, Middx: Penguin 1964)
TT	*These Thirteen* (London: Chatto & Windus, 1974)
TTO	*The Town* (London: Chatto & Windus, 1958)
UW	*Uncle Willy and Other Stories* (London: Chatto & Windus, 1967)
	The Uncollected Stories of William Faulkner, ed. J. L. Blotner (New York: Random House, 1979)
TU	*The Unvanquished* (Harmondsworth, Middx: Penguin, 1955)
TWP	*The Wild Palms* (Harmondsworth, Middx: Penguin, 1961)

1

Dorset: 'the lost sense of home'

Down there I seem to be false to myself, my simple self that was,
And is not now, and I see him watching, wondering what crass
    cause
Can have merged him into such a strange continuator as this

(*Wessex Heights*, 1896)

I should like to begin this study by trying to establish some useful
facts about social change in nineteenth-century rural England, in
order to focus upon its relationship with the novels of Thomas
Hardy. The intimacy of such a relationship, and the importance of
Hardy's awareness of social change in his discovery of subject, may
be gauged from the curious resurrection in *The Mayor of Casterbridge*
(1886) and *Tess of the d'Urbervilles* (1891) of five passages from
Hardy's essay of 1883, *The Dorsetshire Labourer*, published in
Longman's Magazine as one of a series dealing with, in the editor's
words, the condition of 'the peasantry of the various parts of the
kingdom'.[1] For example, when the Durbeyfields of *Tess* are evicted
from Marlott, Hardy explains

> it was the eve of Old Lady-Day, and the agricultural world was in
> a fever of mobility.... The labourers – or 'workfolk', as they used
> to call themselves immemorially till the other word was intro-
> duced from without – who wish to remain no longer in old places
> are removing to the new farms.
>
> These annual migrations from farm to farm were on the
> increase here....
>
> However, all the mutations so increasingly discernible in
> village life did not originate entirely in the agricultural unrest. A
> depopulation was also going on. The village had formerly
> contained, side by side with the agricultural labourers, an
> interesting and better-informed class, ranking distinctly above
> the former – the class to which Tess's father and mother had

1

belonged – and including the carpenter, the smith, the shoemaker, the huckster, together with nondescript workers other than farm-labourers; a set of people who owed a certain stability of aim and conduct to the fact of their being life-holders like Tess's father, or copy-holders, or occasionally, small freehol-ders. But as the long holdings fell in they were seldom again let to similar tenants, and were mostly pulled down, if not absolutely required by the farmer for his hands. Cottagers who were not directly employed on the land were looked on with disfavour, and the banishment of some starved the trade of others, who were thus obliged to follow. These families, who had formed the backbone of village life in the past, who were the depositories of the village traditions, had to seek refuge in the large centres; the process, humorously designated by statisticians as 'the tendency of the rural population towards the large towns' being really the tendency of water to flow uphill when forced by machinery. (*Tess*, pp. 400–1)

The universal flurry of activity on Old Lady-Day, the phrase 'a day of fulfilment', and the explanation of the term 'workfolk', are all drawn from *The Dorsetshire Labourer*; and the whole of the last, lengthy paragraph is an almost verbatim reproduction of the earlier essay's concluding remarks. For a moment the individualised, peculiarly cinematic images of *Tess* have frozen, and Hardy muses over a general and far-reaching social process. The complexity of the rural class structure and the poignancy and bitterness associated with the dispossession of an 'interesting and better-informed class' of life-holders, or 'liviers',[2] are obviously of considerable imagina-tive significance to Hardy, and it is clear, at the end of *The Dorsetshire Labourer*, that he feels for the ousted liviers – whom he has introduced quite gratuitously into his essay – an intimate loyalty and affection absent from his none the less sympathetic descriptions of the agricultural labourer. Both the partisan sensitivity of the essay, and the homeless Tess's wanderings throughout Wessex, are the products of Hardy's long brooding over a period of social upheaval. By deliberately incorporating *The Dorsetshire Labourer*'s earlier sociological images of dislocation and migration in two later novels, Hardy is acknowledging a source of his artistic inspiration. To understand this fact is to arrive immediately at one of the most simple and fundamental of Hardy's many affinities with Faulkner:

it was precisely the disorientating experience of social change in the present that eventually drove the writers of the Southern 'renaissance' to an investigation of their past. During the 1920s, the years when people like William Faulkner, Robert Penn Warren, and Thomas Wolfe were beginning to write and to examine their regional environment, the American South was at last acknowledging the death of its traditional way of life, based on the small farm and the great plantation, and recognising its absorption into the strange new world of industrialism and advanced capitalism.

Disturbance and disorientation are not necessarily bad things however, especially in the field of literature. In a sense, they make possible that analysis of personal motive, the examination of the premises on which our own beliefs and those of our society depend, which is surely one of the characteristic qualities of a good piece of writing.[3]

So it was too with Thomas Hardy. He and William Faulkner may at first appear to have little in common: one born in Dorset in 1840, the other born in Mississippi, dying as recently as 1962. Yet each is the chronicler of a transitional era, and a society in the throes of transformation. Each came from a poor, primitive and isolated rural community, and experienced a period of intense upheaval as his region painfully adapted its traditional way of life to the demands of an industrialised, urbanised, commercialised twentieth century. Both Hardy and Faulkner witnessed the decline of the social class from which they had come, and their novels are therefore concerned with the loss of traditional values and culture, the disintegration of their childhood worlds.

Furthermore, the two writers are themselves examples of what might be desribed as the *transitional consciousness*, a sensibility full of what Hardy called 'the ache of modernism' (*Tess*, p. 163). Each grew up in a traditional rural environment, yet each became estranged from his roots by a common experience of education and formative periods spent in modern cities. Hardy and Faulkner therefore share a profoundly equivocal mood, permeating both the form and content of their novels: they are able to see both the positive and negative aspects of each way of life, tradition and modernity. Fascinated by the process of history and by a certain quality of meditative nostalgia common to their respective regions, they combine a critique of the darker aspects of that past with an interest in the process of change and the transforming social attitudes – to class, sex, marriage or race – which it brings. The chronicles of Wessex and Yoknapatawpha County consequently express a brooding ambivalence, towards man, nature and 'society' – even towards the role of a man of letters – which invites comparative analysis as a powerful literary response to the phenomenon of an engulfing, mechanised and standardised modern way of life.

My aim in this chapter is therefore to investigate the social structure of the changing rural world which Hardy portrays and to attempt to identify the genesis of his subject, before going on to consider the novelistic methods by which Hardy's work brings Angel and Tess's 'ache of modernism' to life.

It is importantly firstly to emphasise the heterogeneity of early Victorian rural society, for its features are frequently oversimplified. Too often traditional 'Wessex', like Faulkner's 'Old South', is obscured by a veil of romantic myth, concealing a more untidy historical reality. Such myths, whether of bucolic English 'peasants' or gallant Southern 'aristocrats', are cherished by a largely urban public today, as yesterday, because they seem to offer an easy nostalgic anodyne, a clear and comforting distinction between a simple, innocent rustic past, and a complex, problematic urban present. But *Far from the Madding Crowd* is an ironic title; if Weatherbury is remote, it contains the same turbulent passions, tragedies and injustices as the city. An obvious point, perhaps, yet treacherous misreadings of Hardy's scrupulous nuances still abound, ironically in view of Hardy's warnings about blithely ignorant generalisations of country life, such as stereotyping of the labouring yokel, that 'pitiable dummy known as Hodge'[4] (another passage from *The Dorsetshire Labourer* to be revived in *Tess*).

A small but significant example of this danger is provided by one otherwise perspicacious critic's claim that, 'It was not until Hardy wrote *Tess* that an educated author was able to identify, unreservedly, with an uneducated village girl.'[5] Of course, Hardy's sympathy for Tess *is* strikingly new and bold in its Victorian context. But the relationship between author and character is not simply one of contrast between two polarised social worlds. Tess's aptitude for her newly authorised education is in fact particularly emphasised in the novel, as is the resulting sense of cultural dislocation (a phenomenon of which Hardy himself was acutely conscious):

> Mrs. Durbeyfield habitually spoke the dialect; her daughter, who had passed the Sixth Standard in the National School under a London-trained mistress, spoke two languages: the dialect at home, more or less; ordinary English abroad and to persons of quality....

> Between the mother, with her fast-perishing lumber of superstitions, folk lore, dialect, and orally transmitted ballads, and the daughter, with her trained National teachings and standard knowledge under an infinitely Revised Code, there was a gap of two hundred years as ordinarily understood. When they were together the Jacobean and the Victorian ages were juxtaposed.   (*Tess*, pp. 48, 50–1)

Far from being 'uneducated', Tess is later to tell Angel that

> I was in the Sixth Standard when I left school, and they said I had great aptness, and should make a good teacher, so it was settled that I should be one. But there was trouble in my family.
>
> (p. 229)

To comment upon Tess's schooling is not merely to cavil over a careless word, for it is precisely because Tess is *not* an ordinary 'uneducated village girl', but an unusually intelligent, sensitive and reflective creature with a 'touch of rarity about her', that her fateful relationship with Angel is set in motion. Tess does not succeed in becoming a teacher (a common source of mobility for ambitious young Victorians from humble backgrounds, such as Fancy Day, Sue Bridehead, Hardy's lover Tryphena Sparks, and his sisters Mary and Kate), but her ability to express in 'her own native phrases – assisted a little by her Sixth Standard training – feelings which might almost have been called those of the age – the ache of modernism' (p. 163), awakens Angel's interest in her transitional consciousness. Had he followed the conventions of his class, and had Tess been an unremarkable village girl such as Betty Priddle, no marriage could have occurred. But their era is one where the traditional boundaries are crumbling, and class definitions become blurred. Simon Stoke, the Northern money-lender, reappears as a Stoke d'Urberville, while a 'decidely bookish, musical, thinking young man' such as Angel unexpectedly chooses to become a farmer, instinctively drawn – like Clym Yeobright or Grace Melbury – 'out of his class' (pp. 163–4), back to the humble life and traditional occupations of the countryside, even as its own accustomed workers are awkwardly struggling towards a new social advancement.

This is a characteristically Hardeian irony, a social paradox which he continually re-examines. It is therefore unfortunate that as the popularity of Hardy's novels continues to grow, so too it seems does a vague public image of his work as a kind of soft-focus, pre-industrial idyll, the pastoral swansong of Merrie England's carefree peasantry. Representative of this view at its most intelligent is Douglas Brown's essay 'The Agricultural Theme', in his study *Thomas Hardy*. Brown's responses to the poetic form and texture of Hardy's work are invariably enlightening, but his thesis of a 'common pattern' in the novels of 'the theme of urban invasion ... a clash between agricultural and urban modes of life', is uncomfortably simplistic. When he declares that 'each of the great Wessex novels treats in imaginative form the defeat of our peasantry and the collapse of our agriculture',[6] it becomes clear that his vision of nineteenth-century English country life is not that of Hardy.

For, firstly, in his summaries of Hardy's two important essays on social change,[7] Brown glosses over Hardy's careful differentiation between the character and fate of different rural classes, to which I shall return. Meanwhile, let us understand that the term 'peasantry' is inaccurate and misleading. Strictly speaking there were no 'peasants' in England, though Victorian writers, very occasionally including Hardy,[8] continued to use the word as a generic term for the lower rural classes.

Secondly, Brown mistakes the nature and chronology of the social upheaval which he believes Hardy to describe. He suggests that the 'Novels of Character and Environment' all 'refer directly or by implication to the contemporary environment ... and the contemporary catastrophe ... the agricultural tragedy of 1870–1902'[9] – that is, to the severe agricultural depression of those years, and the 'exodus of agricultural labourers' which Brown implies was greatly exacerbated in that period. Yet rather than describing the decline of agriculture, or the effects of the late Victorian depression, Hardy's major novels chronicle a gradually accelerating social dislocation, spread like a cancer through the three decades *preceding* Brown's farmers' slump, namely 1840–70; and his fictional exploration of these years is centred around the fate of a quite different class, that of the independent rural craftsmen and tradesmen. I shall return to the class issue; it must first be emphasised that most of the novels to which Brown refers are set twenty or thirty years prior to their date of composition, and do not refer to a contemporary environment at all. By setting earlier 'Novels of Character and Environment' such as *Under the Greenwood Tree*, *The Return of the Native* and *The Mayor of Casterbridge* in the 1840s or 1850s,[10] Hardy could show the transitional era of large-scale disruption in its beginnings – with traditional elements like church quires, reddlemen and idiosyncratic corn-factors still active, the first alien outsiders only just having arrived, and with migration as an isolated rather than universal occurrence. Even in an early work such as *Far from the Madding Crowd*, the effect of Hardy's uncharacteristic choice of a near-contemporary setting – probably 1869–73 – is offset by the story's geographical setting in a corner of Dorset celebrated for its sleepy, unchanged traditional order.[11] It is not until the last three great novels that Hardy examines a countryside seriously ravaged by dispossession, migration and consequent alienation, first in *The Woodlanders*, set about 1857–60;[12] then (by the internal chronology of the novels) in *Jude*, set in 1860–70;[13] and finally in *Tess*, the setting of which is imprecise, though late, being probably the late 1860s or the 1870s.[14]

Thirdly, Brown's 'agricultural theme' stresses a contrast between Hardy's 'dismay at the predicament of the agricultural community ... during the last part of the nineteenth century' on the one hand, and his 'degree of dependence upon an identified and reliable past ... and deep-seated allegiance' on the other. Like Brown's theory of agricultural versus urban modes of life, this is not without a measure of truth; yet ultimately both ideas detract from our understanding of Hardy's ironic insight and wisdom. While cherishing all things historical, Hardy well knew that escape into an imaginative past, whether romanticised or 'identified and reliable', was no solution to present problems. Any suggestion of the 'good old days' in his work is balanced again and again by reminders of the harshness and injustices of that past, sometimes even coiled within a single sentence:

a result of this increasing nomadic habit of the labourer is naturally a less intimate and kindly relation with the land he tills than existed before enlightenment enabled him to rise above the

condition of a serf who lived and died on a particular plot, like a
tree.   (*TDL*, p. 13)

The effect of this sentence is startlingly equivocal, expressing a
fierce determination not to spoon-feed the reader with a half-anti-
cipated, nostalgic image of the outmoded labourer, but instead to
raise awkward questions in his mind. In miniature the passage
typifies Hardy's emphasis upon the complexity of rural change,
the difficulty involved in reaching an objective understanding of its
ultimate consequences, which is the true common pattern of all his
greatest novels.

Some detailed discussion of the different rural classes in Hardy's
day, and of his depiction of them, is therefore required. The most
powerful group, the landowners, ranged from aristocracy down to
local squires, and between them owned perhaps three-quarters of
the nineteenth-century countryside.[15] Where the upper classes are
concerned, Hardy is a far from impartial commentator. His attitude
is a complex one. While one side of him frequently expressed a
prickly hostility towards some of the gentry, especially those
squires who persecuted the cottagers from whom he sprang,[16]
another part of him observed the aristocracy with a frankly
romantic fascination, as attested by his fondness for investigating
their pedigrees. As a successful writer Hardy found the fashion-
able salons of London society open to him, and he evidently
enjoyed mixing with their patrician inmates, especially if they were
female. Such experiences prompted the Kensington and
country-house milieux of *The Hand of Ethelberta*, *A Laodicean* and
A Group of Noble Dames, which demonstrate Hardy's peculiar
mixture of animosity and attraction towards high society. None
of these works show Hardy at his best as a writer, but they
are none the less important evidence that Hardy cannot be categorised as a simple celebrator of vanished country ways. Several
of Hardy's novels contain no gentry: while some representatives, like Felice Charmond or Alec d'Urberville, might be seen
as carelessly unindividualised, close to caricature, if we are de-
manding of Hardy a consistently objective authorial perspective.
Is such a perspective Hardy's intention, however? In 1892, near
the end of his career as a novelist, he explained to a newspaper
reporter that 'I have endeavoured to write from the point of view
of the village people themselves instead of from that of the Hall or
Parsonage.'[17]

If we pause to consider Mrs Charmond and Alec from the socially critical viewpoint of the villagers over whom they exercise their lordly prerogatives, Hardy's characterisations may slip into sharper, more suggestive focus. Hardy's interest in the gentry as fictional material may therefore be understood as an oblique one: he is less concerned with their actual qualities as individuals than with those with which the resentful or awestruck lower orders invest them. George Melbury, for example, feels a foolishly exaggerated and undiscriminating respect for Dr Fitzpiers, solely on account of 'the standing of his family in the country in bygone days' (*TW*, p. 189). One could find many other such examples. The corollary to this theme, of course, is Hardy's didactic interest in suggesting how skin-deep are the distinctions between different classes:

> The two gentleman was not half so far removed from Sol and Dan [a carpenter and house-painter], and the hard-handed order in general, in his passions as in his philosophy. He still continued to be the male of his species, and when the heart was hot with a dream Pall Mall had much the same aspect as Wessex. (*THOE*, p. 219)

These variations upon the theme of class-consciousness suggest that Hardy discovered his own sensitivity to class distinctions to be a powerful imaginative stimulus in his writing. His especial interest in the relativity of class viewpoints adds much to the impression of richness, variety and entanglement in the experience of his stories, and seems to anticipate the multiple perspectives of Faulkner. It was even in his early career a conscious strategem, *The Hand of Ethelberta* (1876) aiming to be a 'drama ... wherein servants were as important as, or more important than, their masters; wherein the drawing-room was sketched in many cases from the point of view of the servants' hall'.[18]

This decision is of a piece with the emphasis placed in 1892 upon studying rural life 'from the point of view of the village people themselves', and the question of the *Hardeian viewpoint* seems to me crucial in learning to appreciate the uniqueness of Hardy's appeal as a novelist. Its effects vary widely. At its crudest the class-conscious perspective expresses a note of unflinching antagonism towards the gentry, resulting in the imaginative anaemia of most of the subjects in *A Group of Noble Dames*. Yet Hardy's partisan sympathies are more often subsumed within a liberating awareness of universal change, an essentially *fluctuating* viewpoint allowing an exhilaratingly wide range of imaginative response. Tess, for example, is captured sometimes with all the intimate apprehensions of a lover – the reader momentarily *becoming* Angel Clare:

> She was yawning, and he saw the red interior of her mouth as if it had been a snake's.... Having been lying down in her clothes she was as warm as a sunned cat.   (p. 210)

while elsewhere we find Hardy himself seeming to appear as spectator regarding her, and speaking tenderly of her as a living, suffering creature:

> Thus Tess walks on; a figure which is part of the landscape; a fieldwoman pure and simple, in winter guise; a gray serge cape, a red woollen cravat, a stuff skirt covered by a whitey-brown rough wrapper, and buff-leather gloves. Every thread of that old attire has become faded and thin under the stroke of raindrops, the burn of sunbeams, and the stress of winds. There is no sign of young passion in her now.   (*Tess*, p. 326)

Or the viewpoint may swing abruptly between a specific awareness of class issues and a magisterial philosophical detachment: Tess's father

> was the last of three lives for whose duration the house and premises were held under a lease.... Moreover, liviers were disapproved of in villages almost as much as little freeholders, because of their independence of manner, and when a lease determined it was never renewed.
>
> Thus the Durbeyfields, once d'Urbervilles, saw descending upon them the destiny which, no doubt, when they were among the Olympians of the country, they had caused to descend many a time, and severely enough, upon the heads of such landless ones as they themselves were now. So do flux and reflux – the rhythm of change – alternate and persist in everything under the sky.   (*Tess*, p. 399)

Not only had Hardy risen out of his own class by becoming a successful man of letters, but he had realised that that class itself was rapidly becoming extinct. Paradoxically, in encouraging us to view Victorian society from the slippery lower rungs of the class ladder, Hardy's writing often transmits to the reader an unexpectedly modern sensation, a distinct impression that we are in touch a seemingly *classless* (and hence very un-Victorian) sensibility.

Hardy's 'village people' are usually drawn from the middle strata of rural classes: he especially delights in portraying the interactions of the minor gentry (such as small squires, provincial clergy, nouveaux riches landlords) with the independent class of cottagers, especially those of livier stock who have 'bettered themselves' by education and travel. Farmers, like ordinary farm labourers, are surprisingly rare in the foregrounds of Hardy's fiction. Indeed, Hardy's chosen 'village people' perspective is firmly at odds with the semi-conscious popular assumption that somehow squires and farmers personify the character of the English countryside. To grasp this point we must study the characteristics of farmers and farming in the Victorian period.

As with every other rural group, class distinctions tended to become blurred at the edges. Prosperous occupiers of several hundred acres might enjoy an almost equal social standing with the humbler of the squires, while those working small farms of 50 acres or less would be virtually indistinguishable from the more substantial among the class of liviers, who commonly owned a smallholding – perhaps an orchard or market garden – as a secondary source of income. Three important social factors require comment.

The first is that the vast majority of farmers in this period were tenants, not owner-occupiers.[19] The typical mid-Victorian farmer rented a farm of between 100 and 300 acres from the owner of a great estate, and showed little desire to own his property, for rents were usually low, and tenure secure.

Secondly, this means that another popular traditional agrarian image, that of the independent English 'yeoman', had little basis in Victorian reality. Few yeomen, in the sense of small farmers cultivating their own land, seem to have survived the period of enclosure in the late eighteenth and early nineteenth century. Hardy seems to have recognised those liviers with substantial trades and smallholdings as the closest Victorian equivalent to the independent 'yeoman' of old, and he uses the term of George Melbury's ancestors, and of Giles Winterborne, in *The Woodlanders*. As with the similarly vague term 'peasant', the word appears to be a chiefly emotional and symbolic usage surviving from an earlier age.

Thirdly, the zenith of Victorian agriculture was reached during the period of 'high farming' in the 1850s and 1860s, intensive farming which relied upon an expanding market. The rapidly increasing population of the Victorian cities provided such a demand for a generation, but after the mid-1870s the mass importing of foreign grain, meat and dairy produce caused a disastrous agricultural depression which lasted up until the First World War. According to the 'nostalgic' reading of Hardy, the 1850s and 1860s should therefore have been the golden age of Victorian rural life, in direct contrast to the bleak final years of the century, but the fallaciousness of this picture, as a social analysis and as a guide to the sources of Hardy's inspiration, should now be clear. As I have explained, none of Hardy's 'Novels of Character and Environment', with the possible exception of *Far from the Madding Crowd*, have a contemporary (i.e. 1873–95) setting. They tend to be set 20 or 30 years in the past, in other words between 1840 and 1870, a fact which Brown overlooks; and the social world which they evoke is a far from happy one. With the exception of *Far from the Madding Crowd*, Hardy's attitude to farmers is generally critical, perennially aware of the economic disparity between 'the well-to-do Farmer Lodge' and his illegitimate son's harsh existence, in the 'The Withered Arm'; between the lives of the hungry Casterbridge poor and the market-day farmers,

> men of extensive stomachs, sloping like mountain sides ... many carried ruffled chequebooks in their pockets which regulated at the bank hard by at a balance of never less than four figures. In fact, what these gibbous human shapes specially represented was ready money – money insistently ready – not ready next year like a nobleman's – often not merely ready at the bank like a professional man's, but ready in their large plump hands. (*TMOC*, pp. 179–80)

Here is the golden age of high farming; and it is significant that Hardy's attitude is to insist upon its darker side. In *The Dorsetshire Labourer*, he recalls that

> It was once common enough on inferior farms to hear a farmer, as he sat on horseback among a field of workers, address them with a contemptuousness which could not have been greatly exceeded in the days when the thralls of Cedric wore their collars of brass.

Hardy is writing in 1883, when agricultural labourers' wages have at least risen, and he dwells upon the ironic reflection that

> if a farmer can afford to pay thirty per cent more wages in times of agricultural depression than he paid in times of agricultural prosperity, and yet live, and keep a carriage, while the landlord still thrives on the reduced rent which has resulted, the labourer must have been greatly wronged in those prosperous times. (*TDL*, pp. 14–16)

As with the gentry, Hardy's novels are usually more concerned with the farmers' effects upon others than with the farmers themselves. Both those who own and those who farm the fields are peripheral to his novels of rural life. But there were other classes, other important groups of country folk:

> Down to the middle of the last century, country villagers were divided into two distinct castes, one being the artisans, traders, 'liviers' (owners of freeholds), and the manor-house upper servants; the other the 'workfolk', i.e. farm-labourers (these were never called by the latter name by themselves and other country people till about 70 years ago). The two castes rarely intermarried, and did not go to each other's house-gatherings save exceptionally.[20]

The commentator is Hardy himself, in a letter of 1927. In three different pieces of writing spread over three decades – an essay, a novel and another letter[21] – Hardy had used the phrase 'the backbone of village life' to describe the liviers, a group of independent craftsmen and tradesmen including carpenters, cobblers, bakers, blacksmiths, tailors, thatchers, masons, wheelwrights, dairymen, dressmakers, brewers, millers, millwrights, butchers, saddlers, barbers, innkeepers, higglers and general dealers. They were the class from which Hardy came, the son of a master-mason occupying a life-hold cottage. The liviers were fiercely proud of their residential and occupational independence, which gave them a slight but palpable social superiority over the mass of workfolk. Culturally as well as economically, the liviers felt themselves to be a village elite; like the Mellstock Quire, they were the inheritors and defenders of the village arts and traditions, while equally responsive to the new advantages offered by education. As Gittings has shown, Hardy's sensitivity on the subject of his own class origins was inflamed to a defensive secrecy by his success in the public eye, which no doubt explains both the lofty tone of authorial detachment in the letter quoted above, and its insistence upon the villagers' 'distinct castes'. Even cursory studies of parish registers of the early nineteenth century show that marriages between liviers and workfolk were common, largely due to the unpredictable hazards of social mobility. The Hardy family was no exception. This is not to deny the nature of important distinctions between the liviers and labourers, merely to emphasise the high rate of cross-over between the two, the precariousness of which the young Hardy and his family must have been all too uncomfortably aware. For nineteenth-century Dorset was an area synonymous with grinding poverty among the lower classes. Sir James Caird, surveying the state of English agriculture in 1850–1, noted that 'The condition of the Dorsetshire labourer has passed into a proverb, not altogether just, as compared with the counties adjoining.'[22] Census returns show that migratory Irish harvest-workers deliberately avoided Dorset in seeking seasonal employment.[23] The agricultural labourers of Hardy's Wessex earned, at mid-century, only seven or eight shillings a week – occasionally only six. Caird was told that on smaller Dorset farms 'even that small sum was in many cases paid partly in inferior wheat',[24] while just over the county border, on Salisbury Plain, 'The lowest rate of wages we met in England, 6s. a week ... was the amount given for ordinary labourers by the most extensive farmer in South Wilts, who holds nearly 5000 acres of land.'[25] Caird's statistics also show that Dorset and Wiltshire had the highest rate of paupers maintained by relief of any English county.

Alexander Somerville, commissioned by the Anti-Corn Law League to write articles on the agricultural England of the 1840s, records interviews with labourers in Hardy's region, where he found the general wage to be actually decreasing. One man to whom he spoke near Salisbury, who supported a wife and two children on eight shillings a week, had been transported for seven years for poaching, and he

wishes, he says, and prays to God, that he could now for himself and his family at home have such an allowance of food as he had in the West Indies when a convict. 'We had *terrible good living* ... by as I ever had for working in England.'[26]

It was the unendurable misery of men such as this which had led to the Captain Swing uprisings of 1830, particularly widespread in north Dorset, and the activities of the Tolpuddle Martyrs, who tried to form an agricultural labourers' union in 1834. Hardy grew up surrounded not by quaint, contented rustics but by hungry, desperate men and women. His own childhood was shielded by his father's flourishing trade, but Hardy's mother and paternal grandmother had both experienced extreme poverty, and they and his father recounted tales of rural hardships and cruelties which the future novelist remembered with a horrified fascination. His writings consequently do not shrink from describing such suffering. Hardy told Rider Haggard, researching for his *Rural England* in 1902, that the condition of the agricultural labourer

> down to 1850 or 1855 ... was generally one of great hardship ... as a child I knew a sheep-keeping boy who to my horror shortly afterwards died of want – the contents of his stomach at the autopsy being raw turnip only. His father's wages were six shillings a week, with about two pounds at the harvest, a cottage rent free, and an allowance of thorn faggots from the hedges as fuel.[27]

Memories such as this were to reinforce the portraits of Hardy's labourers – the hungry poor of Casterbridge, Rhoda Brook and her son, Tess at Flintcomb-Ash, Jude at Marygreen – with a taut, unsentimental authenticity almost unique in Victorian literature.[28]

These then were the classes among whom Hardy grew up, whom he observed and commemorated in his art; and it should now be clear that Hardy chose one particular class, the liviers, as a focus or pivot for the action of his novels. His protagonists invariably spring from this 'interesting and better-informed class' of independent cottagers. Why was his creative imagination so attracted towards this group?

The most obvious answer is of course that his family were liviers, that it was the class whose habits and outlooks he knew most intimately. But it seems equally significant that the 'village people' whose lives he examines – Dick Dewy, Gabriel Oak, Giles Winterborne, Tess – are those most capable of rapid social mobility, either up or down. 'I chose them because there appeared to be so much more dramatic interest in their lives', Hardy explained in 1892; and, 'their passions are franker, for one thing'.[29] In other

words, the precarious social status of the livier and the potential
clash between his unsophisticated but independent and ambitious
character and the inflexibility of Victorian class values, seemed to
offer Hardy the maximum dramatic possibilities for fiction. The
prosperity of those liviers who flourished, like Hardy's father,
exacted a heavy toll in the failure of others. Hardy's lifelong interest
in Darwinian theory and its application to rural society must have
fed upon ready-made examples absorbed from all around him in his
childhood. The population of England and Wales doubled between
1800 and 1850, and had doubled again by 1911;[30] coupled with the
effects of increasing industrialisation and large-scale capitalism, this
massive increase forced the liviers' trades into desperate competition with one another. In 1841, Bere Regis (the d'Urbervilles'
'Kingsbere') had 18 cobblers struggling for survival, in a town of
only 1394 people.[31] Consequently the liviers were frequently forced
out of business, whether through fecklessness, like the haggler John
Durbeyfield, or by ambitiously over-reaching themselves, like the
Caro family of stonemasons in *The Well-Beloved*.

In short, the sweeping social transitions of the mid-nineteenth
century thrust the intermediate livier class into a particularly acute,
Darwinian crisis: they had to drastically *adapt* in order to survive.
Small wonder then that Dick Dewy has some advertising cards
printed 'to kip pace with the times' or that Barber Percomb has 'left
off his pole because 'tis not genteel'. But Hardy's Wessex is, until
Jude, still a transitional world, where old and new uneasily co-exist.
Dick's neighbour Robert Penny, the shoemaker, still keeps to the
traditional liviers' observance that

> advertising in any shape was scorned, and it would have been felt
> as beneath his dignity to paint up, for the benefit of strangers, the
> name of an establishment whose trade came solely by connection
> based on personal respect   (*UTGT*, p. 88)

While we find that, behind Barber Percomb's house

> there was a little yard, reached by a passage from the back
> street, and in that yard was a pole, and under the pole a shop of
> quite another description than the ornamental one in the front
> street. Here on Saturday nights from seven to ten he took an
> almost innumerable succession of twopences from the farm-
> labourers who flocked thither in crowds from the country. And
> thus he lived.   (*TW*, p. 67)

'Perruquier to the aristocracy' by day, and farm-labourers' barber by night, Percomb's is a strange, fragmented way of life. Robert Penny was a craftsman who could identify his fellow parishioners by their boots, which he had made and repaired – 'I can swear to the family voot' – and this kind of proudly localised, integrated work is clearly doomed.

As Hardy gradually became aware of this crisis and of the livier class's many and various reactions to it, he recognised a personal source of imaginative inspiration, one which orders and informs all his greatest novels. Hardy's protagonists are, almost without exception, of this busy, intermediate rural class, ambitious but socially insecure: especially vulnerable in their relationship to house and occupation, those key Victorian definitions of status and moral worth. The figure of the independent livier is faced with an awesome variety of choices: whether to struggle for advancement through traditional occupations or modernised forms of trade; whether to seek fulfilment through education and urbanisation, or marriage, or glamorous daydreams, or private, altruistic ideals. And by deciding on one of these courses, what does he (or she) lose en route? It is an exciting, disturbing and poignant situation, rich in imaginative potential, ironic reversals, the emotional ferment of old loyalties and new ideals. It is the germ of great fiction. Hardy well knew that the agricultural labourer was no dull, characterless 'Hodge', but he realised too that, since social mobility was by mid-century largely denied the ordinary labourer, his dramatic potential in fiction was likewise circumscribed, where that of the livier was fluid, flexible, full of new possibilities.[32] The nicety of the social distinction was beyond most of Hardy's contemporary readers, as Hardy knew, agreeing in 1892 that 'sometimes I am described as the novelist of the agricultural labourer', but significantly adding that 'That is not inclusive, I think ... in my books of rural life I have endeavoured to describe the village community generally.'[33]

Hardy's evocations of the liviers' way of life should therefore be seen as central to his portrayal of rural society. They are distinguished by a deeply elegiac mood: here is the true source of that nostalgic atmosphere in Hardy's novels which critics like Brown strive to identify. However this may be lightened by humour, or balanced by *The Dorsetshire Labourer*'s strenuously fair assessments of social change, an important part of Hardy mourns the passing of a traditional way of life which seemed to draw human activities and natural processes into a fruitful, unpretentious harmony. Thus

Robert Creedle's lament for Giles Winterborne achieves a Shake-spearian purity of resonance, echoed by an elegiac authorial voice:

> 'Forgive me, but I can't rule my mourning nohow as a man should.... I ha'n't seen him since Thusday se' night, and have wondered for days and days where he's been keeping. There was I expecting him to come and tell me to wash out the cider-barrels against the making, and here was he.... Well, I've knowed him from table high; I knowed his father – used to bide about upon two sticks in the sun afore he died! – and now I've seen the end of the family, which we can ill afford to lose, wi' such a scanty lot of good folk in Hintock as we've got. And now Robert Creedle will be nailed up in parish boards 'a b'lieve; and nobody will glutch down a sign for he!'
>
> ... The whole wood seemèd to be a house of death, pervaded by loss to its uttermost length and breadth. Winterborne was gone, and the copses seemed to show the want of him; those young trees, so many of which he had planted, and of which he had spoken so truly when he said that he should fall before they fell, were at that moment sending out their roots in the direction that he had given them with his subtle hand. (*TW*, pp. 352–3)

Hardy seems to have been haunted by a vision of the livier's vulnerability, his imminent descent into poverty, rootless drifting and alienation. Such a fate was no melodramatic fictional ploy; even Hardy's famous tragic coincidences and ironic twists of fate, often dismissed as unrealistic, were unremarkable enough in the context of the harsh unpredictability of the rural life he describes. The rise and fall of Michael Henchard is echoed in Richard Jefferies's essay *Going Downhill*,[34] the story of a farmer who slowly sinks to the position of bailiff on one of the farms of which he was once tenant, while the eclipse of the Durbeyfields reproduces a decline which Hardy detected in his own Dorset relatives, much as Faulkner brooded over the slow decay of the Southern plantation aristocracy. Hardy's uncle, the livier James Sparks of Puddletown, was reduced from a self-employed cabinet-maker to spending his last years as a mere travelling journeyman, dogged by ill-health and eventually dying from a poisoned wound in the hand which he received at work, aged 69.[35] A note in the *Life*, recorded when *Tess* was evidently in gestation, shows us something of the relation between Hardy's observations of the Dorset life around him, and the processes of his creative imagination:

> September 30 [1888]. 'The Valley of the Great Dairies' – Froom. 'The Valley of the Little Dairies' – Blackmoor. In the afternoon by train to Evershot. Walked to Woolcombe, a property once owned by a – I think the senior – branch of the Hardys.
> The decline and fall of the Hardys much in evidence hereabout. An instance: Becky S.'s mother's sister married one of the Hardys of this branch, who was considered to have bemeaned himself by the marriage. 'All Woolcombe and Froom Quintin belonged to them at one time', Becky used to say proudly.... I remember when young seeing the man – tall and thin – walking beside a horse and common spring trap, and my mother pointing him out to me and saying he represented what was once the leading branch of the family. So we go down, down, down.[36]

Hardy's rural world was therefore permeated by an atmosphere of restlessness and insecurity, expressed by a continuing transformation in patterns of trade and economy, and a continual migration to the towns or overseas.

Studies of nineteenth-century rural depopulation show that the most severe effects of a decline in the English population were centred within a region comprising Cornwall, Devon, Somerset, Dorset and Wiltshire – in other words, in Hardy's Wessex.[37] Improved access to the towns, especially by the railways, that in Hardy's novels are seen stretching ever further into the countryside, and the increasing appeal of these towns as apparent sources of glamour, wealth and education, posed an almost irresistible yet confusing temptation to the younger and more restless livier. Consider, for example, the impact of the Great Exhibition of 1851 upon the characters of the short story 'The Fiddler of the Reels':

> For South Wessex, the year formed in many ways an extraordinary chronological frontier or transit-line ... a precipice in Time. As in a geological 'fault', we had presented to us a sudden bringing of

ancient and modern into absolute contact, such as probably in no
other single year since the Conquest was ever witnessed in this
part of the country.   (*LLI*, p. 171)

Accordingly, the themes of the story are enchantment, seduction,
migration, ambition and disillusion, with the mysterious will-of-
the-wisp Mop Ollamoor seeming to personify that glamorous but
elusive promise of the age which lured many villagers towards an
urban business or factory, or a distant colonial future; or, like Jude,
towards frustration and alienation. Meanwhile, those liviers who
stayed in their native communities faced the difficulties of a
declining or fluctuating trade, and growing residential insecurity.
The livier's state of tenure was influenced by the character of his
parish, whether 'open' or 'closed'. A 'closed' parish was one
dominated by a resident landlord, who very frequently deliberately
restricted the size of the village to a small number of regular staff,
perhaps including his tenant farmers' labourers, but few independent villagers. Hence liviers' cottages were pulled down as soon as
the last life expired, driving the homeless cottagers away. Examples
are common in Hardy's novels – Tollamore, Carriford, Faringdon,
Little Welland, Weydon Priors, Little Hintock, Trantridge and
Marygreen are some of the villages, each featured in a different
novel, where cottages are demolished by the squire. There are
several explanations for this persecution. Hardy stresses the
landlords' dislike of the liviers' carefree independence, dryly
remarking that some of them 'were not always shining examples of
churchgoing, temperance, and quiet walking';[38] and he also
suggests a seigneurial arrogance, the desire to extend a park over
the 'eyesore' of higgledy-piggledy cottages;[39] but Hardy fails to
mention another significant factor, that landlords wished to
minimise the number of poor cottagers who might one day
conceivably have to be supported as paupers by parish relief, under
the Poor Law.
  'Open' parishes, by contrast, were distinguished by a heterogeneity of owners, including some small freeholders and many small
tenants. Liviers, therefore, were the dominant class. Such settle-
ments were generally unplanned and sprawling, sometimes
developing outwards from existing freeholders' villages, but often
springing up in the late eighteenth or early nineteenth century in
response to the enclosure movement, the swelling of towns, the
shrinking of 'closed' villages, and the effects of the age's fluctuating

demand for labour. Many such 'open' villages were larger communities than their 'closed' counterparts, but they also occurred as scattered groups of hamlets. Built by squatters, these mushroomed on the outskirts of villages, or by roadsides, or upon commons and heathlands, such as the Egdon hamlets of *The Return of the Native* and 'The Withered Arm'. Included in this category too would be Giles Winterborne's 'One-Chimney-Hut by Delborough', a typical lone squatter's response to eviction, just as Casterbridge's Mixen Lane represents a similar, communal response, albeit in a less attractive guise. Its occupants are largely the remnants of 'that once bulky, but now nearly extinct, section of village society called "liviers"' (*TMOC*, p. 279), torn from their roots in the countryside. We are told that 'The land and its surrounding thicket of thatched cottages stretched out like a spit into the moist and misty lowland' (*TMOC*, p. 278) and the orientation of Mixen Lane towards not the town but the surrounding moorland, like the natural imagery used to describe it, conveys an undertone of stubborn allegiance to the lost way of life. Significantly, its denizens still defiantly live by poaching, a reaction to what the country writer H. J. Massingham called 'the legal crime of enclosing the commons'.[40]

The exact detail of Hardy's fictional settings makes its own quiet but satisfying contribution to his exploration of the relation between character and environment, its ripples of meaning spreading ever outward. For example, when Tess arrives at the 'starve-acre' Flintcomb-Ash, we are told that

> Of the three classes of village, the village cared for by its lord, the village cared for by itself, and the village uncared for either by itself or by its lord (in other words, the village of a resident squire's tenantry, the village of free or copy-holders, and the absentee-owner's village, farmed with the land) this place, Flintcomb-Ash, was the third   (*Tess*, p. 331)

and this information is no mere fortuitous local-colour padding. *Tess* is conceived on an epic scale, the story of a failed livier's daughter whose tragic downward spiral encompasses all manner of emotions, climates, seasons, landscapes, occupations and communities. She has worked in the 'closed' villages of a resident squire (Marlott and Trantridge), and in the more 'open' community of Talbothays; shut out from each, she will now suffer in the bleakest kind of 'closed' – and dying – village, before drifting into the urban

alienation of the 'glittering novelty', Sandbourne. Hardy's knowledge of historical geography and rural sociology structures his
novelistic vision like the map of a drowned landscape, whose islands
are really the peaks of a seldom-remembered country. His
understanding of its contours is part of his unique countryman's
heritage, an awareness both of those visible islands, and of the
flooded, immemorial valleys of a vanishing way of life.

I hope that my discussion in this chapter of Hardy's relationship to
rural change has shown how his vision of that change was identified
not with the decline of high farming, or with the influx of modernistic
outsiders into the Wessex countryside, but with an image of the
dispossessed and estranged cottager, for I think that this vision, and
the interlocking of its effects with Hardy's other fictional purposes, is
as strategically important as it is underestimated or misunderstood.
A recent study of English agrarian history holds that

> The decline in village trades and crafts was perhaps less remarked
> upon by contemporaries because it was gradual, spread over the
> better part of a century, and because at its height it was
> overshadowed by the great depression in farming itself. But it was
> much more than a spin-off of the farmers' decline. It was, in fact,
> one of the long-term consequences which flowed from the
> transformation of Britain into an industrialised and urbanised
> society. As such, it has not attracted much attention from
> historians. But it was, nevertheless, highly significant in the rural
> context, for the going of the miller and the maltster, the dying out of
> the packman and pedlar, and the eventual disappearance of the
> saddler, wheelwright and blacksmith made their own conspic-
> uous contribution to the decay of the old country life.[41]

But it is as an artist that we value Hardy, not as a historian or a
sociologist: his work increasingly attracts attention from readers as
far away as Japan, where a knowledge of nineteenth-century Dorset
cottage life is likely to be scanty. Clearly, Hardy's uprooted livier has
accumulated a complex of universal emotions and meanings. The
transitional experiences of Dick Dewy, Stephen Smith, Ethelberta
Petherwin, Clym Yeobright, Michael Henchard, Giles Winterborne,
Grace Melbury, Tess Durbeyfield and Jude Fawley, each painfully
suspended between the two worlds of rural tradition and disruptive
progress, have become paradigms of modern social change, the
birthpangs of the twentieth century.

Such an achievement would be imposible had Hardy consciously
and rigorously dedicated his art to an unqualified celebration of one
particular social group in the English rural community. Perhaps,
therefore, something should immediately be said about the means
by which he transcends this difficulty, for Hardy's close identification of the liviers' plight with the 'ache of modernism' might seem to
suggest a message of simple, unambiguous nostalgia for a vanished
way of life. This does recur in the novels – Creedle's elegy for Giles is
an eloquent example – yet, as I remarked earlier, Hardy strenuously
avoids any implication that the confused present can meaningfully
be judged against the notion of a rosy, idealised past.[42] In a word,
the crucial tone of Hardy's chronicles of social ferment and
dissolution is one of ambivalence, a characteristic which permeates
his work so consistently and profoundly that few critics fail to allude
to it. I find critical definitions of this quality in Hardy to be full of
interest – not least because it is a quality, and indeed an aesthetic
method, which he shares with Faulkner, a strikingly similar
response to a common study of social disorientation – since each
interpretation must try to capture and identify that sense of divided
consciousness felt by Hardy.

F. R. Southerington, for example, sees *Tess* as the product of two
distinct elements: 'the ballad tale of the maiden seduced by the
dashing young squire forms the basis for the book; this basis is
overlaid by a sombre moral commentary which cannot be
ignored'.[43] This 'ballad tale' gives us a natural, 'pure' girl, the
intimate awareness of a sense of place and of the seasons, the
timeless poetry of *Tess*, while the 'sombre moral commentary'
provides a stream of very Victorian, and hence modern, educated
queries, which hold the 'ballad' up to scrutiny. Southerington is
alarmed by this extreme dualism, 'the most crucial critical problem
raised by Hardy's novels',[44] while Michael Millgate, calling Hardy's
usual attitude a balance between 'intellectual progressivism and
emotional conservatism', praises it as reflecting 'a scrupulous
determination to eschew the kind of blinkered simplification
essential to the politician or to the preacher, and to try instead to see
and present things as they are or were, in all their dense and often
confusing complexity'[45] – an illuminating definition which could
also be usefully applied to Faulkner's technique of multiple
perspectives. John Bayley would seem to be in accord with
Southerington in recognising a 'continuing instability' in Hardy's
prose, constantly fluctuating between 'separates' which he disting-

uishes as the poetic sensibility – vivid, romantic, unconscious and unobtrusive – and the formal Victorian novelist, deliberate, solemn, fussy and self-consciously educated, were it not that Bayley praises this instability as a 'harmony of separates', full of a unique intensity and charm.[46]

Raymond Williams seems to summarise Hardy's dualism most succinctly when he defines Hardy's subject as 'the problem of the relation between customary and educated life; between customary and educated feeling and thought'.[47] Bayley's discussion begins with a study of literary form, while Williams approaches Hardy with an interest in his 'exploration of community', an examination of writers' social and cultural viewpoints. Yet each separately arrives at this Hardeian quality of ambivalence as an essential key to an understanding of the novelist's achievement. What, then, is this ambivalence, and what are its results in the novels?

Its origin appears to be intimately bound up with Hardy's early personal experience, and with a gradual realisation of his desire to express it in literature. The novelist was able to examine the turbulent social transition of Wessex from several different perspectives simply because his whole childhood had been socially and culturally ambivalent:

> Owing to the accident of his being an architect's pupil in a county-town of assizes and aldermen, which had advanced to railways and telegraphs and London papers; yet not living there, but walking in every day from a world of shepherds and ploughmen in a hamlet three miles off, where modern improvements were still regarded as wonders, he saw rustic and borough doings in a juxtaposition peculiarly close.... [He lived] a life twisted of three strands – the professional life, the scholar's life, and the rustic life, combined in the twenty-four hours of one day, as it was with him through these years. He would be reading the *Iliad*, the *Aeneid*, or the Greek Testament from six to eight in the morning, would work at Gothic architecture all day, and then in the evening rush off with his fiddle under his arm ... to play country-dances, reels, and hornpipes at an agriculturist's wedding, christening, or Christmas party in a remote dwelling among the fallow-fields.[48]

Later the instinctive dualism broke out again, at the age of 27, contemplating a literary career:

He considered that he knew fairly well both West-country life in its less explored recesses and the life of an isolated student cast upon the billows of London with no protection but his brains.... The two contrasting experiences seemed to afford him abundant materials out of which to evolve a striking socialistic novel.[49]

Bayley discovers an ambivalence of form in the novels, and Williams celebrates their ambivalence of content. This is no coincidence. The evident evolution of Hardy's true subject of 'customary and educated life', by a date as early as 1867,[50] is closely coupled with an equally ambivalent allegiance of viewpoint, for in his work form mirrors content, and vice versa, to an uncanny degree. A full discussion of this proposition will have to wait until a later chapter; meanwhile, as Williams's essay remarks,

> To see tradition both ways is indeed Hardy's special gift.... He sees as a participant who is also an observer; this is the source of the strain. For the process which allows him to observe is clearly in Hardy's time one which includes, in its attachment to class feelings and class separations, a decisive alienation... [with] spurts of bitterness and nostalgia.[51]

Again, we may be reminded of Faulkner and Mississippi. But what I am most anxious to demonstrate at this point is that Hardy's background as the educated son of a Dorset livier, rising out of a vanishing but culturally vital class during a period of unparalleled social upheaval, placed him in a very sensitive relationship to rural change: one uniquely enabled to experience and assess its effects to the full. With the new insights which detailed biographies have brought into the conflicts, suppressions and vicissitudes of Hardy's personal life, it becomes evident that in describing the painfully insecure and transitional consciousness of a character like Grace Melbury, Hardy is really exploring his own dilemma, a

> peculiar situation as it were in mid-air between two storeys of society

and this impressionable creature, who combined modern nerves with primitive feelings ... was doomed by such co-existence ... to take her scourgings to their exquisite extremity. (*TW*, pp. 246, 325)

Hardy's personal experience of upward mobility seems to have been, if challenging and enlightening, also traumatic. He became a kind of spiritual exile who wrote, as in their different ways Joyce and Lawrence and Faulkner would after him, out of the pain of estrangement from a childhood world perceived by each writer as anachronistic, flawed, and yet fiercely cherished. For example, Gittings's biography suggests that

> In early life [Hardy] had to fight the massive social stratification of the Victorian age. Finally he broke through from one class to another; but one can only guess what violence this did to his own nature.... The gulf between someone with whom he could talk freely in an educated way, and one of his own background, who, however full of simple wisdom, could literally not speak the language which Hardy had acquired, haunted his mind.
>
> In the world of letters and society, he appeared strange and withdrawn, a man nursing an inner secret. In the world of his Dorset upbringing, he appeared, except to his close family, as one who had deserted them.[52]

Like that other Victorian master, Dickens, Hardy obsessively describes over and over again (but with a wonderful variety of means) what might have been *his* fate had he not 'escaped' into literature and a higher class: the homeless and jilted Giles, the exploited and persecuted Tess, the frustrated, defeated Jude. But unlike Dickens's glimpses into the hell of urban poverty, Hardy's protagonists frequently yearn for the traditional life they left behind, only to discover that the native cannot meaningfully return. This too is often a tragic process, but Hardy is not unaware of its comic aspects:

> The fact was that Yeobright's fame had spread to an awkward extent before he left home.... At the age of six he had asked a Scripture riddle: 'Who was the first man known to wear breeches?' and applause had resounded from the very verge of the heath. At seven he painted the Battle of Waterloo with tiger-lily pollen and blackcurrant juice, in absence of water-colours. By the time he reached twelve he had in this manner been heard of as an artist and scholar for at least two miles round. An individual whose fame spreads three or four thousand yards in

the time taken by the fame of others similarly situated to travel six or eight hundred, must of necessity have something in him.

'A man who is doing well elsewhere wouldn't bide here two or three weeks for nothing', said Fairway. 'He's got some project in's head – depend upon that.'

'Well, 'a can't keep a diment shop here', said Sam.   (*TROTN*, pp. 192–4)

One feels here the problematic relationship between 'customary' and 'educated' life, even in its infancy: rendered with great economy, and an alternation of affection and irony. By a further sophistication of psychology anticipating Lawrence, Hardy's protagonists sometimes even seek a bucolic simplicity which they never really knew, for a part of Hardy is identified with Fitzpiers and Angel Clare, as well as with their victims. The novelist's attitude of wry, apparently disinterested empathy remains continually alert to all the ironic consequences of rapid social change:

Dorset labourers now look upon an annual removal as the most natural thing in the world, and it becomes with the younger families a pleasant excitement. Change is also a certain sort of education.... They have become shrewder and sharper men of the world, and have learnt how to hold their own with firmness and judgement.

They are also losing their peculiarities as a class; hence the humorous simplicity which formerly characterised the men and the unsophisticated modesty of the women are rapidly disappearing ... they have ceased to be so local in feeling or manner as formerly, and have entered on the condition of inter-social citizens, 'whose city stretches the whole country over' ... that seclusion and immutability, which was so bad for their pockets, was an unrivalled fosterer of their personal charm.... But the artistic merit of their old condition is scarcely a reason why they should have continued in it when other communities were marching on so vigorously towards uniformity and mental equality. It is only the old story that progress and picturesqueness do not harmonize. They are losing their individuality, but they are widening the range of their ideas, and gaining in freedom. It is too much to expect them to remain

stagnant and old-fashioned for the pleasure of romantic specta-
tors....

Thus ... they have lost touch with their environment and that
sense of long local participancy which is one of the pleasures of
age.... On the other hand, new varieties of happiness evolve
themselves like new varieties of plants, and new charms may have
arisen among the classes who have been driven to adopt the
remedy of locomotion for the evils of oppression and poverty –
charms which compensate in some measure for the lost sense of
home.   (*TDL*, pp. 12–14)

Here, in the condensed form of an essay, is the mercurial
understanding which so richly illuminates Hardy's novels: at once
shrewd and intimate, yet fluid and wide-ranging in its contemplations. One may well intuit that the sensitivity of such insights stems
from a buried identification with those rootless workers, much as
William Faulkner, although himself from a different class, was to
achieve a powerful dramatic empathy with the dispossessed of the
American South, the sharecroppers and destitute tenant-farmers,
like Mink Snopes or the Armstids. Thomas Hardy seems never to
have escaped a sense of regret for his vanished livier heritage, 'my
simple self that was', and the personal pressures caused by this
transition of consciousness were occasionally visible to others, as
attested by the seemingly puzzled remark of a society lady in 1929
that Hardy had changed, over the previous 30 years, from

> a rather rough-looking man, dressed very unlike his fellows, with a
> very keen alert face and a decided accent of some kind ... [to] a
> refined, fragile, gentle little old gentleman, with ... a gentle and
> smooth voice and polished manners.[53]

This provides, I think, a strangely moving contribution to our
understanding of Hardy's life, and of his novels. A chain of imagery
inspired by this 'lost sense of home' and its attendant insecurity can
be located running throughout his work, testifying both to the
subjective urgency of the experience and – of more importance than
any narrowly biographical significance – to the potential value of
Hardy's lonely, uncertain social trajectory as the raw material of
fiction. It was a peculiarly harrowing journey, and no doubt a very
common and representative one in Victorian England. Hardy's
special genius was to make his estrangement the material of great art.

2

Mississippi: 'the implacable and brooding image'

'out of the old time, the old days'
(Go Down Moses, p. 10)

'You would have to be born there'
(Absalom, Absalom!, p. 361)

My general strategy in this chapter will be to examine the relationship between William Faulkner and his regional background, and to consider his knowledge of life in an obscure area of North Mississippi as the inspiration of his novels. Like Hardy's early-Victorian Dorset, the American South in the first quarter of this century provided a peculiarly rich and provocative perspective from which to contemplate a wide range of social and psychological dilemmas, perhaps because, again like Dorset, its anachronistic and essentially frontier conditions seemed to throw them into sharper focus.[1] As in chapter 1 I shall use a socio-historical essay[2] (Faulkner's *Mississippi*, written in 1953) as a starting-point from which to approach the fiction, biography and social history, hoping by this method to arrive at a better understanding of the regional, social and personal origins of Faulkner's inspiration, his 'discovery of subject'.

I apostrophise the phrase to indicate a concept of some importance and complexity, since in Faulkner's writing 'subject' and 'discovery' seem frequently to be synonymous. His novels grew out of his ambivalent relationship with Mississippi, much as Hardy's creative energies were kindled by the difficult engagement of his 'customary' and 'educated' responses to the world of rural Dorset. In an important sense, each man's writing may be understood as a psychological 'return of the native',[3] representing an attempt to define and reconcile conflicting responses. This can be seen very clearly in *Mississippi*, its heavily autobiographical tone delivered in the third person, when the serenity of the narrative voice is jarred by the unexpected declaration, 'Home again, his native land; he was born of it and his bones will sleep in it; loving it even while hating some of it' (*Miss*, p. 36). Faulkner's love–hate relationship with Mississippi life becomes the leitmotif of the remaining six pages, concluding the essay with a paradox of considerable relevance to his novels: 'Loving all of it even while he had to hate some of it because he knows now that you dont love because: you love despite; not for the virtues, but despite the faults' (*Miss*, pp. 42–3).

Faulkner defines in the essay some of the elements of Mississippi life which he values – the richness of its wilderness, the vitality and eccentric individualism of its social texture, the patience and courage of its people. Simultaneously, he evokes its darker side, the destruction of the wilderness, the brutality and intolerance of its society. His tone remains scrupulously balanced, and where a number of other Southern writers, from Thomas Nelson Page through Margaret Mitchell to Erskine Caldwell, might slip into a dogmatic rhetorical insistence upon impeccable Southern virtues, or benighted Southern ignorance and vice, Faulkner chooses to recognise and brood over all of the tensions which characterise his regional subject.[4] In doing this – not just in this essay, of course, but in his novels – Faulkner may be said to have discovered a new subject, one of painful but illuminating ambivalence, among the fragments of decrepit Southern literary and historical stereotypes. In exactly this way, it seems to me, Hardy discovered a new fictional potential in the old sentimental images of quaint rustics and ruined village maidens common to the Victorian English imagination. So the ending of *Mississippi* declares Faulkner's imaginative preference for the equivocal, the compromised, and the ineffable in human experience, rather than the idealised or strictly categorised; a preference which is dramatised in the novels. This discovery finds a striking parallel in Hardy's autobiographical *Life of Thomas Hardy*:

> It is the incompleteness which is loved, when love is sterling and true. That is what differentiates the real one from the imaginary, the practicable from the impossible, the Love who returns the kiss from the Vision that melts away. A man sees the Diana or the Venus in his Beloved, but what he loves is the difference.   (*Life*, p. 239)

Though Hardy's observation is couched in romantic terms, its acceptance of the 'incomplete' or ambiguous qualities in what is loved is discernible not only in the mature love of Marty for Giles, or Giles for Grace, or Gabriel for Bathsheba, but in the acceptance of the harsher side of nature shown by Giles, Marty and Gabriel in their work on the land, just as Faulkner's tall convict or Mink Snopes win our admiration by their stoicism in the face of natural adversity. The struggle to attain equilibrium within a hostile or indifferent environment is also reflected in the social worlds of both writers' novels. Dilsey, Lucas, Gabriel and Marty bravely endure social vicissitudes with patience and steady effort; Elizabeth-Jane and Lucius Priest quietly demonstrate the 'secret ... of making limited opportunities endurable' (*TMOC*, pp. 353–4), 'the ability to cope with environment' (*TR*, p. 103).

This sense of personal equilibrium is, however, a very rare quality among Faulkner's characters. The peculiar tensions of Mississippi life are much more likely to result in violent extremism of one sort or another, or a sense of crippling indecision and conflict, like that experienced by Quentin Compson:

> 'he would seem to listen to two separate Quentins now – the Quentin Compson preparing for Harvard in the South, the deep South dead since 1865 and peopled with garrulous outraged baffled ghosts, listening, having to listen, to one of the ghosts ... and the Quentin Compson who was still too young to deserve yet to be a ghost, but nevertheless having to be one for all that, since he was born and bred in the deep South'. (*AA*, p. 9)

Both subject and tone seem to echo Faulkner's personal remarks about Mississippi, quoted earlier, and it is therefore not surprising that Quentin's final verdict on the South in *Absalom, Absalom!* is a repressed, hysterical scream of 'I dont hate it! I dont hate it!' Part of him, of course, does. A similar, if more creative conflict of feeling seems to be at the very root of Faulkner's writing, as his two introductions to *The Sound and the Fury* make clear ('I have tried to escape and I have tried to indict'),[5] and as several critics have pointed out:

> the aim of all [Faulkner's Yoknapatawpha novels], really, was the same: they were, for him, a way of getting to know his region. Faulkner wanted to embrace the contradictions latent in his background without forfeiting coherence, to describe the mansion and the country store and his own ambivalent feelings about

them in one great variegated portrait; and his stories, or more accurately his gradual invention of Yoknapatawpha County *for* those stories, was his means of achieving this.[6]

> In the world disappearing he saw both grandeur ... and ruthless-ness.... In the world emerging he saw both vulgarity ... and energy.... Thus divided, he began rhetorically to tame not only the mixed world around him but his own mixed response to it ... he wanted to master as well as evoke it.[7]

Like Hardy's Dorset, the world in which Faulkner grew up had very distinctive qualities, and the sense of Southern identity shared by the place and its people was a particularly strong one. Faulkner is trying to 'know' his region through his writing, and he is trying to understand himself as a Southerner; moreover, as a Southern *writer*, a troubled figure who has 'taken the artist in him in one hand and his milieu in the other and thrust the one into the other like a clawing and spitting cat into a croker sack'.[8]

In seeking an understanding of some of the reasons for, and effects of, this peculiarly tense and ambivalent relationship between Faulkner and his region, one must first appreciate that the South in which Faulkner grew up was, in comparison with the mainstream of American life, a distinctly foreign place. Its uniqueness is perhaps most readily established by indicating four historical features of Southern life that were especially applicable to Faulkner's Mississippi: these were the influences of agricultural monopoly, poverty, defeat and slavery, or later, segregation.

The Deep South generally, and Mississippi in particular, remained committed to an unwieldy and oppressive system of agriculture long after the rest of the USA had begun widespread industrialisation. 'King Cotton' spread westwards rapidly after about 1820, its dominance assured by the invention of the cotton gin, the vast area and fertility of land, and the availability of black slave labour, an institution which had until this point been in gradual decline, and which was now dramatically revived.[9] Other than the arrival of cotton mills, the anticipated post-war industrial-isation of the Deep South failed to materialise until the twentieth century. Meanwhile the universal adoption of the invidious system of sharecropping as a replacement for the gang system of slavery ensured that large cotton plantations survived, even expanded, and that the class of independent yeoman farmer declined in both number and prosperity.[10] The practice of crop-lien and chattel mortgage established by this monopoly of cotton plantations resulted, in fact, in a new form of slavery which increasingly affected white sharecroppers as well as black.[11] The effects of this monolithic system of agriculture during Faulkner's lifetime were economic stagnation and social injustice.[12]

The effects upon Faulkner, meanwhile, were to instil in his writing a deep sympathy with the landless dispossessed, admiration for the dogged efforts of those who treat the land with respect rather than rapaciousness, and sympathy for the victims of a harsh agricultural system. The theme is explored through different personae and voices, and, as always in Faulkner's work, the accent is one of ambivalence, falling sometimes upon the unbearable hardships of an anachronistic way of life, sometimes upon a rueful celebration of the traditional virtues. The parallels with Hardy here need little emphasis:

> was it any wonder that a man would look at that inimical irreconcilable square of dirt to which he was bound and chained for the rest of his life, and say to it: *You got me, you'll wear me out because you are stronger than me since I'm just bone and flesh. I can't leave you because I can't afford to, and you know it. Me and what used to be the passion and excitement of my youth until you wore out the youth and I forgot the passion, will still be here next year with the children of our passion for you to wear that much nearer the grave, and you know it; and the year after that, and the year after that, and you know that too. And not just me, but all my tenant and cropper kind that have immolated youth and hope on thirty or forty or fifty acres of dirt that wouldn't nobody but our kind work because you're all our kind have.* (TM, p. 88)

Mink Snopes is clearly a victim, crucified like Tess Durbeyfield by an oppressive social system which he recognises, but cannot change.

Common to many of Faulkner's portrayals of farming in Yoknapatawpha is a pervasive sense of economic and social stagnation, with widespread poverty. The South has been the poorest region of the USA ever since the Civil War, and Mississippi has been consistently its most disadvantaged state.[13] The consequences of this poverty during Faulkner's lifetime were similar to phenomena described in Hardy's *The Dorsetshire Labourer* – intensive urban migration, a social atmosphere of disorientation and decline, and a questioning of traditional values, the resultant changes seeming the more traumatic because of their long-belated appearance. The 'New South' was popularly assumed to have come into being amidst the restlessness and optimism of the 1920s, exemplifying, in the words of W. J. Cash,

> the infection of the general spirit of the times. With the patriotic faith in Progess already drilled into them for forty years, with every platform and newspaper full of Prosperity and the dream of the greater South to come, all the ambitious sort, in industry and on the land alike, entered into the prevailing romantic belief and feverish expectancy.

> [T]he immediate effect of almost sudden contact with [the modern ideology] was apt to be the collapse of old standards without the creation of adequate new ones.[14]

This febrile atmosphere is remarkably similar to that evoked in Hardy's descriptions of mid-Victorian Wessex, for example in 'The Fiddler of the Reels', which stirred his restless young protagonists into unfocussed yearnings for another life much as Bayard Sartoris, Darl Bundren, Lena Grove or Joe Christmas travel, in their different ways, without arriving. The dream of prosperity and the collapse of old standards is also obviously closely related to the rise of the Snopeses and the eclipse of traditional craftsmen, such as Giles Winterborne or the blacksmith Trumbull, whose bewildered customers are greeted one morning by the new lessee, the voluble I. O. Snopes:

> Well, gentlemen, off with the old and on with the new. Competition is the life of trade, and though a chain ain't no stronger than its weakest link, I don't think you'll find the boy yonder no weak reed to have to lean on once he catches onto it.   (*TH*, p. 61)

Here one recognises the triumph of a shallow, alien modernism and empty 'words' over traditional taciturnity and 'doing'. The contrast, and Jack Houston's contempt for the new regime, are sharply reminiscent of Gabriel Oak's scorn of Sergeant Troy's slipshod farm management. Faulkner reports the old blacksmith's departure with laconic pathos:

He drove through the village with his wife, in a wagon loaded with household goods. If he looked toward his old shop nearby, nobody saw him do it – an old man though still hale, morose and efficient.... They never saw him again.   (*TH*, p. 61)

The reader's sympathy for Trumbull, and appreciation of the underlying social significance of the change, is encouraged by one further felicitous detail. The evicted smith has left his successor, in place of the can of coal oil used to light the forge, a rusty can of 'hog piss'; but Snopes cannot tell the difference (*TH*, pp. 58–9).

It is important to note that the rise of the Snopeses is at first a *qualitative* type of social change – Frenchman's Bend, after all, still requires a blacksmith – and in Faulkner's novels it is this sense of inharmonious disturbance and deterioration which prevails, rather than a truly violent and wholesale intrusion of modernism. For Mississippi, like Dorset, remained stubbornly impervious to the modern world: during Faulkner's lifetime it maintained an astonishing contiguity with the nineteenth century. A recent Mississippi historian, John Ray Skates, suggests that the watershed between traditional and modern eras in the state's history was as recent as 1940.[15]

Another crucial factor in the South's unique and troubled history was its experience of tragedy and defeat in the Civil War, unknown to the rest of the USA until the era of Vietnam. While the rest of America enjoyed a century of moral and ideological complacency, the post-war South contemplated failure, economic decline and the dream of its former greatness.[16]

Faulkner's novels explore this intense awareness of the past through a variety of personae, each of whom reacts to the experience in different ways. Gavin Stevens, for example, is a lawyer of an intellectual and philosophical cast of mind. Explaining to his nephew what it means to be a Southerner, he remarks that

It's all *now* you see.... For every Southern boy fourteen years old, not once but whenever he wants it, there is the instant when it's still not yet two o'clock on that July afternoon in 1863; the brigades are in position behind the rail fence; the guns are laid and ready in the woods...waiting for Longstreet to give the word...because you escape nothing, you flee nothing...and tomorrow night is nothing but one long sleepless wrestle with yesterday's omissions and regrets.   (*IITD*, pp. 187–9)

The passage's sense of the all-pervasive influence of the past, and of past actions, is characteristic of Southern culture generally; but the conscious echoes of *Macbeth* are Faulkner's own, and add to the reader's knowledge of Gavin Stevens.

The Civil War was not the only skeleton in the Southern closet. The fourth distinguishing feature of Southern historical experience was a buried awareness of guilt and insecurity aroused by the institution of slavery. White inhabitants of the Old South profited by the exploitation of black slaves, but their gains were undermined by a regional psychology emphasising human imperfection, guilt and vulnerability. Perhaps, indeed, Faulkner's frequent echoes of *Macbeth* are regional rather than personal in origin. W. R. Taylor's study *Cavalier and Yankee* convincingly establishes a recurrent theme of imminent apocalypse and doom in Southern ante-bellum literature, exemplified by images of ruined plantations and 'neurasthenic' gentlemen-heroes, the ancestors of Quentin Compson.[17] Taylor sees the prevalence of Southern fatalism as intimately related to self-doubts concerning slavery, and fear of black insurrection.[18] This sense of secret racial guilt and insecurity began to be reflected in Southern novels as early as the 1830s,[19] and it represents another regional characteristic which would become an important imaginative resource in Faulkner's fiction. Slavery might have been formally abolished in 1865, but its economic and psychological effects were perpetuated for another century by the abandonment of Reconstruction and by the establishment in the later nineteenth century of black disenfranchisement, Jim Crow laws and a concept of white supremacy to which all classes of the white South paid allegiance.[20] Somehow, of course, meaningful relationships between black and white Southerners still persisted, and they find their place in Faulkner's work. But the social climate in which he lived his life, and in which his novels are set, was uncompromisingly one of institutionalised racism, and his work expresses a belief that the ultimate victims of this sytem were the white racists themselves.

Mississippi vehemently denounces the state's condonement of racial 'intolerance and injustice ... inequality' (p. 37), while its warmest affection is lavished on Caroline, 'matriarchal and imperial', the ex-slave who was Faulkner's surrogate mother.[21] She is Caroline Barr (1840–1940), to whom he dedicated *Go Down, Moses*, a cycle of related stories which explore the many varieties and repercussions of racial guilt. While this quality can be detected as an undercurrent in early Southern literature, it was more often defensively repressed,[22] or concealed by layers of sentimental romance and comedy.[23] In *Go Down, Moses* Faulkner directly confronts and uses these evasive responses: the South's traditional racial stereotypes are continually probed, and their underlying reality distinguished from their surface appearances. The founder of the McCaslin dynasty is revealed as a heartless egotist who seduced his own black grand-daughter; the McCaslin with most self-possession and dignity is a black bootlegger; the greatest wisdom is to be found in an obscure half-breed hunter.

'Was', the first story, shows us the McCaslin plantation in 1859. Uncle Buck and Buddy's attitude to slave ownership is one of disquiet, concealed by a ritualised lifestyle of gentlemanly ceremony. They disapprove of slavery and allow considerable freedom to their slaves, yet maintain nominal control by locking them up at night in a house with no back door (*GDM*, p. 200). They hunt their runaway slave Tomey's Turl with dogs, though well aware that he is actually their half-brother, 'that damn white half McCaslin' (p. 11). But the dogs desire only to lick rather than bite a familiar companion, and the aim of this 'good race' is to protect Buck from the unwelcome attentions of a predatory spinster at Turl's destination, rather than to punish the runaway. Despite their efforts, Buck is eventually outwitted by an unholy alliance of the slave and the Beauchamp womenfolk, the supposedly inferior and powerless. The rueful tone of the story is that of a po-faced tall tale, deliberately drawing attention to the bizarre irony of its characters' self-deceptions:

> He reached out and tilted the lampshade, the light moving up Tomey's Turl's arms that were supposed to be black but were not quite white, up his Sunday shirt that was supposed to be white but wasn't quite either, that he put on every time he ran away just as Uncle Buck put on the necktie each time he went to bring him back. (*GDM*, p. 29)

The overall effect of this tone, like the characters' behaviour, is highly equivocal. One responds to the story's quasi-legendary humour, yet flinches at its underlying implications. The apparent brutality of slavery is softened by whimsical rituals, yet it is clearly degrading in its effects upon both races. Buck and Buddy demonstrate one eccentric, unsatisfactory way of coping with racial problems: later generations of the family will dramatise other experiences. Meanwhile in 'Was' Faulkner has rearranged the familiar stock images of plantation slavery to form a wholly new and bewildering picture.

One general premise of my comparative analysis is that Faulkner's exploration of the human damage caused by racial injustice finds a thematic parallel in Hardy's examination of the effects of class prejudice. In each case an inflexible code of attitudes and conduct is shown to cripple sensibilities and to warp relationships, in fiction which combines great authenticity of social detail with a tragic and expressionistic vision of suffering humanity. The affinity is primarily emotional and humanistic, and it would be misleading to gloss over the differences of subject and literary treatment which obviously exist. In Hardy's Wessex, a livier can move from one social class to a higher (or lower) one, albeit with difficulty. But the choices of Faulkner's black characters are more drastically limited, for they cannot change the colour of their skin,[24] and caste restrictions are therefore immutable. Similarly, Hardy came himself from humble livier stock, but Faulkner could never know what it was like to be a black man in Mississippi. Hence – perhaps wisely – he never fully internalises a black character's consciousness: Darwin Turner remarks that as Faulkner's career progressed, 'he learned to comprehend Blacks better or – which is as important – to understand that he did not know them as well as he once thought he had'.[25] We can see this awareness, for instance, in Quentin's reflection that black people

> come into white people's lives ... in sudden sharp black trickles that isolate white facts for an instant in unarguable truth like under a microscope; the rest of the time just voices that laugh when you see nothing to laugh at, tears when no reason for tears.   (*TSATF*, p. 154)

Hardy, coming from a society where social divisions were, however severe, not insuperable, did not have to contend with the psychological tensions facing the white Southern writer, comprising the inherited experiences of slavery and defeat in Civil War, and a literary mythology devoted to glamorisation and nostalgia. A Wessex vicar who marries his parlour-maid may commit 'social suicide' (*LLI*, p. 41), but he is spared the extreme intolerance and violence (lynch mobs, legally sanctioned segregation) which characterised Mississippi in Faulkner's day and which, towards the end of his life, seemed to be nearing a crisis point.[26] This dissimilarity in social climate is probably of relevance to the final dissimilarity of Hardy and Faulkner's literary careers. The course of Hardy's art after *Jude* lay towards poetry, the development of a quiet, ironic and essentially *private* vision of human foibles. The pressures on Faulkner were rather different, and in the 1950s he felt it increasingly his duty to adopt the public role of spokesman on racial matters for a lonely brand of Southern liberalism. Accordingly, later novels, such as *Intruder in the Dust*, *Requiem for a Nun* and *A Fable*, reflect this overtly didactic role.

However, I am chiefly concerned here with Faulkner's major novels (which I would define as ending with *Go Down, Moses*). Within their scope, I would point to two important ways in which Hardy's preoccupation with class separation and Faulkner's with racial separation can be usefully seen to converge, in the expression of a sense of human loss and waste, and the refutation of social stereotypes.

Irving Howe identifies a 'central image...of memory and longing' in Faulkner's treatment of black characters,[27] indicative of an urge to break down inter-racial barriers. Much of the troubled energy underlying works like *The Sound and the Fury*, *Absalom, Absalom!* and *Go Down, Moses* clearly derives from Faulkner's awareness of the tragic results of his society's racism, including an emotional deprivation often unconsciously exposed by white characters' fond memories of the inter-racial friendships of their childhood.[28] This seems to be emotionally akin to Hardy's 'lost sense of home', particularly that recurrent nostalgia for a simpler, humbler existence associated with rural childhood felt by Angel or Ethelberta.[29] The two sensations have different origins but both express an uneasy dissatisfaction with the social status quo, and a longing for some lost innocence.

The novels of Hardy and Faulkner continue this critique by expressing the hollowness of social stereotypes based upon class or racial discrimination. Sometimes Hardy comments authorially upon the universality of human emotions and talents, regardless of status;[30] sometimes his characters' crass remarks are self-condemnatory. The first reactions to Tess of both Alec and Angel, for example, reflect the condescending stereotypes of a class-consciousness which deems itself superior: 'what a crumby girl' (p. 72), 'What a fresh and virginal daughter of Nature' (p. 158). Such impoverished assessments can only impede their understanding of

Tess, who combines both of these things and much more besides.[31]

Faulkner's novels censure caste-stereotypes in a closely comparable way, suggesting that an obsessive insistence upon caste status
and the supposed inferiority of blacks actually betrays the secret
insecurities and inadequacies of those vociferous whites. A citizen
of Mottstown, where Joe Christmas is pursued and killed, significantly complains that, 'He never acted like either a nigger or a white
man.... That was what made the folks so mad' (*LIA*, p. 263). The
deputy in 'Pantaloon in Black' is 'a little hysterical' as he protests to
his unconcerned wife that 'them damn niggers ... aint human
... when it comes to the normal human feelings ... they might just as
well be a damn herd of wild buffaloes' (*GDM*, pp. 121–2). But the
understated, beautifully controlled story convinces the reader that
the black protagonist's inconsolable grief for his dead wife betrays
an all-too-sensitive humanity, in pointed contrast with the emotional poverty of the deputy's existence. Moreover, it seems
possible that the deputy has dimly intuited this unacceptable truth,
and that the callous tone of his narrative merely conceals his
'hysterical' suspicions. His wife, however, is not listening; she
wants to clear the table and get to the picture show (*GDM*, p. 125).

The qualities of introspection, isolation, poverty and racial
self-consciousness which set the South of Faulkner's childhood
apart from the rest of the USA also encouraged a peculiar
defensiveness in its regional outlook. The guilt induced by slavery,
the indignation aroused by Northern abolitionism, and the fear of
Yankee domination had a strong unifying effect upon the Old South
before and during the Civil War. A pride in Confederate gallantry
and bitter resentment of Reconstruction continued the process. One
important manifestation of this defensiveness was a sectional
solidarity uniting classes whose interests were otherwise antipathetic – the emergence of the 'Solid South',[32] in which poor-white and
rich planter made common cause in their hatred of meddling
Yankees and in their vaunted racial superiority to blacks. The
cynical use of the Negro as a racial scapegoat who conveniently
deflected attention from uncomfortable class issues characterised
Southern politics from Reconstruction until the 1960s, producing a
uniquely unpleasant breed of racist demagogues celebrated in
Faulkner's Senator Clarence Egglestone Snopes.

Another expression of Southern defensiveness was an increasing
'tendency toward unreality'. W. J. Cash, whose phrase I use here,
relates the origins of the Southerner's 'romanticism' and 'hedonism'

to the extravagant landscape and climate, the easy possibilities of subsistence farming, the cultural interrelation with the Negro, and the Southerner's large admixture of Celtic, 'Scotch–Irish' ancestry.[33] What is more certain is that the South's political and cultural insecurity from about the 1830s onwards accelerated this nascent fondness for mythicising its own image, expressed chiefly in the cotton planter's claim to the rank of aristocracy. This claim was almost wholly bogus, as Cash has convincingly shown.[34] Most of the South was not far removed from rough frontier conditions in ante-bellum days, and this was especially true of Mississippi. The typical Mississippi planter was an adventurer from the Carolinas, like Lucius Quintus Carothers McCaslin or Jason Lycurgus Compson I, possessing courage, luck and determination rather than a glorious lineage. Nevertheless, the myth of an authentic Southern aristocracy remains significant in that, while bogus, it was widely accepted not only by Southerners themselves but by the victorious Yankees: the courtly Southern gentleman provided a highly convenient and attractive focus for romantic dreams of a vanished agricultural, pre-industrial past.[35] The Southern penchant for romanticised self-delusions was to provide Faulkner with another potent area of subject-matter, beginning with the careful ambivalences of *Sartoris*:

> Virginia Due Pré ... told them of the manner of Bayard Sartoris' death prior to the second battle of Manassas. She had told the story many times since ... and as she grew older the tale itself grew richer and richer, taking on a mellow splendor like wine; until what had been a hare-brained prank of two heedless and reckless boys wild with their own youth had become a gallant and finely tragical focal point to which the history of the race had been raised from out the old miasmic swamps of spiritual sloth by two angels valiantly fallen and strayed....
>
> That Carolina Bayard had been rather a handful even for Sartorises. Not so much a black sheep as a nuisance.... His high-colored face wore that expression of frank and high-hearted dullness which you imagine Richard First as wearing before he went Crusading. (*Sartoris*, pp. 6–7)

Faulkner's immediate subject here is not the past itself, but 'old tales and talking' (*AA*, p. 303): we are being shown a highly subjective form of history. Faulkner's tone maintains a nice equilibrium between involvement and detachment, between surges of rhetoric and sudden dips into bathos. *Sartoris* is written from a wholly authorial perspective; Faulkner's use of multiple narrators and viewpoints does not begin until his second Yoknapatawpha novel, *The Sound and the Fury*. But his deliberate portrayal of Bayard III and Horace Benbow as different, extreme types of romantic Southern escapists – the one seeking oblivion in gratuitous violence, the other in futile dreams and rhetoric – shows a growing ability to adapt the strange contortions of the Southern psyche to his own creative purposes.[36]

The third important manifestation of Southern defensiveness, closely related to the tendencies toward retrospection and unreality, was a violent intolerance of all dissent from Southern conventions, especially those of race. Originating in hatred of abolitionism, this intolerance quickly spread to prohibit any form of intellectual or religious free thought, any sign of racial or sexual irregularity, until by the end of Reconstruction it formed 'the savage ideal ... where-under dissent and variety are completely suppressed and men become, in all their attitudes, professions, and actions, virtual replicas of one another'. Writing in 1941, Cash compares this totalitarian atmosphere to that 'in Fascist Italy, in Nazi Germany, in Soviet Russia'.[37] Yet unlike these nations, totalitarianism in the South was not directed or maintained by a strong central government, but by the spontaneous will of the mass of the (white) population, and expressed through a welter of popular institution-alised violence – lynchings, beatings, ostracism and murder.[38] The worst period for these atrocities was during the 1890s, the decade of Faulkner's birth. *Mississippi* fiercely declares that 'most of all he hated the intolerance and injustice: the lynching of Negroes not for the crimes they committed but because their skins were black (they were becoming fewer and fewer ... but ... there should never have been any); the inequality ... the bigotry' (pp. 37–8).

During his career as a novelist, Faulkner's work was, like Hardy's, to become increasingly critical of reactionary social institutions and a repressive social conformity. A major theme of his novels from the later 1920s onwards is therefore that of a search for justice, struggling against racial and class prejudice and the corruption which accompanies it. Horace Benbow attempts to save Lee Goodwin from a lynch mob, and to aid the despised Ruby Lamar; Joe Christmas searches in vain for a secure racial identity, while Charles Bon seeks acknowledgement from his white father,

Thomas Sutpen, who is himself obsessed by a 'design' conceived to combat the planter oligarchy; Isaac McCaslin tries to make restitution to the exploited black members of his family; Chick Mallison saves Lucas Beauchamp from a lynch mob. Even the most cursory consideration of these protagonists' histories shows that Faulkner is no smug liberal composing agreeably complacent protest novels. Like Jude Fawley, his dissidents are idealists with a lot to learn, and Faulkner is as keen to explore their internal development or disillusion as he is to chronicle their actions. Rebellion and reform are therefore examined as ambivalently as the failings of society. Horace Benbow, for example, fails to save Goodwin and remains baffled and rebuked by Ruby. He is traumatised by the glimpse into evil which Temple's narrative affords him, responding with a poetic but wholly impotent death-wish reminiscent of Quentin Compson, and he numbly returns in the end to the empty repetitions of his life with the two Belles.

The best sustained example of the destructive Southern tendency to judge by appearances is probably represented by Jason Compson's section in *The Sound and the Fury*, a *tour de force* of prejudice, cruelty and self-delusion.[39] Jason's bigotry reappears in many different guises in Yoknapatawpha. Some of Faulkner's saddest and bitterest episodes examine the oppressive atmosphere of a small Southern town as most (but never all) of its citizens abdicate their individual consciences in a mindless celebration of intolerance and sadism. Gossip, bigotry and boredom explode into mob violence in *Sanctuary*, *Light in August*, *Absalom, Absalom!*, 'Dry September', *The Wild Palms*, *Go Down, Moses* and *Intruder in the Dust*, and provide an ominous undercurrent to events in many other stories. It is perhaps worth emphasising that Faulkner's depictions of such violence tend to under-represent, rather than exaggerate, its actual occurrence in his local environment, and that his narrative technique deliberately avoids gruesome descriptions.[40] The novelist's intention is not to arouse sheer sensation but to examine psychology and motivation. Joe Christmas's horrible death is presented indirectly, even poetically in its evocation of a crucifixion, and is preceded by a long, dispassionate analysis of his 'too sincere ... humourless' murderer, Percy Grimm, a masterful and prophetic case-history of the psychology of a 'Nazi Storm Trooper', written in 1932 (*LIA*, pp. 338–50).[41]

Light in August also establishes the tragic relationship between this tendency towards self-righteousness and violence, and the repressive, life-denying character of Southern Protestant religion. Faulkner once remarked that, 'I think that the trouble with Christianity is that we've never tried it yet'.[42] His novels, often employing religious imagery, make it clear that Faulkner values the basic teachings of Christ while denouncing the perversions of his Church's dogma: like Hardy, he may be understood as a humanist who respected Christ without deifying him. It is a measure of Faulkner's exceptional wisdom and humanism that when his greatest novels confront intolerance and violence, they move and persuade the reader without becoming mere crude vehicles of protest, and – even more remarkably – without sacrificing a residue of compassion for the perpetrators of these horrors, like the fanatical Percy Grimm. Rather, his attitude of 'loving it even while hating some of it' emerges in a steadfast opposition to any system which regards people as abstractions, as things, rather than as complex, vulnerable humanity.

It should perhaps be stated at this point that I have no wish to fall into the trap of glibly portraying the Mississippi of Faulkner's lifetime as a consistently wretched region of wholesale misery and cruelty, especially since Faulkner's work vigorously enacts the uniqueness of experience and the transcendence of stereotype. His Yoknapatawpha contains an astonishing variety of personalities, lifestyles and attitudes. In part this may be seen as a reaction, not only to that native urge falsely to idealise Dixie, but also to the crudity of that image of Mississippi which obtained elsewhere in the United States. Faulkner's novels try, like *Mississippi*, to make sense of the real tensions and complexity of life in the region, and he is well aware that in the popular American imagination Mississippi represented a distillation of everything Southern, usually meaning an ambiguous, largely negative complex of associatior.s combining fact and myth, as Skates explains:

> Before World War II ... it was ... a symbol of poverty, ignorance, and cultural backwardness. After World War II, the civil-rights movement thrust Mississippi to national notice as a symbol of the worst of the South, a grotesque relic of racism, poverty, ruralism, and violence.... In the minds of some uninformed modern liberal puritans, the state is a symbol of the darkest forces in American history. In the view of unreconstructed romantics, it is a dreamy, contented land filled with Uncle Remuses, devoted mammies, and a white gentry.'[43]

It is easy to see why Mississippi attracted these sensationalised images, for its history abounds in extremes. As stated earlier, it has consistently remained the poorest state in the USA. In Faulkner's lifetime it also had a higher proportion of black inhabitants than any other state – three blacks for every two whites in 1900; about numerically equal in 1940.[44] This ubiquitous black presence doubtless intensified the latent feelings of racial self-consciousness and tension among the white populace, stimulating defensive myths of contented black Sambo figures – such as the role which Quentin finds Deacon playing to Southern students (*TSATF*, pp. 91–3) – which clash uncomfortably with Mississippi's fearsome reputation for racial violence and unyielding white supremacy.[45]

C. V. Woodward suggests that 'the South seems to have been one of the most violent communities of comparable size in all Christendom',[46] and Mississippi was, at the time of Faulkner's birth, arguably its most bloodthirsty state. Life was held exceedingly cheap: in 1890, 106 homicides were recorded in Mississippi compared with only 16 in Massachusetts, 'for all its cities and slums and unassimilated immigrants'.[47] Faulkner's father Murry nearly died from pistol and shotgun wounds resulting from a ludicrously petty quarrel in 1891. His father, trying to avenge the attack, suffered the indignity of misfiring his pistol six times and being shot in the hand: their assailant was acquitted.[48] Earlier in the day on which the Faulkner family moved house to Oxford in 1902, 7000 citizens watched the public hanging of two men who had murdered a federal officer investigating illegal distilling.[49] Mob sadism and violence were to be major themes in Faulkner's fiction, and it is interesting to speculate upon the similarity between his knowledge of this and other local examples of public brutality[50] and Hardy's horrified fascination with public executions in Dorchester during his childhood. Certainly the casual violence which punctuates Faulkner's narratives must be recognised as an accurate reflection of everyday Mississippi reality.[51]

Another, more crucial, relationship between the novels of Hardy and Faulkner concerns their common interest in those figures who felt most keenly the 'ache of modernism', as their respective regions changed. Faulkner's Yoknapatawpha consciously embraces a wide variety of social classes, and the social scene is, of course, complicated by the intricacies of race, but it remains evident that Faulkner focusses in particular upon two traditional class roles which have inspired the mind of the South since colonial days. One of these is the figure of the small yeoman farmer, self-sufficient and contented on his few acres. As Skates has shown, independent yeoman farmers formed the dominant class, numerically, in nineteenth-century Mississippi, though the ascendancy of cotton and the large plantation ensured a steady decline in their number and prosperity, especially in this century, along with the wilderness upon which their lifestyle was based. The other Southern figure is represented by the concept of the gentleman-planter, squire, or feudal aristocrat, supervising his domain with a benevolent paternalism.[52] The colonists who began arriving in Virginia in the seventeenth century considered these ideal roles to have been eclipsed in England, and they vigorously sought to revive them amidst the rich wilderness of the South, enthusiastically described by a settler in 1705 as

> so delightful, and desirable; so pleasant, and plentiful; the Climate, the Air, so temperate, sweet, and wholsome; the Woods, and Soil, so charming, and fruitful; and all other things so agreeable, that Paradice itself seem'd to be there, in its first Native Lustre.[53]

The pioneers' confidence in these ideals and in their new Southern paradise was bolstered by the use of this kind of pleasant pastoral imagery. But the reality of civilising the wilderness proved more problematic, for the settlers were aware of two uncomfortable presences in the Edenic garden: the Indian, embittered by the whites' encroachment on his territory, and the black slave, whose exploitation made the wilderness profitable. The two agrarian ideals of the Old South and their associated qualities of idealism and repressed guilt therefore provided Faulkner with powerful material for fiction. He fashions these traditional figures into a series of ambivalent paradigms of the Southern experience, and Faulkner's treatment of them, in particular that of the small farmer, invites close comparison to Hardy's use of the livier class in the Wessex novels. Both Southern classes are shown in the Yoknapatawpha novels to be in a state of gradual decline, just as Hardy's liviers are. While the figure of the aristocratic planter in Faulkner's work is always dogged, even arguably 'cursed', by his exploitation (actual or inherited) of blacks, Faulkner's treatment of the small farmer is generally warmer and more intimate, though an ambivalence remains present. The MacCallums and Lucas Beauchamp are probably the most attractive examples of the type, which shades into an ambitious merchant and landlord class at one extreme (the

Varners) and landless poor-whites at the other (Ab Snopes, Wash Jones).[54] The best of Faulkner's small farmers, like Hardy's livier-craftsmen, are resourceful, shrewd, adept in many traditional rural skills, and proud of their independent class status, their ways of life demonstrating a simple dignity. The description of Bayard Sartoris's stay with the MacCallum family in *Sartoris* provides one of the novel's most memorable episodes. Its lovingly-evoked scenes, of hunting in the frosty December hills and of the rough hospitality of the bachelor household in its rambling log-chinked home, full of dogs underfoot, corn whiskey and talk of familiar things, offer an elegiac reminder of all the rich traditional folk-life from which Bayard's modernistic despair excludes him. Virginius MacCallum's contempt for his sons' intention of buying a turkey for Christmas dinner reflects the true consciousness of the independent yeoman, and he speaks in a voice which, dialect notwithstanding, is recognisably Hardeian:

> 'Buyin' turkeys,' Mr MacCallum repeated with savage disgust. 'Buyin' em. I mind the time when I could take a gun and step out that ere do' and git a gobbler in thutty minutes. And a ven'son ham in a hour mo'. Why, you fellers don't know nothin' about Christmas. All you knows is sto' winders full of cocoanuts and Yankee popguns and sich.'   (*Sartoris*, pp. 248–9)

Faulkner clearly sympathises with the modest virtues of this way of life, and it is perhaps significant that after he bought a farm in the 1930s, he enjoyed describing himself as a farmer rather than a writer, and chose to raise on it corn, hay and mules (not very successfully) rather than cotton.[55] Yet Faulkner maintains a certain detachment from his small farmers: they are usually secondary rather than primary figures in his fiction. One reason for this is probably biographical. The gulf between the intellectual who loves the country from a distance, and uneducated country people who take for granted their intimacy with the land, is an ironic reflection of the ache of modernism found in both novelists' work and lives. Hardy and Faulkner both uneasily suspected that they had substituted *writing* about their regions for the more intimate and unselfconscious integration which they might otherwise have enjoyed.[56] This particular sense of loss was expressed in Hardy's wistful desire to have been a country archi-tect, or Faulkner's repeated use of metaphors of carpentry to describe the writer's craft,[57] as well as in a succession of idealistic intellectuals like Clym, Fitzpiers, Angel, Bayard, Horace and Hightower, who find that assimilation into traditional rural life and society is not as easy as they had hoped. Faulkner's brother John comments that

> I think Bill liked to talk about hunting almost as much as he liked hunting itself. He'd stop by the places where his hunting cronies worked and talk to them by the hour, usually working himself into a fidget to get back to the woods. But as the years passed he seldom got around to actually going ... he collected literature about farming and really studied it. He talked well about crops, though he had never actually made one.[58]

A second and more important reason for Faulkner's tangled attitudes toward Southern farmers is contained within his view of the history of his region. His fiction boldly synthesises two aspects of Mississippi's colonisation, massive land claims and chattel slavery, as interrelated elements in a single process of cultural corruption. This is both historically justifiable and philosophically persuasive. It is a historical commonplace that the South's determined retention and even extension of the institution of slavery in the nineteenth century doomed the region to a sense of isolation from the rest of the world which exacerbated the slide towards Civil War.[59] It is much less widely appreciated that Mississippi's long-established reputation for its own special sense of isolation arguably originates in the huge land cessions, amounting to two-thirds of the state, wrung from the Choctaws and Chickasaws between 1820 and 1832 by the US Government's use of 'bribery and drink ... threats and promises ... [of] only two alternatives – extinction or forcible removal'.[60] Thus Skates considers that these sordid transactions

> set Mississippi on a different road ... that led not only to secession and civil war but, afterwards, to a peculiarity and insularity remarkable for its persistence.... The Indian cessions tripled the public lands available for settlement and provoked explosive changes.... As the nation moved toward industrialization, Mississippi's agrarianism prospered. As the nation became more critical of slavery, Mississippi's slave population zoomed upward.... Education ... remained dormant.... The promising

development of some urban life was curbed by the availability of cheap new public lands. Towns ... failed to grow, a pattern that for a century after 1830 would keep Mississippi one of the most rural states in the nation.[61]

Of course, other states seized land from Indians and experienced booms in land speculation and slavery. But the suddenness, scale and repercussions of Mississippi's 'flush times' were unusually dramatic, causing an enormous expansion of land settlement, especially that involving cotton plantation and slavery, in a very short time.[62] Skates concludes that the social patterns and conflicts which would dominate Mississippi life for more than a century were established by 1840, and changed little thereafter.[63]

The violence and unscrupulousness of these patterns of settlement are reflected in Faulkner's chronicle of Yoknapatawpha. His theme of dual exploitation consists of a betrayal of the land, by buying and selling it for greed and self-aggrandisement, and a betrayal of man's common humanity, through the crime of slavery. This process resembles a mythic paradigm of man's Fall, conceived in Southern terms but of universal application. The results of the land's exploitation are as damaging to the perpetrators as the psychological recoil of racism: what man imposes on his victims, he does ultimately to himself. Faulkner makes the point explicitly in *Go Down, Moses*,[64] but its impact is often more powerful when the sense of modernistic futility is conveyed dramatically by objective correlatives, like the grimly identical 'matchboxes' of bungalows spreading over the former grandeur of the 'Compson Mile', or the chaotic obsolescence of Doane's Mill:

> gaunt, staring, motionless wheels rising from mounds of brick rubble and ragged weeds with a quality profoundly astonishing, and gutted boilers lifting their rusted and unsmoking stacks with an air stubborn, baffled and bemused upon a stumppocked scene of profound and peaceful desolation, unplowed, untilled, gutting slowly into red and choked ravines beneath the long quiet rains of autumn and the galloping fury of vernal equinoxes. (*LIA*, p. 6)

Man has created his own wilderness; and indeed Faulkner's novels explore what might be called a wilderness of human nature. The uncertain conditions of frontier Mississippi and the strange vicissitudes of its history encouraged distinctively wild and idiosyncratic tendencies among its inhabitants. In *Mississippi*, the state is defined as a 'land of individualists' exemplified by the farmer who, during floods, 'patrolled his section of levee with a sandbag in one hand and his shotgun in the other, lest his upstream neighbour dynamite it to save his (the upstream neighbor's) own' (*Miss*, p. 25). The novels are full of such fiercely independent characters. If one seeks a common pattern in the behaviour of Faulkner's 'individualists', it may be said to reside in the qualities of tenacity and capriciousness which were the heritage of the frontier. Hence the 'dreamlike' and slightly sinister encounter with the 'mud-far-mer' of Hell Creek is richly comic, while also revealing the crafty opportunism and fierce pride of back-country life (*TR*, pp. 73–8). Miss Reba's tale of the Memphis police commissioner discovered upstairs in her brothel 'bucknekkid, dancing the highland fling. A man fifty years old, seven foot tall, with a head like a peanut', similarly testifies both to the raffish individualism of the Southern temperament, and to Rèba's own boozy self-esteem ('He was a fine fellow. He knew me') (*Sanctuary*, p. 114). Miss Emily Grierson's ghoulish preservation of her faithlesss suitor's corpse expresses the equal potential for tragedy, lurking in an individualistic will turned rank by years of introspection. More representative is a marked tendency to watchful, stoical resourcefulness, exemplified by Mrs Littlejohn's prompt dispatching of the wild pony which invades her porch, or Mannie Hait's revenge upon I. O. Snopes and his mule.[65]

These two latter examples serve to indicate Faulkner's regional debt to the Southwestern humorists, and his ability to reshape traditional genres, as did Twain, for his own creative purposes. The Snopes trilogy in particular deftly integrates scenes of backwoods violence and humour with those of the most impassioned poetry, so that the reader's perspective upon the characters never quite remains fixed; they prove, indeed, to be almost as elusive as the creatures of the wilderness. This slippery narrative quality represents one of the particular pleasures of reading a Faulkner novel, and I would emphasise its uncanny resemblance to Hardy's fluctuations of tone. The shifting and unpredictable character of the Faulknerian narrative may also be seen as related to the essential moral ambiguity and social complexity underlying so many forms of behaviour in Yoknapatawpha. The dilemmas faced by Faulkner's protagonists (and those of Hardy) take on a special urgency, poignancy and ambiguity because their choices of response are so often unbalanced by the tensions of their transitional environment.

In other words, I am arguing that Faulkner discovered powerful universal archetypes and paradigms of the transition from a traditional to a modern society lying latent in the instability of frontier and post-frontier Mississippi society, much as Hardy did in Dorset, and that the character of these regional exemplars helped to shape both his narrative style and his moral vision. Faulkner recognised that the primitive conditions of Mississippi demanded particular qualities, and that the peculiarities of the region's history and culture influenced the development of its society in specific ways. Settlers of a wild, anarchic land needed to possess courage, determination, self-reliance and pride; but inevitably these pioneering qualities included a darker side, expressed in the abuses of slavery, greed for land and agricultural profits, social inequalities and Cash's 'savage ideal'. Much of the tragedy in the Yoknapatawpha cycle derives from the fatal ease with which the original pioneers' bold qualities can be equally well defined as self-perpetuating ruthlessness and exploitation. The 'design' of Thomas Sutpen provides perhaps the most comprehensive example of this process.

Sutpen's childhood in the mountains of West Virginia possesses Edenic overtones associated with the settlement of an ideal New World, since

> where he lived the land belonged to anybody and everybody ... he didn't even know there was a country all divided and fixed and neat with a people living on it all divided and fixed and neat because of what colour their skins happened to be and what they happened to own   (*AA*, p. 221)

When Sutpen is ten, his family move down into Tidewater, plantation Virginia, and he begins to notice racial and class distinctions, though in his 'innocence' he considers them due to 'luck'. One day he is sent to deliver a message to a rich planter's house. He wears shabby old clothes, and a sneering black house-servant tells him 'never to come to the front door again but to go around to the back' (p. 232). Sutpen experiences a traumatic epiphany, recognising how he and his family appear to other more privileged Southerners, 'as cattle, heavy and without grace' (p. 235). Nevertheless, Sutpen is intelligent enough to attribute his humiliation not to the slave but to the caste system of his owner, and to see that to combat them you got to have what they have ... land and niggers and a fine house.... He left that night ... rising from the pallet and tiptoeing out of the house. He never saw any of his family again.

He went to the West Indies.   (p. 238)

Sutpen's 'design' is conceived to 'combat' this caste system, and although details of how he hopes to do this remain unclear, it evidently involves the democratisation of relationships between landowner and dispossessed.[66] But in his dangerous 'innocence', he seeks to implement this 'design' by emulating the men whom he opposes, and having by superhuman courage and will-power acquired slaves and a huge plantation, his original aim is wholly obscured by egotistical dynastic ambitions. Tragic ironies become increasingly apparent to the reader. The deadly simplicity with which the boy could abandon his family in pursuit of an abstract idea is repeated in a series of heartless rejections. Sutpen 'puts aside' his first wife, and subsequently refuses to acknowledge their son, because their part-Negro blood is not 'incremental to the design' (p. 240); and he finally rejects his illegitimate white daughter because his 'design' required a male heir. Each of these rejections has, ironically, re-enacted the original contemptuous dismissal which provoked his 'design'. Thus, the minor injustice which occurred in Virginia in 1817 is seen to spread its repercussions across the rest of the South and on into the twentieth century.[67] Thomas Sutpen is arguably a conventionally flawed tragic hero, possessing some interestingly close correspondences with Hardy's Michael Henchard, which I shall examine in a later chapter. The issue which I want to stress here is the delicate moral ambiguity of Faulkner's 'individualists', and the way in which this can be seen to grow out of, and explore, aspects of Faulkner's particular Southern experience.

One further example should help to illuminate this complex relationship: the role of the Snopes clan. Faulkner uses the career of these poor-whites to dramatise his worst fears about modernistic 'progress' in the New South. Originally redneck sharecroppers, they follow the ambitious Flem Snopes's migration into the small towns of Yoknapatawpha, gaining an insidious control over the community by ruthless commercial activity and a total lack of ethics. The Snopeses combine the worst extremes of corruption and racism with a lust for cosmetic respectability, and Faulkner records their rise with profound distaste. But as with most generalisations about his work's meanings, one must immediately balance this damning interpretation of the Snopeses with mitigating factors.

First, the modernistic intruders only gain power because, as in Hardy's rural society, the traditional order was vulnerable through its own innate inadequacies. As Lyall Powers's *Faulkner's Yoknapatawpha Comedy* points out,

> Snopeses appear wherever they can take advantage of human frailty, human weakness.... They represent Evil in an ambivalent way: they are apparently evil themselves ... but in addition to that their presence indicates that human evil (or at least the distinct tendency or liability to do evil) was already present before them. Faulkner spoke of them as being 'like mold on cheese'.[68]

The sinister Snopes aptitude for sharp practice in trade, for example, is not a purely modernistic phenomenon, but has its roots in the traditional system of rural barter and quick-witted individualism which obtained on the frontier. What is significant is that Flem and his tribe develop this art to a new and inhuman degree of perfection. In *The Hamlet* we learn that Jody Varner had frequently short-changed customers in his store, but everyone expected this and, more importantly, he always gave them credit when needed. But when Flem takes over as clerk, he is never found to make mistakes:

> 'You mean ain't nobody ever caught him *once* even?'
> 'No', Bookwright said. 'And folks don't like it. Otherwise, how can you tell?'   (*TH*, p. 53)

To the reader, this is mildly amusing, but it also signifies ominous changes in the quality of traditional life, sharply reminiscent of the contrast in business methods between Henchard and Farfrae.[69] And Flem Snopes refuses to give anyone the accustomed credit (*TH*, pp. 53–4).

To appreciate the full significance of the impact of the Snopeses upon Yoknapatawpha, one must also consider Faulkner's admiration for the occasional decent Snopes like Eck or Wallstreet Panic, alongside his disapproval of the deracinated upper-class establishments of the Compsons and Sartorises, whose abdication of moral leadership allows them to thrive. Secondly, one must acknowledge his growing inclination to stir the reader's sympathies for such dubious Snopeses as Ab, Mink, Montgomery Ward, and even the arch-villain Flem. In the powerful story 'Barn Burning' Ab appears as a violent and ruthless figure, driven like Sutpen by fierce resentment of rich plantation owners and the black servants who symbolise their power. Ab's 'design', however, is arson. The reader sees Ab through the confused and apprehensive eyes of Sarty, his young son: 'he looked again at the stiff black back, the stiff and implacable limp which ... had ... that impervious quality of something cut ruthlessly from tin, depthless' (*DM*, p. 16). Faulkner's exploration of Sarty's ambivalent loyalties, aided by quiet authorial observations, achieves the remarkable effect of blending the reader's instinctive revulsion for Ab's foulmouthed antagonism with a reluctant sympathy for his 'wolf-like independence' (p. 13). Ab habitually burns small domestic fires, 'niggard, almost, a shrewd fire' (p. 13). This is ostensibly the result of Ab's furtive career as a horse-trader during the Civil War, hiding in the woods, but Faulkner adds that, had Sarty been older, he would have intuited

> the true reason: that the element of fire spoke to some deep mainspring of his father's being, as the element of steel or of powder spoke to other men, as the one weapon for the preservation of integrity, else breath were not worth the breathing, and hence to be regarded with respect and used with discretion.   (*DM*, pp. 13–14)

Even an Ab Snopes must preserve some integrity, albeit through arson. As with Thomas Sutpen, courage and independence are disfigured by inflexibility and cruelty: the commitment to an individualistic sense of honour, so highly developed in the South, is double-edged.

Ab, the founder of the Snopes dynasty, remains a countryman, and, significantly, Sarty's sole experience of serenity is when he listens to his father and his companions telling 'long and unhurried' stories of crops, animals and horse-trading (*DM*, pp. 25–6). Ab's oldest son Flem, however, gets out of farming and into urban businesses as swiftly as possible, a pattern which mirrors the similar fragmentation of Hardy's Wessex. It is notable that in both writers' work, the very real vices of traditional rural characters, such as Ab Snopes or Michael Henchard, are contrasted with, and frequently exceeded by, the rather difficult failings of modernistic successors, such as Flem Snopes or Donald Farfrae. In each case an excessively personalised violence and egotism is supplanted by a more calculating form of pragmatism, blander, but arguably more damaging to the human spirit through its new social acceptability and insidiousness.

These contrasts exemplify the clash of different social or psychological 'worlds' upon which Hardy and Faulkner's plots usually revolve. They both grew up during eras when their *national* cultures were full of enthusiasm for 'Progress', a phenomenon viewed by both writers with deep suspicion and distrust. And it was exactly at the point when the two men began to write novels (in 1860s Dorset, in 1920s Mississippi) that their remote and still-intact *regional* cultures began truly to feel the impact of this disorientating stimulus from the larger world outside. Astonishing as it may at first seem, the insularity of 1920s Mississippi was remarkably comparable to that of Dorset in the 1860s, owing – in Cleanth Brooks's useful phrase – to 'the cultural lag of the South',[70] historically isolated by sectionalism and Civil War in a far more profound and long-lasting way than Victorian Dorset. Each writer's regional environment in those formative years stimulated what Allen Tate has called 'the curious burst of intelligence that we get at a crossing of the ways'.[71] The comparable insularity and vulnerability of the two environments is aptly demonstrated by the influx of modern transport, and by the writers' reaction to it – in Hardy's case to trains, and in Faulkner's to automobiles and aeroplanes.[72] Each novelist treats the incursion of these symbols of modernism into his primitive rural world with an ambivalent mixture of disturbance and fascination, balancing the potential of new freedoms with the sad loss of accustomed intimacies and parochialisms.[73]

Both the *Mississippi* essay and *Requiem for a Nun* dramatise the onslaught of modernism by a panoramic succession of innovations. The decline of the small 'self-consumer' farmer, and images of rural depopulation, inevitably demand comparison with Hardy's *The Dorsetshire Labourer*: the obsolete figures of the old shepherd and the uprooted livier are paralleled in Mississippi by the mule and the black sharecropper, 'both gone now: the one, to the last of the forty- and fifty- and sixty-acre hill farms inaccessible from unmarked dirt roads, the other to New York and Detroit and Chicago and Los Angeles ghettos' (*RFAN*, p. 206). Faulkner dramatises the full shock of modernism on the nerve-ends in Mink's return to Memphis after release from Parchman, where, like Hardy's John Lackland, he finds that you can't go home again, 'because the Memphis he remembered from forty-four years back no longer

existed' (*TM*, p. 263). Another parallel between Hardy and
Faulkner in the treatment of this theme concerns the remarkable
similarity of the meditative responses shown by Tess and Mink to
the 'hissing' trains that they watch: the unity of incident and
emotion seems almost beyond chance (and possibly is, since we
know that Faulkner had read and brooded over Hardy's work).[74]
Each passage contrasts a humble bucolic consciousness with a train
symbolising disdainful and disruptive modernism, leaving confusion in its wake.[75]

Many of the most powerful examples of this paradigmatic clash of
different 'worlds' relate to conflicts between different social classes
or races. I have already remarked upon the tensions of the
white/Indian frontier, and upon the poor-white/rich planter
relationship. The latter was, of course, often characterised by real
loyalty or genial familiarity instead of (or, sometimes, as well as)
hostility and resentment. Here it is instructive to consider Wash
Jones's dog-like trust in the ageing Thomas Sutpen, and his
eventual fury when his idol is found to have feet of clay. Cash
comments upon the 'working code of the Old South' which
expressed in everyday life 'the old basic democracy of feeling ... this
tradition of the backcountry ... a sort of immense kindliness and
easiness',[76] and this may be seen as another important, and very
attractive, feature of Southern individualism. Faulkner clearly
values the egalitarian aspects of Mississippi society which survived
from frontier days, especially the simple courtesy, hospitality and
refusal to conform to the more artificial distinctions of class (or,
occasionally, racial) discrimination: one thinks of Bayard's Christmas dinner with the black sharecropper's family, the easy hospitality of the MacCallums, or Saucier Weddel's punctilious manners.[77]
In each of these encounters too, though, the clash is felt, and
meaningful communication is difficult.

More often, the confrontation of Southerners of different
backgrounds is uncomfortable, or openly violent. Faulkner commonly uses such incidents to create moments of potential
epiphany, when a character's innermost perceptions are laid bare
or enlarged. A large proportion of these moments feature relationships between black and white Southerners. Perhaps wisely,
Faulkner never directly internalises a black consciousness, but
concentrates upon exploring the masks and roles which characters
adopt to deal with racial tensions, and upon the mixture of
confusion, guilt and inadequacy experienced by his white protagon-

ists when the mask momentarily slips, to reveal common humanity beneath.[78] Quentin's reflections upon blacks in *The Sound and the Fury* provide an instructive example of this sort of uneasy awareness. When he first goes north to college, Quentin resolves to rely upon the stereotypes of contemporary racial etiquette, telling himself that 'a nigger is not so much a person as a form of behaviour; a sort of obverse reflection of the white people he lives among' (*TSATF*, p. 82). But the uncharacteristic callousness of Quentin's tone suggests that this is less a belief than a consciously artificial strategy, which is counterpointed and ironically outmatched by the behaviour of Deacon, a black campus factotum who preys upon the paternalism of the Southern freshmen whom he greets at the station in 'a sort of Uncle Tom's cabin outfit, patches and all' (p. 91). Quentin's usual attitude to blacks is that of a conventional upper-class Southerner, condescending and affectionate, associating them with traits like 'childlike ... incompetence' and his own aching nostalgia for the South (p. 83). But he is also capable of great emotional sensitivity and intuition, and on the day he commits suicide his jumbled, homesick thoughts suggest an ability to discern the inner, secret lives of others. Hence, when he talks with Deacon, whom he has come to like, Quentin seems momentarily to recognise Roskus, the Compsons' shrewd old servant, looking out from behind Deacon's defences:

> His eyes were soft and irisless and brown, and suddenly I saw Roskus watching me from behind all his [Deacon's] white folks' claptrap of uniform and politics and Harvard manner, diffident, secret, inarticulate and sad. 'You ain't playing a joke on the old nigger, is you?'
> 'You know I'm not. Did any Southerner ever play a joke on you?'
> 'You're right. They're fine folks. But you can't live with them.'
> 'Did you ever try?' I said. But Roskus was gone. Once more he was that self he had long since taught himself to wear in the world's eye, pompous, spurious, not quite gross. (p. 93)

Deacon's remark is unexpectedly honest and direct, besides being horribly ironic (for Quentin, too, has found that he can't live with Southern folks). For a moment he and the old black man have established a fleeting communication. Equally penetrating is

Quentin's memory of Dilsey, growing out of a moment of compassion for his mentally subnormal brother Benjy:

> O Benjamin. Dilsey said it was because Mother was too proud for him. They come into white people's lives like that in sudden sharp black trickles that isolate white facts for an instant in unarguable truth like under a microscope; the rest of the time just voices that laugh when you see nothing to laugh at, tears when no reason for tears.   (p. 154)

This moving description of Dilsey is all the more impressive when contrasted with Jason's responses to her; and it is, of course, by exactly this kind of multiple juxtapositioning that Faulkner's novels unfold their meanings. Jason boasts:

> after things got quieted down a little I put the fear of God into Dilsey. As much as you can into a nigger, that is. That's the trouble with nigger servants, when they've been with you for a long time they get so full of self-importance that they're not worth a damn. Think they run the whole family.   (p. 186)

The reader meanwhile ironically perceives that it is Jason who is full of self-importance, that Dilsey is already full of a genuine reverence for God, and that she does indeed run the whole family.

Despite the injustice, violence and tragedy which pervades his Yoknapatawpha stories, Faulkner's work is full of examples of human decency and – to use Hardy's term – simple loving-kindness. This may easily be overlooked by those with the vaguest conceptions of Faulkner (especially in Britain, where he is respected but not much read) as a 'Deep South' writer, a tag likely to prompt associations like 'difficult', melodramatic, grotesque, exaggerated, over-emotional or obsessive. All these epithets are not without a certain restricted relevance, but it must be emphasised that in his huge range of characters Faulkner does achieve a characteristic balance. Lena Grove travels alone through a territory seemingly full of harshness and violence, yet she finds that 'folks have been ... right kind' (*LIA*, p. 12). Yoknapatawpha is peopled by the likes of Mrs Armstid, who appears to be 'manhard ... savage and brusque ... her face like those of generals who have been defeated in battle' (p. 15), yet whose formidable exterior is shown to conceal a good heart as, with 'a single shattering blow', she breaks open a small china effigy of a rooster with a slot in its back' to give Lena her egg-money (*LIA*, pp. 18–19). Similarly, the reader tends to take Nub Gowrie for the tough racist hillbilly which he appears to be, and probably is, and may therefore be surprised, along with Chick Mallison, to discover that Gowrie too is susceptible to grief, and therefore to love (*IITD*, p. 156).

Despite its unique characteristics, life in Mississippi displays qualities of human behaviour which are universal, and it is these which are Faulkner's ultimate interest: 'I was trying to talk about people, using the only tool I knew, which was the country that I knew. No, I wasn't trying to – wasn't writing sociology at all ... just the human heart, it's not ideas.'[79]

In examining the relationship between Faulkner's regional environment and his work, one must therefore guard against the danger of exaggerating the sensational and less attractive aspects of Mississippi's peculiar culture. Faulkner certainly is not guilty of any such exaggeration. At the same time, subjective impressions are not without their own kind of relevance: Mississippi has attracted lurid stereotypes for many generations and has silently made them a part of its 'implacable and brooding image' (*AILD*, p. 38), adding to both its complexity and fascination. I hope that my discussion has already begun to show how Faulkner's work draws its vitality from a conscious refashioning of this mingled body of history and legend. In chapter 1 I discussed the idealisation and stereotyping which sometimes distorts understanding of Hardy's Wessex, and it is interesting to note that Faulkner's vision of Yoknapatawpha has suffered comparable misinterpretations. Some have been misled by a partisan preoccupation with the sociological aspects of the novels, many of his contemporary fellow-Southerners attacking his work for allegedly portraying Mississippi as a wholly brutal and benighted region;[80] while another school of thought identified Faulkner's outlook as deeply conservative and supportive of the traditional Southern status quo.[81] Both interpretations fail to take account of Faulkner's essential ambivalence, and mistakenly seek to identify the author's viewpoint with that of some of his characters.

Other critics have sometimes complained that Faulkner's imaginative work is too exaggerated or cruel. This overlaps with the first, 'benighted-South' reading, but also rests upon a moral or aesthetic distaste oddly reminiscent of some of the contemporary criticism of *Tess* and *Jude*. Hence the *New York Times* editorial commenting upon Faulkner's Nobel Prize award declares that

His field of vision is concentrated on a society that is too often vicious, depraved, decadent, corrupt. ... Incest and rape may be common pastimes in Faulkner's 'Jefferson, Miss.' but they are not elsewhere in the United States.[82]

A variation of this approach objects that Faulkner's novels are far-fetched, unrealistic, much as Hardy was attacked for being too pessimistic. Wyndham Lewis's essay, subtitled 'The Moralist with the Corn-Cob', found Faulkner's characters 'demented' and his plots dominated by a kind of melodramatic quasi-Hardeian 'notion of fatality ... controlling human life'.[83] Again, the critic is confusing Faulkner's authorial viewpoint with the consciousness of a character like Quentin Compson or Rosa Coldfield; it is rather like complaining that Hamlet has written a very implausible autobiography.

Three other rejoinders to these critiques should swiftly be mentioned. One is to note Faulkner's frequently overlooked use of humour to leaven the tragic elements of his stories, for laughter is an important antidote to Snopesism or those like Jason Compson, while it simultaneously warms us to the human fallibility of the Reporter or Byron Bunch; and Faulkner can be a very funny writer indeed. Secondly, one must not underestimate the influence of the decent characters in Faulkner's stories, as I suggested earlier, for it is through the quiet humanity of a voice like that of Cash Bundren that the more extreme or 'demented' viewpoints, *pace* Lewis, are set into a meaningful overall perspective:

> Sometimes I ain't so sho who's got ere a right to say when a man is crazy and when he ain't. Sometimes I think it ain't none of us pure crazy and ain't none of us pure sane until the balance of us talks him that-a-way. It's like it ain't so much what a fellow does, but it's the way the majority of folks is looking at him when he does it. (*AILD*, p. 184)

Cash's concern with 'balance', with 'doing' rather than talking, and with the relativity of viewpoints, point to some essential Faulknerian themes which I shall discuss later. As Waggoner points out, it seems significant that Cash has the last word in *As I Lay Dying*, as Dilsey does in *The Sound and the Fury*, for both personify a sympathetic and 'committed' response to the problems of existence.[84]

A third answer to the charge that Faulkner's novels lack realism is simply that, like Hardy, Faulkner does not pretend to be a naturalist, although both men's work frequently includes splendid naturalistic description. Faulkner's aim is clearly to transcend straightforward factual objectivity in favour of a mode of fiction which approaches that objective world obliquely, by exploring different subjective versions of reality. These he continually contrasts and reassesses, in search of a larger truth than that available to any single consciousness, whether that of protagonist or author.[85] The tangle of ambivalent attitudes and associations posed by Mississippi's unusual history and culture may usefully be seen as a major, perhaps germinal, example in Faulkner's experience of the elusiveness of 'truth'.

To conclude this comparative discussion of the influence of the regional environment, I would like to look at an actual reminiscence of Hardy's childhood, and a fictional counterpart by Faulkner, the story 'A Justice', for the two pieces illustrate with great dramatic force the role of those ambivalent feelings for their native cultures which so fascinated and teased both novelists' creative instincts. Faulkner once explained that

> it was not my intention to write a pageant of a county. I simply was using ... what I knew best ... the locale where I was born and had lived most of my life ... just like the carpenter building the fence – he uses the nearest hammer.[86]

For the reader, this is to beg important questions about why and how 'pageants' of great fiction grow, as Hardy's and Faulkner's did, consciously or unconsciously, out of localised experiences similar to those suggested in the following examples. Millgate's biography of Hardy tells us that in 1888 Hardy recorded these memories of life on the Kingston Maurward estate during the late 1840s:

> A farm of Labourers, as they appeared to me when a child in Martin's time; in *pink & yellow Valentine hues*: Susan Sq–, & Newnt (e.g. leaning & singing at harvest-supper) their simple husbands: Newnt's lovers; Ben B's wife, & her lover, & her hypocrisy; T. Fuller – the schoolmaster, far above his position in education, but a drunkard; also wife – the lech–'s boy T. M.... s. Also Walt, Betsy, & Eliza. The school kept by latter, & their chars, sensuous, lewd, & careless, as visible even to me at that time – all incarnadined by passion & youth – obscuring the wrinkles, creases, & cracks of life as then lived.[87] [emphasis as in original]

It is a remarkable passage; and the nature of its creative pressures upon Hardy's imagination become clearer as Millgate immediately relates it to a note for a possible poem in the same 'Poetical Matter' notebook: 'Cf. Theocritus & the life at Bockn when I was a boy – in the wheatfield, at the well, cidermaking, wheat weeding, &c.'[88] The reference to Theocritus and pastoral activities expresses a bookish man's urge to idealise his memories of a vanished way of life, and those carefully chosen, italicised *'pink & yellow Valentine hues'* are a conscious documentation of the haze of sentimental nostalgia which accompanies them, like stage-coaches on a modern Christmas card. At the same time, Hardy acknowledges his recognition, even as a boy, of the ambiguous nature of village life, now plainly seen by adult eyes in all its squalid and cheerful crudity. But the epithets 'sensuous, lewd, & careless' betray the double-edged nature of Hardy's memories, and while he cannot overlook the 'wrinkles, creases, & cracks' in the pastoral tableau, the writer can still see the slatternly wives and their fuddled, cuckolded husbands as they once appeared to an impressionable boy, 'all incarnadined by passion & youth'. The romantic magic of his original response has been overlaid by an equally absorbing cluster of uneasy equivocations, and Hardy's imagination is always stirred by such bitter–sweet ironies. As Millgate comments, the juxtaposition of the two notes reveals a 'conflict ... which troubled Hardy all his life'.[89] One regrets that the poem was apparently never written, though the wry flavour of the reminiscences seems related to the world of *Far from the Madding Crowd*.

Faulkner's story 'A Justice' grows out of a similarly retrospective view of a child's bewilderment, whether actual or imaginary. Despite its understated tone, it is a work of considerable power and condensation, consisting of a double-framing device whereby the ostensible story, of Indian life *c.* 1800, is framed within the impressions of its audience, the 12-year-old Quentin Compson, now recollecting them at a later date. This relationship reflects the importance which Faulkner, like Hardy before him, attached to 'old tales and talking', 'out of the old time, the old days': for both writers, oral folklore and legend represented a vital means of insight into the history and psychology of their regional worlds. The nominal story is told by Sam Fathers, and passes on what Sam heard in turn from Herman Basket, concerning the last corrupted era of Choctaw (in later stories, Chickasaw) Indian life as it began to be disrupted by contact with the white frontier and the institution of slavery.

Quentin learns of Sam's parentage by a Choctaw warrior named Crawfish-ford and a black slave woman, and of the rivalry between the woman's black slave husband and the Choctaw, resulting in Sam's original name, Had-Two-Fathers.

The true significance of the story lies less in these remote events than in the apparent effects of Sam's tale upon the 12-year-old Quentin. The situation may have some biographical source, since the young Faulkner and his brothers frequently visited their grandfather's farm a few miles north of Oxford, where John Faulkner remembered William habitually spending his time talking to the Negro blacksmith – 'He would be the last one back when Grandfather rounded us up to go home.'[90] Be that as it may, here is the beginning and the end of 'A Justice', told by Quentin:

> Until Grandfather died, we would go out to the farm every Saturday afternoon.... The farm was four miles away. There was a long, low house in the grove, not painted but kept whole and sound by a clever carpenter from the quarters named Sam Fathers ... they said he was almost a hundred years old. He lived with the Negroes and they – the white people; the Negroes called him a blue-gum – called him a Negro. But he wasn't a Negro. That's what I'm going to tell about.... I would always bring him some tobacco. Then he would stop working and he would fill his pipe ... and he would tell me about the old days ... his face was still all the time, like he might be somewhere else all the while he was working.

Sam tells Quentin the story of his parentage, his birth and naming. Eventually,

> Grandfather called me again. This time I got up. The sun was already down beyond the peach orchard. I was just twelve then, and to me the story did not seem to have got anywhere, to have had point or end. Yet I obeyed Grandfather's voice, not that I was tired of Sam Fathers' talking, but with that immediacy of children with which they flee temporarily something which they do not quite understand.... 'What were you and Sam talking about?' Grandfather said.
> We went on, in that strange, faintly sinister suspension of twilight in which I believed that I could still see Sam Fathers back there, sitting on his wooden block, definite, immobile, and

complete, like something looked upon after a long time in a preservative bath in a museum. That was it. I was just twelve then, and I would have to wait until I had passed on and through and beyond the suspension of twilight. Then I knew that I would know. But then Sam Fathers would be dead.

'Nothing, sir,' I said. 'We were just talking.'   (*TT*, pp. 107–8, 123–4)

The ending is unmistakably sombre; but on a first reading the overall effect of the story may seem strangely opaque, rather like the impression which Quentin claims was left by Sam's tale ('the story did not seem to have got anywhere'). But the longer one reflects upon 'A Justice', especially in relation to Faulkner's other work, the more clearly one perceives dark and incipiently tragic depths. It seems wise to examine the story with the observations of Louis D. Rubin in mind:

> the reason Faulkner's version of experience is not acceptable to many of his fellow Mississippians is that he depicts it in the kind of ultimate dimension of tragedy, a dimension not apparent to those who are busy living the life that he writes about. People do not customarily see their lives as a moral drama of the soul's own bitter travail, nor do they see themselves as living in history. All the same, one must insist, that is precisely what life was for Faulkner as an artist. And it is the function of his art to delineate the lines of meaning that lie concealed in the confusion of everyday life.... The novel is not merely life; it is life ... *charged with purpose.*[91]   [Emphasis as in original]

What then are the 'lines of meaning' drawn in Faulkner's story, and how can they usefully be related to Hardy's reminiscences? I have three common themes in mind: a contrast between a child's and an adult's view of the world; an ambivalent fascination with the 'old days' of a vanished culture; and an uncertain response to the effects of time and change. The contrast between the voices of innocence and experience is perhaps the strongest first impression given by the story, not only that contrast between the 12-year-old Quentin and the venerable Sam Fathers, but also that subtler distinction between the boy Quentin and his older self now telling the whole story in present time, whose age remains unstated. Quentin 'does not quite understand' at 12, and if he does now, he remains silent. As a young boy, Quentin realises that 'I would have to wait'. But one may suspect that he has since begun to become aware of some of the darker mysteries of life touched upon in Sam's story.

These include, firstly, the problematic subject of Southern race relations, for Quentin tells the story to explain Sam's mysteriously blurred racial identity – 'that's what I'm going to tell about'. This itself is a vaguely troubling task, for Sam does not neatly fit into any clear-cut racial category, and to the sensitive Quentin he has an uncomfortably frank way of dealing with the subject ('a Choctaw chief ... sold my mammy to your great-grandpappy', *TT*, p. 108).

Secondly, Sam's story focuses upon notions of social justice and honour in the 'old times', which were, to say the least, somewhat arbitrarily administered. Quentin can doubtless see that any 'justice' established by the treacherous and opportunistic Indian chief Doom is not worth much, however amusing the grim old Sam Fathers finds it; and he is probably disturbed by the story's casual violence.[92]

Thirdly, if we relate the story to Quentin's other appearances in Faulkner's fiction, Sam's story may be seen to throw a harsh light upon the bitterness of sexual rivalry, in the shape of the slave and Crawfish-ford; and this will soon become all too familiar to Quentin in his relationship with his sister Caddy. Lastly, the story concentrates Quentin's mind upon the sense of loss and finality associated with the passing of time, another subject of his later obsessions, and especially upon death. At the end of the story, he anticipates the death of Sam, whom he regards with both awe and affection, while the story opens with an abrupt image of childhood security disrupted by the death of his grandfather. The story is thus enclosed by images of mortality.

Faulkner's story also shares with Hardy's reminiscences an ambivalent fascination with the 'old days', though the responses of Hardy or his protagonists to the shadows of their regional past are seldom quite so fraught as those of Quentin appear ultimately to be. Nevertheless, Quentin is a fundamental example of that key figure in both men's fiction, the sensitive transitional man with access to both traditional and modern worlds, who is torn helplessly between them. When afforded a unique glimpse of authentic Mississippi frontier life, Quentin seems to find the experience decidedly disturbing. Though he internalises rather than expresses his feelings, something of his uneasiness emerges in the 'strange, faintly sinister' quality which he attributes to the twilight, and in his equally ominous image of the ancient, immobile Sam Fathers 'like something ... in a museum', with its connotations of Egyptian mummies. A sense of traumatic shock experienced by a boy or youth encountering the savagery concealed beneath the surface of Southern history occurs repeatedly throughout Faulkner's novels, and obviously relates closely to his own sense of divided loyalties towards the region.

Finally, both of the examples under discussion (and, for that matter, all of the novels) are energised by a profound ambivalence towards the effects of time and change, particularly social change, and the processes of history. Growth from inquisitive childhood to adult maturity brings loss as well as gain, as Quentin's opening and penultimate sentences acknowledge. It is interesting, too, to recall at this point the sensation felt by Hardy as a boy, that 'Reflecting on the experiences of the world so far as he had got, he came to the conclusion that he did not wish to grow up'[93] – and that Hardy later attributed precisely this experience to his most sensitive hero of all, Jude Fawley.[94] If one relates Quentin's reactions in 'A Justice' to those which he displays elsewhere, one can recognise what will indeed be Quentin's greatest problem – coping with the painful change and knowledge which comes with adulthood. So the reader may claim to identify in this story (and in its twin, 'That Evening Sun') the earliest manifestations of Quentin's tormented consciousness. For Quentin is an over-sensitive idealist, and those with whom he comes into unsettling contact, Sam Fathers and Nancy, have not lived in very ideal or sensitive worlds.[95] When one meets him again in *Absalom, Absalom!*, Quentin is increasingly haunted by the voices of Southern history; and on 2 June 1910, the dilemmas of the 'loud world' of *The Sound and the Fury* finally overwhelm him. His hysterical denial at the end of *Absalom, Absalom!* is also foreshadowed here, since Quentin finds himself unable to share his bewildered thoughts with any sympathetic member of his family ('Nothing, sir'). Quentin must go alone into that 'faintly sinister suspension of twilight', which may well symbolise adolescence, always a time of trauma and initiation in Faulkner's fiction: 'I would have to wait until I had passed on and through and beyond the suspension of twilight. Then I knew that I would know. But then Sam Fathers would be dead.'

Quentin is faced with the end of childhood innocence, and the necessary acceptance of painful adult knowledge. Yet as the story ends, he is *looking back* in his mind's eye, as if desperately to prolong

Sam's life ('in a preservative bath in a museum') and his own innocence; and the story he tells is elaborately retrospective. Even a stranger to Faulkner's work must intuit that something is badly wrong here, while the readers of his other fiction will grieve for Quentin, recognising that he will never emerge from that 'suspension of twilight' into which he travels. One cannot, I think, doubt that the solemn tone of Quentin's last paragraph denotes some level of experience which must have been shared to a significant degree by a young and sensitive William Faulkner, just as Jude and Hardy share important moments of discovery. Quentin and Jude represent other selves, equally plausible hypothetical fates. The South at the beginning of the twentieth century was a society of extraordinary tensions, of a kind peculiarly challenging to writers, as I hope this chapter will, however cursorily, have established. Luckily Faulkner, unlike Quentin, discovered that he could explore, analyse, and even exorcise his own ambivalent responses to Mississippi in fiction, 'loving it even while having to hate some of it'. By creating Yoknapatawpha out of his own twilight confusion, the artist could give order and meaning to the voices of Mississippi, Sam Fathers, poor doomed Quentin and many more, which spoke so eloquently within him.

3

'A full look at the worst'

I was, perhaps, after all, a paltry victim to the spirit of mental and social restlessness that makes so many unhappy in these days
(*Jude the Obscure*, p. 345)

I'm interested primarily in people, in man in conflict with himself, with his fellow man, or with his time and place, his environment
(*Faulkner in the University*, p. 19)

Hardy's evolving paradigms of social change indicate a growing preoccupation with the latent tragedy within his protagonists' lives. This tragic quality was, of course, always inherent in his writing. The 'small bird that was being killed by an owl in the adjoining wood, whose cry passed into the silence without mingling with it', and the duplicity of Fancy Day's 'secret she would never tell' in *Under the Greenwood Tree* (pp. 166, 208) are subdued but telling prefigurations of the symbolism of trapped animals in *Tess* or the artful wiles of Arabella Donn and their consequence in *Jude*. But as Hardy's instinctive recognition of his most powerfully felt themes grew surer, so his emphasis upon the origins of tragedy shifted. Hardy's three definitions of tragedy in the *Life* all posit a fundamental incompatibility between a character and his environment, but this may result from one of many different tensions between the rival claims placed upon man by the forces of nature (including 'human' nature) and society: for man is both a natural and a social animal. Gradually, Hardy's perception of a rift between the two influences grew clearer and starker. My purpose in this chapter is to identify and examine the methods which Hardy and Faulkner adopt to express the tragic 'tendency of the age'[1] encouraging man's alienation, and to look at what are perhaps the two writers' darkest novels. Hardy's note of April 1878 declares that

A Plot, or Tragedy, should arise from the gradual closing in of a situation that comes of ordinary human passions, prejudices, and ambitions, by reason of the characters taking no trouble to ward off the disastrous events produced by the said passions, prejudices and ambitions.[2]

Here tragedy is accounted simply the result of human nature and its failings, although the mention of 'prejudices and ambitions' may quietly imply some related confusion of social conditioning, such as lies at the heart of the recently completed *The Return of the Native*. Clym and Eustacia's vulnerability has its origin in their innate self-righteous wilfulness; but it is inflamed and made truly lethal by the collision of her romantic illusions of glamorous society with his altruistic ideals.

In November 1885, while working on *The Woodlanders*, Hardy declared that 'a tragedy exhibits a state of things in the life of an individual which unavoidably causes some natural aim or desire of his to end in a catastrophe when carried out'.[3] Here the culprit is no longer 'natural' feelings, but an enigmatic 'state of things', whose various manifestations can best be understood when we apply Hardy's statement to the plot of the contemporaneous novel. Marty South aims to raise money for her ailing father by selling her hair, but the 'state of things' ensures that by so doing she renounces her one sexual advantage over Grace Melbury, her rival for Giles's love; and, incidentally, helps to ensure Fitzpiers's attraction towards Felice Charmond. What is at fault here? Some play of cosmic irony, perhaps, and certainly irrational human nature – specifically, the blindness of sexual selection; while elsewhere the story's tragedy springs directly from class division and its blighting effects of snobbery, excessive propriety and alienation. George Melbury wishes not only, quite reasonably, that his daughter should be well educated, but also that this should make her superior to his kind, and that she should then marry 'well'. Giles feels forced to express his love for Grace not by a passionate consummation, or even declaration, but – in atonement for his 'social sin' of kissing her while knowing her to be another man's wife – by a selfless renunciation, insisting that she occupy his hut alone. The tragically exaggerated regard for social propriety which is shown to have infected these two woodlanders constitutes Hardy's first explicit and sustained attack upon the tyranny of Victorian social conventions, more outspokenly articulated in the last two great novels, and echoed in his third definition of tragedy, a reaction to the reviews of *Jude*: 'Tragedy may be created by an opposing environment either of things inherent in the universe, or of human institutions.'[4]

The kinds of personal incompatibility portrayed in *The Woodlanders*, *Tess* and *Jude* are, of course, likely to be exacerbated during an era of rapid social change, disruption and migration, which I have suggested as a vital source of Hardy's inspiration; and even in early novels, such as *Desperate Remedies* and *A Pair of Blue Eyes*, social innovations and observances tend to operate divisively upon character and environment. Yet even while defending *Jude*, Hardy scrupulously maintained that tragedy sprung not from social injustices alone but from universal causes, from 'things inherent in the universe', a philosophical dialectic which helps save *Jude* from an excess of didacticism. Again, we are touching upon an aspect of Hardy's essential dualism, in this case the peculiar fluctuations of his philosophical and intellectual sensibility.

Hardy in fact claimed to 'have no philosophy – merely … a confused heap of impressions, like those of a bewildered child at a conjuring show.… It is my misfortune that people *will* treat all my mood-dictating writing as a single scientific theory.'[5] The origins of these 'confused impressions' may, I think, become clearer when we contemplate the twin modes of Hardy's thought, his feeling for both 'customary' and 'educated' life. To be properly understood, this dualism should again be related to the world in which Hardy lived. His own disorientating experience of social mobility must be largely responsible for what one essay on 'Hardy's Philosophy' calls 'the paradox that one of the most thoughtful and thought-provoking of our greater writers often spoke as if thought was a curse'.[6] So the explanation of the paradox may seem quite simple; that Hardy's 'impressions' alternated between the instinctively emotional, intuitive countryman's view of life which he inherited, and that of the reasoning autodidact, with a lifelong interest in philosophical and intellectual speculation, which he became. Yet, curiously, Hardy's ability to explore these seemingly disparate worlds in the creation of his fiction depends upon a further philosophical paradox, that within the void between them he discovered a dour, uncharted region of thought where 'customary' and 'educated' life unexpectedly converged. Perhaps only Hardy, with his 'life twisted of three strands, the professional life, the scholar's life, and the rustic life',[7] could have perceived and exploited this common area. He had early observed that the rhythmical patterns of Dorset country life bred a traditional folk-philosophy of fatalism, rooted in a belief in custom, superstition, folklore and a fascination with hereditary traits. Such a view of life depended most of all upon a simultaneous familiarity with and reverence for the mysterious processes of nature, teaching an uncomplaining acceptance of life's habitual harshnesses. It is this fatalism which reconciles the other milkmaids to Angel's choice of Tess – 'such supplanting was to be' – or perpetuates the woodlanders' dogged planting of vegetables beneath dripping trees, 'year after year with that curious mechanical regularity of country people in the face of hopelessness' (*Tess*, p. 186; *TW*, p. 152).

Quaint and unsophisticated as this creed may have seemed to outsiders, to the young Hardy who studied *Essays and Reviews*, Darwin, Spencer, Huxley and Mill during the 1860s, unexpected similarities must have been apparent, ironic connections made. The school of modern scientific pragmatism, and in particular the development of Darwin's discoveries, revealed with shocking force to the mid-Victorian intellectual a brutal new world of continual competition for survival, wholesale violence and extinction, a world of random process where moral purpose seemed to count for naught. Hardy must have reflected that the cottagers and labourers of Dorset would remain unshaken at such news. Joan Durbeyfield could have answered Tennyson's agonisings over 'Nature, red in tooth and claw' with an unflinching 'Well, we must make the best of it, I suppose. 'Tis nater, after all, and what do please God!'[8]

Hardy himself was denied even the consolation of belief in God. It is difficult today to appreciate the distress involved in the Victorians' loss of faith and consequent metaphysical anxieties. Their realisation of the implications of Darwinian theory to human society at first caused widespread philosophical panic – 'Society must fall to pieces if Darwinism be true' proclaimed the *Family Herald*.[9] Agnostics sought new forms of faith, while Christians struggled to accept evolution and natural selection as the workings of divine providence.[10] The creed of 'Social Darwinism', Hardy's relationship to which I shall discuss later, appealed to many Victorians, though Darwin himself never endorsed it. Such an acceptance of the concept of the survival of the fittest seemed to offer justification for the age's busy capitalism and ruthless economic competition.[11] Others, such as George Eliot, turned to a stern devotion to Duty and Responsibility, while Hardy evolved an ideal of simple humanism, the 'religion of loving-kindness and purity' (*Tess*, p. 377) At the same time he recognised the moving force of life as a quite separate, blind and morally neutral 'Immanent Will', which manifests itself through nature. Those humble characters closest to nature, such as Giles and Marty, who know 'the tongue of the trees and fruits and flowers themselves' – much like Faulkner's Sam Fathers – are those most meaningfully in touch with the hidden sources of life; but even for them, nature remains largely inscrutable and unpredictable (*TW*, p. 358). So man's relationship with nature is a mysterious and problematic one; Hardy's own attitudes to it seems to have varied at different times, and his protagonists' responses to it often tell us more about their individual characters than about Hardy's own 'mood-dictated' speculations.

It is, however, clear that from his mixed experience of 'customary' and 'educated' life, Hardy inherited a unique and richly suggestive combination of philosophical 'impressions' wherein traditional rural fatalism and modern scientific determinism fused into a new and potent vision of man's predicament. One of the most perspicacious commentaries upon this compound vision is that of Walter Allen, in *The English Novel*:

> It was not an easy or harmonious marriage, but its tensions were part of its strength. Without the philosophical interpretation of what he saw and felt his work might have approximated in scope to the traditional ballad; but if he had not seen human beings in depth, in their relation to traditional skills, the work and rhythm of the seasons, and the force of the great nonrational, instinctual urgencies, he would probably not have been the superior of other novelists of the same time, Gissing in England and Dreiser in America, who interpreted man according to the deterministic philosophy of the day. They, for all their pity for mankind, do not achieve more than the pathetic: Hardy rises to tragedy, and his tragedy is an arraignment of the nature of the universe as he saw it.[12]

In a particularly bold example of this tragic vision, Hardy presents to the reader an urban intellectual protagonist, perilously suspended over a sheer cliff-face:

> Haggard cliffs ... are not safe places for scientific experiment upon the principles of air-currents, as Knight had now found, to his dismay.
> He still clutched the face of the escarpment – not with the frenzied hold of despair, but with a dogged determination to make the most of his every jot of endurance....

He reclined hand in hand with the world in its infancy. Not a blade, not an insect, which spoke of the present, was between him and the past. The inveterate antagonism of these black precipices to all strugglers for life is in no way more forcibly suggested than by the paucity of tufts of grass, lichens, or conferrae on their outermost ledges.

... At first, when death appeared improbable, because it had never visited him before, Knight could think of no future, nor of anything connected with his past. He could only look sternly at Nature's treacherous attempt to put an end to him, and strive to thwart her.

... By one of those familiar conjunctions of things wherewith the inanimate world baits the mind of man when he pauses in moments of suspense, opposite Knight's eyes was an embedded fossil, standing forth in low relief from the rock. It was a creature with eyes. The eyes, dead and turned to stone, were even now regarding him ... separated by millions of years in their lives, Knight and this underling seemed to have met in their place of death....

The creature represented but a low type of animal existence.... The immense lapses of time each formation [of the cliff's strata] represented had known nothing of the dignity of man. They were grand times, but they were mean times, too, and mean were their relics. He was to be with the small in his death.

... However, Knight still clung to the cliff.

To those musing weather-beaten West-Country folk who pass the greater part of their days and nights out of doors, Nature seems to have moods in other than a poetical sense: predilections for certain deeds at certain times, without any apparent law to govern or season to account for them. She is read as a person with a curious temper; as one who does not scatter kindnesses and cruelties alternately, impartially, and in order, but heartless severities or over-whelming generosities in lawless caprice. ... In her unfriendly moments there seems a feline fun in her tricks, begotten by a foretaste of her pleasure in swallowing her victim.

Such a way of thinking had been absurd to Knight, but he began to adopt it now. He was first spitted on to a rock. New tortures followed. The rain increased....

Knight perseveringly held fast. Had he any faith in Elfride? Perhaps. Love is faith, and faith, like a gathered flower, will rootlessly live on.

... Knight ... knew that his intellect was above the average. And
he thought – he could not help thinking – that his death would be
a deliberate loss to earth of good material, that such an
experiment in killing might have been practised upon some less
developed life.   (*APOBE*, pp. 239–43)

Nature here *seems* 'treacherous', 'heartless', a cosmic agency 'eager
for conquest'; the sun appearing as a 'a red face looking on with a
drunken leer'. But Hardy is careful to disassociate himself immediately from this impression by adding that, 'We colour according to
our moods the objects we survey.' What is certain is that Hardy's
nature cares nothing for science, for history or for intellect, and the
shocking revelation of its power serves to humble Knight's pride.
Previously we have seen him exercising a haughty superiority over
Elfride, and implicitly – by his 'scientific experiment' intended to
impress her – over nature; now he is to be saved by the young girl
whom he had humiliated. But first he learns that there are more
things in heaven and earth than he had dreamed of in his urbane
and rationalistic philosophy.

One of the major themes of *A Pair of Blue Eyes* examines the
process (and the cost) of 'bettering oneself', in a race where the
stakes are the closely related prizes of class status and marriage.
Hardy now dramatises this Darwinian struggle in Knight's predicament, its bizarre horror readily symbolising man's slippery foothold
in a world where everything is becoming increasingly transitory,
ambiguous or unknown, the old verities overturned, only the blank
cliff-face of purposeless circumstance before one. And at this point
Hardy introduces one of his characteristic objective correlatives, one
of those 'familiar conjunctions of things', the fossil which seems to
stare at Knight with a nightmarish microcosmic significance. It
provides a macabre Darwinian reminder of the unimportance of one
small life when viewed against the full spectrum of time and nature,
of the theory of natural selection and the survival of the fittest which
haunted the mid-Victorians. Hardy has swept us into that world
where his imagination always excels itself – a tableau of a small
human figure set against a vast, timeless landscape, bringing
sudden unexpected insights.

Knight muses therefore over new realisations. One is that nature,
far from being a mere pleasant, rather romantic backdrop to man's
activities, is at best indifferent and perhaps even actively hostile to
humanity, with its own deadly 'moods in other than a poetical

sense': a rustic superstition which he had previously found 'absurd'. Furthermore, while held at nature's mercy, he is introduced to 'an entirely new order of things' in which heartfelt subjective emotions assume a new urgency. Paramount among these is his admission of love for a fellow-creature, a 'novelty in the extreme' for this coldly taciturn intellectual.

Whether Knight recognises Hardy's final inference is unclear. But Hardy shows the reader at least that, despite man's relative insignificance, Knight is enabled to survive by a combination of courage, reasoning ability and faith in Elfride's loyalty; and this triumph is an assertion of 'the dignity of man'. His desperate experience should serve to prove how much human beings need one another, but though Knight admits to being saved by Elfride, he cannot maintain any vision of their human interdependence. When he in his turn can finally 'save' Elfride, by sacrificing his rigid social proprieties (just as Elfride had done, by removing her clothes to rescue him) he refuses, able to 'reason her down' even though he still loves her (*APOBE*, p. 364). The lesson offered upon the Cliff without a Name goes unheeded, and though it is Elfride who dies, the withering of simple human compassion by an inflexible decorum is very much Knight's tragedy too, exactly as it is later to mar the careers of Angel Clare and Faulkner's Thomas Sutpen.

In following this path of philosophical speculation, one arrives at a further point where traditional rural fatalism and Darwinism touch, marking another essential premise in Hardy's work: the belief that all life's phenomena share in some invisible interrelation. To Hardy this was a source of wonder, frequently celebrated by bursts of imagery which seem to be only semi-consciously aware of their cumulative and multiple patterns of significance:

It was a typical summer evening in June, the atmosphere being in such delicate equilibrium and so transmissive that inanimate objects seemed endowed with two or three senses, if not five. There was no distinction between the near and the far, and an auditor felt close to everything within the horizon. The soundlessness ... was broken by the strumming of strings.

they wandered in the still air with a stark quality like that of nudity....

The outskirt of the garden in which Tess found herself had been left uncultivated for some years, and was now damp and rank with juicy grass which sent up mists of pollen at a touch; and with tall blooming weeds omitting offensive smells.... She went stealthily as a cat through this profusion of growth, gathering cuckoo-spittle on her skirts, cracking snails that were underfoot, staining her hands with thistle-milk and slug-slime, and rubbing off upon her naked arms sticky blights which, though snow-white on the apple-tree trunks, made madder stains on her skin....

Tess was conscious of neither time nor space.... She undulated upon the thin notes of the second-hand harp, and their harmonies passed like breezes though her, bringing tears into her eyes. The floating pollen seemed to be his notes made visible, and the dampness of the garden the weeping of the garden's sensibility. Though near nightfall, the rank-smelling weed-flowers glowed as if they would not close for intentness, and the waves of colour mixed with the waves of sound. (*Tess*, pp. 161–2)

This remarkable passage fuses together Tess's overall sense of place and event with all the more immediate, fragmentary impressions thrown off by her sensibility. Her awed fascination with Clare and her instinctive, feline sensuality are marvellously conveyed through Hardy's startling juxtapositions. Musical notes are related to 'stark ... nudity', or to 'floating pollen', while the reader's sense that this is a special, memorably poetic moment is actually enhanced rather than undercut by the association of Tess's rich but quite unselfconscious aura of 'pure' and therefore 'natural' sexuality not with the roses of cliché but with the wonderfully unexpected imagery of 'damp ... rank ... juicy grass', 'weeds', 'slug-slime' and 'sticky blights' upon her 'naked arms', natural details which are charged with both symbolic and matter-of-fact persuasiveness. Hardy here achieves a striking anticipation of Faulkner's emotive and rhetorical evocations of nature in *The Hamlet*.

The reverberations of these images carry on into later pages. For example, our several impressions of Tess, as a 'pure', natural, spontaneous girl, as a member of a once noble but now unkempt family gone to seed, and as the defenceless victim of social laws, are all encouraged by the subdued but recurrent association of her situation with an imagery of plant life. Irresistibly falling in love, moral misgivings overwhelmed by natural emotions, she

rose from table, and, with an impression that Clare would follow her, went along a little wriggling path, now stepping to one side of the irrigating channels, and now to the other, till she stood by the main stream of the Var. Men had been cutting the water-weeds higher up the river, and masses of them were floating past here – moving islands of green crowfoot, whereon she might almost have ridden.   (*Tess*, p. 221)

The weed-image is briefly held up to our view, and then discarded, one of many similar Hardeian effects contributing to the reader's sensation of glimpsing, semi-consciously but at first hand, something of the interrelations and wholeness of life. The simple pantheism of a Tess or a Gabriel Oak is a natural, 'customary' vehicle for such an experience. As a philosophical or 'educated' tenet, Hardy's awareness of the oneness of life also bred more problematical reflections:

Altruism, or 'The Golden Rule', or whatever 'Love Your Neighbour as Yourself' may be called, will ultimately be brought about I think by the pain we see in others reacting on ourselves, as if we and they were a part of one body....
    The discovery of the law of evolution, which revealed that all organic creatures are of one family, shifted the centre of altruism from humanity to the whole conscious world collectively.[13]

Such a belief is obviously capable of a philosophical, even moral imperative, the theory that all actions and events are interrelated, and hence have inevitable consequences upon one another. This belief is comparable with the Buddhist concept of 'karma', the process by which one's present behaviour determines one's fate in the next incarnation, and the suggestion of some karmic system of interrelation everywhere at work is featured in the lives of many of Hardy's – and Faulkner's – characters as a painfully acquired realisation that to discount the consequences of even trivial actions is folly:

I have learnt that there are some derelictions of duty which cannot be blotted out by tardy accomplishment. Our evil actions do not remain isolated in the past, waiting only to be reversed: like locomotive plants they spread and re-root, till to destroy the original stem has no material effect in killing them.   (*LLI*, p. 76; from 'For Conscience' Sake')

In Hardy's work this belief (which can once again be related both
to the traditional fatalism of the countryside and to contemporary
Darwinism) not only informs subtle studies of man *vis-à-vis* his
surroundings (Knight and the fossil, Tess and the weeds) but also
encourages the construction of the novel's plot as a 'great web of
human doings' in which strange and unexpected relationships may
become apparent, between those apparently divided by time,
distance, or (often) social class:

> Hardly anything could be more isolated or more self-contained
> than the lives of these two walking here in the lonely hour before
> day, when grey shades, material and mental, are so very grey.
> And yet their lonely courses formed no detached design at all, but
> were part of the pattern in the great web of human doings then
> weaving in both hemispheres from the White Sea to Cape
> Horn.   (*TW*, p. 52)

It is, of course, in these patterns of universal interrelation that we
can recognise the *raison d'être* of Hardy's tragic 'coincidences'
which have earned him so much critical ridicule as impossibly
'unrealistic'. But to complain that such a Hardeian device as the
undelivered letter (Clym's letter of appeasement to Eustacia, Tess's
confession to Clare) is an 'impossible coincidence' is to mistake
Hardy's mode of realism, which despite a skill for exact physical
description was not ultimately naturalistic, but metaphysical in its
intentions:

> The Realities to be the true realities of life, hitherto called
> abstractions. The old material realities to be placed behind the
> former, as shadowy accessories....
>   The exact truth as to material fact ceases to be of importance in
> art – it is a student's style – the style of a period when the mind is
> serene and unawakened to the tragical mysteries of life; when it
> does not bring anything to the object that coalesces with and
> translates the qualities that are already there, – half hidden it may
> be – and the two united are depicted as the All.[14]

Hardy's coincidences should therefore be understood as motifs
indicative of the labyrinthine interrelations and 'tragical mysteries'
of life. Hardy's skill at interweaving trivial, microcosmic incident
with its eventually catastrophic consequences adds greatly to the

poignancy and persuasiveness of his plots. When Elfride vacillates in her impulse to elope with Stephen, and 'overwrought and trembling ... vowed she would be led whither the horse would take her' (*APOBE*, p. 141), or when Bathsheba frivolously sends Boldwood a valentine bearing the inscription, 'Marry Me', hidden series of repercussions are set in motion which prove just as disastrous as Henchard's drunken sale of his wife at a fair. In each case a small but dangerous flaw – indecision, coquetry, recklessness – acquires a lethal ascendancy in the circumstances of a small group of lives, its destructive effects spreading over outwards. As I shall discuss later, this is precisely the philosophical patterning which obtains in Faulkner's *Absalom, Absalom!* The tragic flaws of Hardy's protagonists are invariably universal human failings, but it is significant that their deadly effects gain a new momentum from the unprecedented and uncontrollable tide of social change which sweeps through Hardy's mid-Victorian Wessex, where characters' sense of the wholeness and purpose of life is undermined by the drifting instabilities of an alienating modernism. This, too, is exactly reproduced in Faulkner's Yoknapatawpha.

It should therefore be clear that throughout Hardy's career as a novelist an important element in his work is devoted to a persistent questioning of the role of social processes and institutions, considered against the touchstone of the natural and the traditional communal life of the countryside. Again, I must stress the ambivalence of Hardy's attitudes, for social change is not *always* held to be pernicious, nor traditional usages to be unmitigatedly admirable, as I shall try to show. The passage above simply represents an exceedingly common but not exclusive Hardeian viewpoint. Meanwhile, some important recurrent patterns of plot and character which Hardy uses to set up a potentially tragic situation may now become apparent. Three of the most fundamental, which I would like to discuss, can be characterised as the figure of the modern outsider, and (a refinement upon the former) that of the returned native; and the theme of sexual versus social pressures.

The figure of the modern outsider may at first sight seem to offer a valuable key to unlocking the inner meaning of the Wessex novels. One thinks of Sergeant Troy, Dr Fitzpiers and Alec d'Urberville, and sees them menacingly superimposed upon an otherwise tranquil and unchanging rural landscape. Certainly, one

school of critical thought has viewed such figures as a dialectical part
of a 'common pattern' in Hardy's greatest novels:

> His protagonists are strong-natured countrymen, disciplined by
> the necessities of agricultural life. He brings into relation with
> them men and women from outside the rural world, better
> educated, superior in status, yet inferior in human worth. The
> contact occasions a sense of invasion, of disturbance ... the theme
> of urban invasion ... it is a clash between agricultural and urban
> modes of life.[15]

As I suggested in the first chapter, such an explanation is rather too
pat. Brown applies it only to five major novels, and this perhaps
suggests its blurred inadequacy as a meaningful exegesis of Hardy's
work as a whole; an inadequacy which becomes clearer when one
examines the 'urban invaders' themselves.[16] Where Brown's
approach is indisputably accurate is in identifying a common
formative element of social disturbance in Hardy's plots – indeed,
his work must be acknowledged as a pioneering attempt to make
sense of the novels by reference to the actual social world (or worlds)
in which Hardy had lived. It is true, also, that Hardy's vision of that
social disruption included a powerful feeling of revulsion for the
tawdry artificialities of modern urbanised life and their corrupting
influence upon the traditional rural scene. But to attribute a
consistent scale of values, laudatory or pejorative, to Hardy's
portrayal of rural and urban influences is to deny much of the wry
sensibility which distinguishes his perspectives.[17] To figure the
matter differently, it would be equally possible, and equally
misleading, to view Faulkner's work as a committed 'nostalgic'
treatment of Southern social life. While Faulkner's novels regret the
decline of many traditional features, they are not simply an
extended apologia or elegy for the Old South. Indeed, the South's
former, vanishing way of life is probed sceptically and often
mercilessly, alongside the dissected mores of a modern Popeye or
Snopes. I hope firmly to establish ambivalence as a crucial, and
indeed enriching, ingredient in both writers' transmutations of
social change into literature.

Who then is Hardy's modern outsider, or 'alien invader' in
Brown's phrase, and what is his/her role? I take the tag to indicate
one who has been brought up and/or educated in a modern,
probably urban, setting quite unfamiliar to the rural protagonists,

who suddenly and unexpectedly projects himself or herself into a traditional rural community in a manner that threatens to disrupt it. This disruption is invariably dramatised by romantic or sexual inroads into the community, and also, in Hardy's later, fully developed, versions of the theme, by some ideological (moral, philosophical or economic) challenge to the traditional status quo. When we study these criteria, I think an important distinction emerges between these disruptors of the traditional order who are intrinsically outsiders, and those who are natives returning after long absence to the communities from which they sprang. This distinction illumines once again Hardy's growing awareness of his special thematic interests and technical requirements as an observer of country life who is at once detached and involved, for the returned native readily enables a complex, ambivalent assessment of both modern and traditional worlds to be presented through the troubled consciousness of one suspended between them.

The vast majority of Hardy's intrinsic outsiders fall naturally and easily into three groups: suave, shallow lady-killers; self-indulgent *femmes fatales*; and thoughtful idealists.[18] Aeneas Manston introduces this first group in Hardy's first published novel, his predatory charms directly foreshadowing those of Troy, Wildeve, Fitzpiers and Alec d'Urberville. His victim, Cytherea Graye, finds herself helplessly wondering '"how is it that man has so fascinated me?" ... She was interested in him and his marvellous beauty, as she might have been in some fascinating panther or leopard' (*DR*, pp. 169, 172).

The primary role of this type of 'invader' is clearly one of simple sexual encroachment, and only in its two final incarnations (Fitzpiers and Alec) does the Don Juan develop a significant parallel connotation of social violation; although as early as *Far from the Madding Crowd*, the potential social symbolism is present in embryo. Troy's characterisation on two or three occasions hints at the notion of a specifically modern destructive consciousness, without developing the theme;[19] and so while Brown schematises him as 'the invader from without', Troy surely remains an essentially timeless and universal symbol of rootless irresponsibility, the carefree roving soldier of ballad and folklore. The image is as traditional as that of Gabriel's faithful shepherd. In addition, Hardy tells us that Troy grew up in Weatherbury and Casterbridge, so his characterisation can scarcely be regarded as that of an 'alien invader' in any carefully formulated scheme; like Damon Wildeve, Troy's measure of alienation from the community is simply the lack of any consideration for the consequences of his impulsive actions (*FFTMC*, p. 143; *TROTN*, p. 70).

Hardy's treatment of the lady-killer type is extremely flat and detached; from Manston to Alec, they are seldom realised through glimpses of internal consciousness, as are the true Hardeian protagonists, but obliquely, through exact and vivid descriptions of their actions and effects upon others. Troy's sword-exercise is probably the classic example; again, the reader senses Alec less through clear perceptions of personal detail than through intimations of his effect upon Tess. At their most perfunctory, these characterisations may therefore appear thin and insubstantial, for Hardy's creative interest is generally engaged elsewhere. This is also true of his *femmes fatales* to some extent. While Eustacia is captured unforgettably (thought not without some sense of creative strain), Lucetta Templeman and Felice Charmond – who share common traits of exotic background, emotional self-indulgence and irresponsibility – often seem exceedingly mediocre characterisations. As one critic remarks, 'whenever [Lucetta] appears the writing becomes slack, conventional and at times melodramatic',[20] though this often appears to be a habitual Hardeian modulation of form to emulate content.

The third significant group of outsiders comprises a much more highly individualised and heterogenous trio of characters; at this point, generalisation becomes dangerously arbitrary. Yet it does seem indisputable that Henry Knight importantly anticipates Angel Clare, and that both share common aspects of the character of Clym Yeobright, their equally misguided intermediary. All three are sober, highly educated, reflective and well-intentioned young men, whose apparently commendable idealism masks a savage and unyielding moral dogmatism.[21] Just how much the disastrous repercussions of their moral idealism are attributable to their hypothetical 'modernism' is less obvious. Although they are all clearly 'outsiders' in the rural milieux in which they find themselves, largely due to a common intellectual sophistication, the primary cause of each one's fatal rejection of his lover has its basis in sexual rather than cultural dissension. Yet each of their discarded women's sexual 'falls' can be traced to her social vulnerability; as so often in Hardy, sexual and social response is felt to be entwined in a complex, dynamic relationship.[22]

It may be objected that my third grouping of 'modern outsiders' is

anomalous, for Clym does not conform to my definition of the type –
rather, he is a returned native. This is quite true, and the distinction
I think reveals how Hardy gradually, carefully felt his way towards a
symbolic figure which would fully project his instinctive themes.
Slowly the returned native becomes a paradigm of Hardy's
ambivalent feelings about social change, the focus of inner torment
and discord. In *Desperate Remedies*, Edward Springrove moves
through both traditional rural and modern urban worlds with
relative equanimity, betrayed only a certain brusque outspokenness. Fancy Day manages to accommodate herself back into the
traditional community, while it is quite clear that the increasingly
supercilious Stephen Smith will not. Ethelberta Petherwin is the
first Hardeian native to suffer real agony when she finds herself,
through her own driving ambitions, irreconcilably cut off from her
social and cultural roots;[23] and Clym is the next of the line.

From Clym onwards, Hardy concentrates his creative energies
upon those characters who find themselves 'in mid-air between two
storeys of society' (*TW*, p. 246), whether they are natives who have
literally migrated and returned like Clym and Grace, or whether –
like Henchard, Giles and Tess – they find their domestic and
vocational security eroded from without, and themselves unable to
'return' to their former social equilibrium. Even Angel represents a
synthesis of the detached outsider and the alienated countryman,
for he is a middle-class Dorset native who longs to return spiritually
and vocationally to a simpler, wholesome agricultural existence:

> Unexpectedly he began to like the outdoor life for its own
> sake ... he made close acquaintance with phenomena which he
> had before known but darkly – the seasons in their moods
> ... winds in their different tempers, trees, waters and
> mists. (*Tess*, pp. 156–7)

By the time of *Tess*, the 'ache of modernism' has become universal
– Tess, Angel and Alec are all restless and dissatisfied, in their own
different ways; and in the world of *Jude* there is nothing for the
natives to return to – Jude, Sue and Arabella have all become totally
estranged from their rural origins. Hardy's minor fiction of this final
period similarly dwells upon the theme of the native who finds, in
Thomas Wolfe's phrase, that 'you can't go home again'. George
Barnet, Sophie Twycott and Jocelyn Pierston long to 'return' to their
old lovers of a former, simpler time,[24] while the aptly-named John

Lackland, like Nicholas Long and George Barnet,[25] arrives back in his native village after years of absence to find that the only place in which he feels at home 'amid the village community that he had left behind him five-and-thirty years before' is in the churchyard, amid the gravestones of those former villagers whom he remembers. Soon, 'ghost-like', he disappears, and is not seen again. Lackland is Hardy's contemporary;[26] both story-tellers and protagonists are drawn almost exclusively from the livier class; and the orally-told anecdotes encompass both dark and sunny aspects of traditional village life. In its own modest, subdued way then, the miscellany of tales and the framing chronology of 'A Few Crusted Characters' offers a sensitive and affecting analogue to the Wessex novels in miniature.

The third important pattern continually found in Hardy's tragic drama involves the relationship between sexual and social pressures. By this I mean a theme in which Hardy examines the problems of a man/woman relationship, whether latent or actual, which cuts across barriers thrown up by class, or convention, or social conditioning. What was originally merely a rather obvious basis for a romantic plot along the lines of 'the poor man and the lady', at its shallowest verging upon a sexual fetish of class (I am thinking of *An Indiscretion in the Life of an Heiress*, or the overworked device of the secret marriage in *A Group of Noble Dames*) becomes in its more subtle manifestations a convincing and richly suggestive means of exploring the areas of social dilemma and choice which seem to have most stimulated Hardy's imagination. His novels therefore constantly inquire into the relationship of sexual and social pressures, seeking the cause of romantic attraction; asking what makes a good marriage; questioning whether one's primary loyalty is to one's inherited status – one's parents, class, social conformity – or to one's own instinctive choice of lover; enquiring which is the most important, respectability or romance; ambition or love; wealth and education, or a life of contented obscurity.

By the time of *The Woodlanders*, these questions are being posed as an explicit and fundamental feature of the novel's structure: sexual attitudes have become a vital index to the modern age's tendency towards fragmentation and separation. But in the early novels too they are to be seen growing quite spontaneously out of the quandaries of the wide range of figures embodying Hardy's theme: the humble but educated and/or ambitious livier who loves a 'lady', or (a little later) the poor girl who loves a man of superior status; the girl with several lovers, each on a different social level; the lover who chooses wrongly; the girl who marries for convenience; the patient, enduring lover who loves on through adversity. There is at the same time a notable continuity of theme. Henry Knight, Clym Yeobright and Angel Clare are clearly-related versions of a man who falls very agreeably in love with an image, without making any attempt to see the beloved as she really is, a complex individual. Similarly, Fancy, Elfride, Bathsheba, Eustacia, Grace and Sue all combine a somewhat uncertain and isolated status with a vacillating, irresponsible attitude to important decisions, which can prove devastatingly destructive. Millgate has remarked upon the theme of parental failure in the lives of Hardy's heroines, 'through selfishness, insensitivity, or death', concluding that

> as Jane Austen, Thackeray and George Eliot had earlier realised – some removal or disqualification of parental direction is indispensable to the presentation of young women acting and choosing independently.[27]

It seems important to add, firstly, that Hardy's version of this parental failure is commonly related to the mid-Victorian process of violent social change, and, secondly, that the theme of inadequate parents is one shared by Faulkner's novels, to which I shall return. Clearly, the generation gap between Hardy's young protagonists – in particular his heroines – and their parents is an unprecedentedly wide one: the two generations appear to be living simultaneously in two radically different 'worlds'. Geoffrey Day and George Melbury isolate their daughters from the traditional community by educating them to marry out of their class; Parson Swancourt is too busy with his financial speculations to care adequately for Elfride. Mrs Yeobright's inflexible determination on her son and niece 'doing well' contributes to their uncertain aims and disastrous marriages. Reckless social ambition drives Henchard to sell his wife and to mock Elizabeth-Jane's provincialisms, while Tess's early misfortunes can be blamed upon lack of normal parental guidance, itself attributable not only to the Durbeyfields' innate fecklessness but also to the chasm dividing Tess's Victorian and her mother's 'Jacobean' consciousnesses. Thus the tragic careers of Hardy's young lovers are commonly shown to originate in their uncertainty of status and in their fragmented, confused responses to new social pressures – of education, migration, 'bettering oneself' – and to vital personal choices, the most crucial of which is the choice of a lover. Throughout his life Hardy remained imaginatively fascinated by the tensions of a love affair between two members of different classes. How then is the antagonism of sexual and class motivations developed as a theme in the Wessex novels?

The most important development, closely corresponding to Hardy's shift of emphasis in his definitions of tragedy, is a growing insistence upon the perniciousness of social and class pressures in perverting spontaneous expression of 'loving-kindness' in personal relationships, sexual or otherwise. In other words, while in the earlier novels 'natural' folly plays an important and clear-cut role in causing tragic errors, Hardy's tendency is increasingly to suggest that society is largely to blame for the failure of man/woman relationships, while simultaneously pointing to the difficulty of ever adequately understanding the origin of much of life's suffering. Such a theme can be recognised as directly comparable to Faulkner's treatment of individual versus social loyalties, the social barriers in the Mississippian's case generally being those of race rather than of class. The Yoknapatawpha novels shows us the instinctive loyalties of blood, of family, undermined by the social pressures of a racial caste system, and Faulkner consequently probes the causes and effects of Southern racism, much as Hardy finds himself radically questioning the role of marriage and the effects of sexism in English society, in works which frequently offer a ferocious indictment of social oppression: 'The Son's Veto', *Tess of the d'Urbervilles*, *Jude the Obscure*.

In two early novels, *Under the Greenwood Tree* and *Far from the Madding Crowd*, the lovers are eventually able to reconcile their differences of class and conditioning in marriage (though the former novel's last words may seem to cast doubt upon Dick and Fancy's future happiness, and Gabriel and Bathsheba are united only after much suffering). A more positive final note is made possible in *Under the Greenwood Tree* only by the resilience of the traditional community in absorbing change – and the modern Fancy Day – without losing its identity. There is an air of balance and compromise in the closing chapters: Dick is trying 'to kip pace with the times' and dresses in 'a painful style of newness' on his wedding day, just as Fancy acquiesces in walking the bounds of the parish (pp. 186–7, 198). As a different solution, Gabriel and Bathsheba discover an eventual stability in a love which has developed through *working* together, 'knowing the rougher sides of each other's character, and not the best till further on' (*FFTMC*, p. 419); and it is indicative of Hardy's growing preoccupation with 'the tendency of the age' towards estrangement and isolation that when in *The Woodlanders* we find a similar potential match between working partners, Giles and Marty, the union is frustrated by Giles's yearning for a woman of superior status – who is herself persuaded to marry above her.

The precariously balanced love affairs of *Under the Greenwood Tree* and *Far from the Madding Crowd* are shaken by the destructive impetus of a natural force, the irrationality of sexual desire. But by the time of writing *The Return of the Native*, Hardy is viewing his lovers' incompatibility as a more complicated matter. Admittedly, the affairs of both Eustacia and Thomasin with Damon Wildeve are doomed simply by the universal human error of falling in love with love, as revealed in Thomasin's foolishly romantic visions of the dryly ironic Wildeve:

'Here I am asking you to marry me; when by rights you ought to be on your knees imploring me, your cruel mistress, not to refuse you, and saying it would break your heart if I did. I used to think it would be pretty and sweet like that; but how different!'
'Yes, real life is never at all like that.' (*TROTN*, p. 72)

But the more extravagant and finally tragic self-deceptions of Clym and Eustacia are examined in a rather different light. Each creates a self-delusory fantasy about the other, based upon wistfully idealistic daydreams of other social worlds and possibilities. Eustacia finds herself 'half in love with a vision' of exotic Parisian sophistication before she has even seen Clym, while he is quite undeterred by the obvious differences of temperament and philosophy which their first extended conversation reveals:

'I have come to clear away these cobwebs', said Yeobright. 'Would you like to help me – by high class teaching? We might benefit them much.'
'I don't feel quite anxious to. I have not much love for my fellow-creatures. Sometimes I quite hate them.'

'Still, I think if you were to hear my scheme you might take an interest in it. There is no use in hating people – if you hate anything, you should hate what produced them.'

'Do you mean Nature? I hate her already.'   (*TROTN*, p. 209)

Though previously warned by Sam that Eustacia is 'quite a different sort of body' from the potential school-teacher he has hoped for, it is clear that Clym has already made up his mind about what sort of person he will have the glamorous stranger be. Such is the power of their mutual wish-fulfilment that Eustacia believes that Clym will eventually carry her away to some cosmopolitan boulevard, while he, ludicrously, can claim to his mother that the romantic beauty 'would make a good matron in a boarding-school', a vision at which the mind boggles furiously (p. 215).

Hardy seldom established more firmly the ineluctable antipathy of the claims of nature and human society than in the affair of these two emotional extremists. Through inconspicuous but cumulatively persuasive patterns of incident he invests each of their characters with some symbolic reference to the conflict of the two forces. Clym, whose face we are told showed 'the mutually destructive interdependence of spirit and flesh' (p. 162), intends to bring a new social reformism to the heath; yet very soon wild nature claims him back absolutely, the description of him cutting furze being notable for its connotations of dehumanisation:

> This man from Paris was now so disguised by his leather accoutrements, and by the goggles he was obliged to wear over his eyes, that his closest friend might have passed by without recognising him. He was a brown spot in the middle of an expanse of olive-green gorse, and nothing more....
>
> His daily life was of a curious microscopic sort, his whole world being limited to a circuit of a few feet from his person. His familiars were creeping and winged things, and they seemed to enrol him in their band.   (*TROTN*, p. 273)

Clym has virtually *become* an insect, and for a moment we can sympathise with his 'educated lady-wife', who weeps to see that 'he did not care much about social failure'. There is indeed something peculiarly unsettling in the way in which a relish for the more primitive aspects of nature forces its way quite illogically into Clym's otherwise radical desire for progress:

he could not help indulging in a barbarous satisfaction at
observing that, in some of the attempts at reclamation from the
waste, tillage, after holding on for a year or two, had receded
again in despair, the ferns and furze-tufts stubbornly reasserting
themselves.   (*TROTN*, p. 198)

Hardy's marvellously vibrant yet unobtrusive symbolism quietly
drives home the realisation that one cannot expect to enjoy a way of
life which is both savagely 'natural' and educated. Meanwhile
Eustacia, who avowedly hates nature, yearns to escape from Egdon.
Yet it is tragically ironic that Hardy's 'Queen of Night' does in fact
possess, in this wild, dramatic landscape, a superbly apt setting in
which to exercise her physical and emotional charms, without once
realising it: indeed, in her brooding, enigmatic solitariness she often
seems an unconscious personification of the heath's secret qualities.[28] Hence it is not surprising that when Eustacia dances in the
pagan revel at East Egdon she feels an instinctive delight in the
'tropical sensations' of the evening. The reader recognises that,
spiritually and aesthetically, she is utterly suited to the form of this
wild, unselfconscious celebration of the senses – 'a new vitality
entered her form.... Her beginning to dance had been like a change
of atmosphere' – yet any joy she may naturally feel is checked by her
social inhibitions at finding herself a stranger, out of her class:
'joining in became a matter of difficulty' (*TROTN*, pp. 281, 283).
    There is an air of great pathos in the way in which we see Clym
and Eustacia helplessly stranded on the periphery of the vivid, if
primitive, society of Egdon; necessarily so, for *The Return of the
Native* seems to take its whole shape and texture from a Darwinian
vision of incompatibility and extinction. Immured within the
sparse, remote hamlets of Egdon, its scattered inhabitants are
forced to lead lonely and isolated lives, splendidly dramatised by
images of tiny figures set in a huge, bare landscape, and continually
reinforced by significant social details: the prevalence of 'obsolete'
features such as reddlemen and witchcraft; the lack of regularly-at-
tended church services, of a standard time, of a school; and –
perhaps most importantly – the lack of compatible suitors. In a
district where 'coldest and meanest kisses were at famine prices' (p.
96), the health and survival of the community is at risk, and can only
be maintained by a kind of flexible, rough-and-ready adaptability
accepted by Egdon's humbler folk but scorned by the more genteel
natives. The viability of social – and in particular, romantic –

relationships is therefore made a crucial theme. It seems highly significant that Captain Vye and Mrs Yeobright are haughtily stand-offish, both towards the heath-folk and each other, and that Eustacia and Wildeve are yet more contemptuous of Egdon life. Even Clym is misunderstood by the villagers with whom he wishes to communicate.[29] Thomasin and Diggory Venn, however, manage to adapt themselves with relatively little difficulty to the natural conditions of the heath, and to their changing social circumstances, which eventually makes their marriage possible. And theirs is the only union on Egdon which is depicted as both socially and (though not very convincingly, due to Diggory's confused characterisation)[30] romantically compatible.

By contrast, Clym and Eustacia have evolved into two types of consciousness quite different from those of the Egdon natives, and quite different from each other, though sharing a common unrealistic and romantic idealism. When, therefore, they are placed in the unyielding environment of the heath, it is small wonder that Clym finds that 'the rural world was not ripe for him' (p. 196), or that Eustacia cannot reconcile herself to it; or that in their lonely and confused positions they seize upon the almost irresistible temptation of a passionate affair. On their prolonged honeymoon at Alderworth, Clym and Eustacia utterly seal themselves off from the outside world, 'consuming their mutual affections at a fearfully prodigal rate' (p. 261). This ominous self-absorption is at once a dangerous excess of 'natural' sexual passion, and a disastrous effect of the lovers' lack of meaningful social outlets for their talents (or, perhaps, of the self-knowledge and confidence with which to create suitable opportunities). The contrast between their secret social ambitions and the actual conditions of their lives has become unbearable, and since Clym and Eustacia cannot adapt to their circumstances with the resourcefulness of Diggory and Thomasin, they cling for a little while, incompatibly and destructively, to each other.

The Return of the Native, therefore, offers an intermediary example of Hardeian tragedy, midway between the 'natural' tragic workings of *Far from the Madding Crowd* and the explicitly 'social' agonies of *Tess* and *Jude*. Like the otherwise very different and much less self-assured *The Hand of Ethelberta* which preceded it, *The Return of the Native* represents a further clarification of Hardy's evolving tragic vision of a state of social and personal fragmentation in which natives cannot truly return, or agree upon what, in Mrs Yeobright's term, constitutes 'doing well', or heal the 'ache of modernism' through happy marriages. One notable innovation, for example, is that Clym yearns for *downward* social mobility in search of an envisaged bucolic simplicity, as Grace and Angel are later to do. Another, more important, index of this sense of separation is the failure of most man/woman relationships, one indeed that orchestrates Hardy's entire oeuvre; and it seems necessary to examine Hardy's final treatment of the relationship between sexual and social pressures in *Jude the Obscure*, his bleakest tragedy.

Reading *Jude* can be a peculiarly distressing experience, and it is perhaps instructive to consider why this is so. Unlike *Tess*, I think that *Jude* affects the reader less through the protagonist's individual fate than through Hardy's insistence upon the relentless fragmenta-tion and dissociation of *all* aspects of human life, from the first chapter's picture of the official vandalisation of the original church at Marygreen, to the brutal, quasi-cinematic, effects which close the story, cutting between the dying Jude hearing the cheers of the Remembrance games and the uncaring Arabella hurrying away down sunlit alleys towards her admirers. *Jude* takes its bitter flavour and its shape from this merciless quality of separation – separation of man from his accustomed environment, of talent from opportun-ity, of compassion from convention, of love from marriage. Each influence which affects man – social convention, class, religion, intellectual endeavour, even nature – is shown to be antipathetic to his humanity, and to each other. The erstwhile sustaining power of traditional rural culture is seen to be broken; and Jude and Sue are themselves incompatible fragments doomed to an imperfect communion. The most effective and probably the most disturbing aspect of this process is the way in which Hardy piles up so much of the novel's oppressive weight of moral and social dilemma upon the fulcrum of sexual choice, like pressure on a nerve-end. Jude's first proud intellectual ambitions are thwarted with pitiful ease simply by the eagerness of a 'handsome country wench...to take a walk with him in her Sunday frock and ribbons' (p. 65), an impulsive yielding to desire which ends in his unintended and highly unsuitable marraige. Hardy shows these seeds of tragedy to be first scattered by a natural impulse and then nourished by inflexible social institutions, 'the fundamental error of their matrimonial union...[which] based a permanent contract on a temporary feeling' (*Jude*, p. 90). Desire for a woman similarly overcomes Jude's later religious aspirations when he recognises that his love for Sue will frustrate his plan to be ordained, for the 'human was more powerful in him than the Divine' (*Jude*, p. 227).

Jude's two lovers are expressive of a further division, between crudity and fastidiousness, both of sexuality and of personal moral consciousness in general,[31] the symbolic contrast threatening a potential clumsiness which the finely drawn characterisation of Arabella and Sue in fact transcends. They succeed in encapsulating that schizoid Victorian attitude to female sexuality which made woman into an impossibly ethereal, sexless image and yet simultaneously required that the streets of London be literally teeming with prostitutes,[32] while still impressing the reader as entirely credible and convincing creations. This is achieved by a confident handling of details of personal idiosyncracy and dialogue, and a characteristically Hardeian ambivalence of attitude towards the two women, which affords us a balanced perception of the reasonableness of Arabella's opportunism, and the wilful selfishness of Sue's idealism.

A good example of this division and of Hardy's fluctuating responses to it is provided by the chapter in which Arabella and Sue first meet, and the latter tries to prevent Jude from going out in the rain to speak to his ex-wife. Sue protests that Arabella is a 'low passioned', 'coarse' creature: yet her objections are really grounded not in ethics but in simple sexual jealousy, as she later realises: 'love has its own dark morality when rivalry enters in' (p. 286). Jude's attitude to Arabella's plight, in pointed contrast to Sue's, is one of dispassionate sympathy towards 'an erring, careless, unreflecting fellow creature', and his subsequent argument with Sue ironically tips the scales of their unresolved relationship towards Sue's admission of her love for Jude and of her tacit yielding to their sexual consummation. Arabella's presence is thereby made the indirect agent of a new honesty in Sue, the admission of her sexuality and of her involvement in that 'dark morality' of love which Jude's ex-wife so thoroughly personifies in its most primitive and negative aspects.

Moved by one of her characteristic inconsistencies – 'strange and unnecessary penances' – Sue goes the next morning to enquire after Arabella at the inn; and the exchange between the two is rich in a typically low-keyed Hardeian comedy, based not only upon the obvious contrast between the prim, hesitant Sue and the blowsy, worldly-wise Arabella, but also upon the irony of their buried similarities as sisters beneath the skin. Owing to their common attitude of sexual jealousy, Sue is secretly pleased to note Arabella's 'frowsiness', while the latter lies on the bed making dimples in hope that her visitor is Jude; and, when disillusioned, quickly intuits Sue's lack of sexual confidence:

> 'I don't know what you mean,' said Sue stiffly, 'he is mine, if you come to that!'
> 'He wasn't yesterday.'
> Sue coloured roseate, and said 'How do you know?'
> 'From your manner when you talked to me at the door. Well, my dear, you've been quick about it and I expect my visit last night helped it on – ha-ha!' (*Jude*, p. 288)

Arabella continues in this vein of blandly confidential pragmatism, advising Sue to 'coax' Jude into marriage:

> 'Life with a man is more business-like after it, and money matters work better. And then, you see, if you have rows, and he turns you out of doors, you can get the law to protect you, which you can't otherwise, unless he half runs you through with a knife, or cracks your noddle with a poker. And if he bolts away from you – I say it friendly, as woman to woman, for there's never knowing what a man med do – you'll have the sticks of furniture.... Ah, yes – you are a oneyer too, like myself.... Bolted from your first didn't you, like me?'
> 'Good morning! – I must go,' said Sue hastily.
> 'And I, too, must up and off!' replied the other, springing out of bed so suddenly that the soft parts of her person shook. Sue jumped aside in trepidation. 'Lord, I am only a woman – not a six-foot sojer!' (*Jude*, pp. 288–9)

Sue is discomfited rather in the matter of a self-congratulatory philanthropist who is unexpectedly taken aback by the canniness of the riff-raff she is patronising. But beneath the comedy of class differences, this episode is designed to emphasise the ominous gulf separating the sexuality of Arabella from that of Sue – as the latter seems wistfully half-aware: 'O Jude – I've been talking to her.... I wish I hadn't! And yet it is best to be reminded of things.... I – I can't help liking her – just a little bit! She is not an ungenerous nature' (*Jude*, p. 290). For where Arabella is thoroughly 'coarse' and – if of necessity – self-seeking, Sue is infuriatingly idealistic and 'fastidious', and Jude is destroyed largely by the warfare of these two types of consciousness, his sensitivity repelled by the former's indifferent animalism and lured towards Sue's enigmatic spirituality only to find her 'epicene tenderness' (and later, her tender piousness) 'harrowing' (p. 173). The separation is rigid and insurmountable. Since the Hardeian novel is an 'impression, not an argument', Jude's role is to question and probe this state of separation without ultimately finding a solution:

> Is it ... that the women are to blame; or is it the artificial system of things, under which the normal sex-impulses are turned into devilish domestic gins and springes to noose and hold back those who want to progress?

> I am in a chaos of principles – groping in the dark – acting by instinct and not after example.... I perceive that there is something wrong somewhere in our social formulas: what it is can only be discovered by men or women with greater insight than mine.   (pp. 238, 346)

Hardy's purpose in voicing these speculations is not to formulate an ideology, but to explore the difficulties and repercussions of acting upon this kind of social dissent. Consequently we are shown how the decision of Jude and Sue to live together, and Phillotson's resolution not to oppose them, are brave actions which allow all three to attain new and radical flashes of insight into the flawed workings of society,[33] but only at the cost of inexorable social exclusion and hostility (a curiously exact parallel to this plot is explored in Faulkner's *The Wild Palms*). Phillotson loses his post at Shaston, Jude is pushed out of the Artizans' Mutual Improvement Society, and Little Father Time is ostracised at school. As social outcasts, Jude and Sue are forced to adopt a 'shifting, almost nomadic life' (p. 328); by a skilful interlocking of his characteristic social and sexual themes, Hardy creates the image of a vicious circle wherein marital nonconformity exacerbates the domestic and cultural instability which already undermines the whole social world of *Jude*. It is therefore wholly fitting that the fragmentary remnants of the Fawleys' livier heritage (which Jude has never really known) pointedly provide the background to climactic scenes of Jude and Sue's descending spiral of separation. Jude is literally, and Sue is virtually, an orphan; after the death of his great-aunt Drusilla, and increasingly as their troubles accumulate, it is noticeable how the cousins turn to the Widow Edlin as a kind of surrogate aunt:

Jude decided to link his present with his past in some slight degree by inviting to the wedding the only person remaining on earth who was associated with his early life at Marygreen – the aged widow Mrs. Edlin, who had been his great-aunt's friend and nurse in her last illness. He had hardly expected that she would come; but she did, bringing singular presents, in the form of apples, jam, brass snuffers, an ancient pewter dish, a warming-pan, and an enormous bag of goose feathers towards a bed.

(p. 300)

She is, significantly, the novel's sole representative of the positive qualities of that traditional rural world from which Jude and Sue have been cut off, her gifts a moving reminder of their livier origins: yet all her kindnesses and commonsense bring only momentary comfort to the complex alienation of the two young lovers. Eventually they are forced to sell his 'great-aunt's heavy old furniture ... much as he would have preferred to keep the venerable goods', in an auction at which Jude and Sue, isolated in a bare upper room, overhear the bidders gossiping about them, prompting Jude to reflect that 'We must sail under sealed orders, that nobody may trace us.... We mustn't go to Alfredston, or to Melchester, or to Shaston, or to Christminster. Apart from those we may go anywhere' (pp. 324–7). Equally suggestive is the setting of their last, agonised meeting in the new, spiritually and aesthetically barren church at Marygreen, where

Everything was new, except for a few pieces of carving preserved from the wrecked old fabric, now fixed against the new walls. He stood by these; they seemed akin to the perished people of that place who were his ancestors and Sue's.   (p. 407)

Each of these scenes is shot through with a sense of loss, pointing to the protagonists' desperate need of the stable, humane and practical values which in earlier novels Hardy had identified with the traditional world of cottage-life at its best, as personified by William Dewy or Marty South. In *Jude*, the sense of that vanished world only filters through a few scattered, cryptic images of impotence and pathos – the obliterated buildings of Marygreen, the three stale buns in Aunt Drusilla's shop-window, the obsolete furniture, the goose-feathers for an unmade marital bed, Mrs Edlin's troubled sympathy; or else it appears through its less attractive legacies, such as the pig-killing which nauseates Jude, or the worthless trickster Physician Vilbert. As in *Tess*, the example or memory of that former world can no longer provide a practial redemption from the dilemmas of the present. Jude and Sue have sought meaningful values instead in the frail refuge of their relationship, with its urge to 'be joyful in what instincts Nature afforded us' (p. 358); or, failing that, in the uniformly sterile worlds of anachronistic Christminster, archaic Hellenism, or a self-lacerating fundamentalism. But the lovers' natural instincts towards self-delight are everywhere opposed by social law and by 'circumstance': and those various '-isms' are not only innately ineffectual as creeds, they are also mutually antagonistic, as Sue perceives. It is to be an ironic refinement of the lovers' tragedy that while Jude gradually frees himself from all forms of blinkering dogma, partly under Sue's influences, she eventually succumbs to an especially bigoted dependence upon the social, religious and even sexual conformism which she had once derided.

Jude heroically maintains his faith in the integrity of the love which he and Sue had enjoyed, and to the end he refuses to give credence to Sue's reactionary visions of retribution: his struggle is solely 'against man and senseless circumstance' (p. 362). But he is doomed to fail because his life has no stable centre, strive though he may to find one. Jude is Hardy's ultimate exemplar of modern, lost, alienated man, as starkly eloquent a portrayal as that of Little Father Time is diffident and overly allegorical. Such is the air of finality surrounding the tragedy of Jude, and the continual emphasis upon fragmentation which reverberates throughout its world, that it is difficult to see in what direction Hardy might have moved had he chosen to continue his novelistic career. This is not to imply that Hardy had exhausted the inspiration behind his fiction, for variations and reworkings of his familiar themes would doubtless have been possible; rather it is to suggest that Jude, like Tess, inherits the dramatic status and the burden of accumulated significance of one who is self-evidently the last of his line.

Tess *became* a homeless migrant: Jude has always been restless, for he does not belong to Marygreen, however often he returns there. As one critic has remarked, he is simply 'dumped there one dark night' off a train,[34] much as his son is later to be dispatched to Aldbrickham. Just as the titles of the book's six 'parts' testify to Jude's restless wanderings – 'At Marygreen', 'At Christminster', 'At Melchester', etc. – so the things which shape his quest fall apart, the centre cannot hold. He is constantly driven to adopt new 'lives': 'It was a new idea – the ecclesiastical and altruistic life as distinct from the intellectual and emulative life' (p. 148).

There is an unyielding barrier between Jude's true creativity and his 'dream' of it, as he once fleetingly realised in the stonemason's yard, perceiving the true dignity of his own skilled craftsmanship; but he cannot sustain 'the true illumination.... This was his form of the modern vice of unrest' (p. 104). It is this invisible barrier, this 'modern vice', which is the novel's true tragic subject, for Jude is a man of considerable potential talent, able to do several different things well – stonemasonry, baking, classical study – yet he never manages consistently to direct his full creative energies into any one channel. That he can by no means be wholly blamed for this wastage of promising material simply increases the sense of tragic pathos aroused by the devotion which Jude puts into building a model of Cardinal College, or making gingerbread 'Christminster cakes' in the shape of 'windows and towers, and pinnacles' (p. 331); culminating in the reader's final heartbreaking glimpse, across Jude's open coffin, of

old, superseded, Delphin editions of Virgil and Horace, and the dog-eared Greek Testament on the neighbouring shelf ... roughened with stone-dust where he had been in the habit of catching them up for a few minutes between his labours. (pp. 427–8)

In response to questions about his work, Faulkner frequently described his essential story as one of people 'coping', or failing to cope, with 'conflict'. These two words occur repeatedly in his interviews; thus in the 1950s he spoke of the novelist's duty to tell

the story of human beings in conflict with their nature, their character, their souls, with others, or with their environment.

a story ... of people, with their aspirations and their struggles and the bizarre, the comic, and the tragic conditions they get themselves into simply coping with themselves and one another and environment.[35]

These ideas seem to me to interlock in a number of suggestive ways with the essential features of Hardy's 'Novels of Character and Environment'. Both men's stories place a high value upon the ability to 'cope' through simple stoicism. Hardy's most cherished heroes and heroines are those who endure tragic vicissitudes of natural and social misfortune without complaint; similarly, Faulkner defined his favourite literary characters as those who 'coped with life, didn't ask any favours, never whined', like Mrs Gamp, Mercutio, Sut Lovingood or Don Quixote, also citing Lena Grove and the Bundren family as examples of his own characters who 'coped pretty well'.[36] Clearly, the two writers' familiarity with the harsh experience of Dorset liviers and labourers, or Mississippi hill-farmers, encouraged a common admiration for the virtues of imperturbability and endurance.

Faulkner's choice of favourite literary characters indicates the close relationship which he envisaged between tragedy and comedy. His frequent affectionate references to Don Quixote, whom he regarded with 'admiration and pity and amusement',[37] suggest that the latter's quest helped to form Faulkner's vision of man as a harried, bemused creature whose plight is both terrible and funny.[38]

Faulkner's stories perhaps insist more thoroughly upon the equivocation of comedy and tragedy than do those of Hardy, which tend in their tragic climaxes towards a more purely elegiac tone. Nevertheless, Hardy's habitual irony is a double-edged weapon which even in his most impassioned tragedies is frequently used to undercut the pathos of his protagonists' experiences. The effect is often very funny: Sue Bridehead's proud attack upon the tyranny of marriage vows, bolstered by quotations from her recent reading, wrings from her husband the querulous rejoinder: 'What do I care about J. S. Mill! ... I only want to lead a quiet life' (*Jude*, p. 244). The essential similarity between the two writers' balancing of tragic and comic responses to life can be effectively demonstrated by a comparison of the endings of *The Woodlanders* and *Light in August*. Both novels adopt a humorous coda with which to modulate the tone of the final pages. The tragedies of Giles, Marty, and the incipient tragedy of Grace's doomed marriage as foreseen by her father, are balanced by the farcical incident of Grace, Fitzpiers and the man-trap, and by the blunt commentary upon events supplied by Melbury's rustic companions in the inn at Sherton Abbas (*TW*, pp. 389–92). The tragedies of Joe, Joanna and Hightower are balanced in a remarkably similar way by the travelling salesman's ribald account of Byron Bunch's persistent courtship of Lena (*LIA*, pp. 371–81). The parallel is additionally fascinating in that both codas supply a detached commentary revolving around a grudgingly admiring male perspective upon the sagacity and determination of women, qualities which unobtrusively sustain much of the two novels' meaning:

> 'Tis so with couples: they do make up differences in all manners of queer ways.'

> 'What women do know nowadays! ... You can't deceive 'em as you could in my time.'
>   'What they knowed then was not small.... Always a good deal more than the men!'   (*TW*, pp. 390–1)

> 'You cant beat them'. He lies in the bed, laughing. 'Yes, sir. I be dog if you can beat them... *All she needed to do was wait. And she knew that.*'   (*LIA*, pp. 379–80)

By encouraging the reader to view the relations of the sexes as bizarre, even comic, Hardy and Faulkner in no way detract from the reader's sense of tragedy aroused by the two novels' successive portraits of tragically ill-fated affairs (Giles and Marty, Giles and Grace, Grace and Fitzpiers, Hightower and his wife, Joe and Joanna); rather, the latter are given additional depth and meaning as the narrative gains in light and shade.

There seems little risk of controversy in suggesting that, beyond this fruitful ambivalence of tone, both novelists' imaginations responded most passionately and creatively to tragic experience. Hardy's 'full look at the worst' is echoed by Faulkner's remarks that

> the good, shining cherubim to me are not very interesting, it's the dark, gallant, fallen one that is moving to me.

> it's man wishing to be braver than he is, in combat with his heart or with his fellows or with the environment, and how he fails.[39]

Both men's art is ultimately moral and philosophical in scope, being concerned to find 'a way to the better' by exploring human folly, nobility and tragedy. My main premise in the remainder of this chapter will be that Faulkner's art, like his life, was dominated by an instinctive quest to find means of coping with conflict, for a sense of equilibrium which would balance jarring forces. This compulsion may have sprung in part from his early awareness of familial disharmony, as I shall discuss; certainly it must be related, with some consciousness on Faulkner's part, to his awareness of regional tensions, 'loving it and hating it'. My interest at this point is less in the sources of this desire to achieve balance, fascinating though they are, than in the ways in which that instinct can be seen to function as a structural principle in Faulkner's fiction; and in the ways in which it forms a close counterpart to the tension between the 'customary' and 'educated' facets of Hardy's divided consciousness.

I want, therefore, to examine some of the recurrent character-types, plots, themes and narrative techniques that Faulkner uses to explore man's lack of, and need for, balance; and I hope thereby to reach some tentative conclusions about the moral, philosophical and aesthetic implications of Faulkner's work. But the most important of these conclusions can be confidently stated at the outset. It is simply that, like Hardy's 'jumbled heap of impressions', Faulkner's 'philosophy' is not easily reducible – rather, the content of his greatest novels is best approached by a study of their form. And here the importance of the concept of Faulknerian 'balance' should become immediately apparent, in the unique characteristics of his prose style – the polyrhythmical, contorted and highly-wrought language which strains to gather many different aspects of an experience into a single whole; the successive layers of narration and perspective which seek, like the 'comic' codas discussed above, to establish a multivalent version of 'truth'.[40]

The Faulknerian concern with the balancing of jarring forces and with the causes of tragic conflict is obviously related closely to the peculiar tensions of his Mississippi society, and its oppositions are accordingly reflected in a rich variety of characters. As in Hardy's 'Novels of Character and Environment', certain significant patterns of characterisation and behaviour are apparent.

One obvious tragic flaw is the alarmingly obsessive nature of many of Faulkner's characters, resulting in a dangerous lack of equilibrium. If one bears in mind Faulkner's 'verities of the human heart', which include courage, honour, pride, love, pity, compassion and sacrifice,[41] one sees that the tragedy in his stories often occurs when a powerful or talented character possesses *most* of these qualities, but with some disastrous atrophy or exaggeration of one or two elements. Thus Thomas Sutpen and John Sartoris unwittingly frustrate their great designs through a lack of compassion; Quentin's sensitivity and idealism is doomed by insufficient courage and endurance; Hightower's talents are wasted by his over-developed pride and under-developed concern for the feelings of others. In each case, the lack of one essential quality interacts with the hypertrophy of a dangerous personal obsession. This might seem a truism applicable to most forms of tragic literature, except that these characters' tragic imbalances are closely interrelated with the wider failings of their regional environment (Sutpen's and Sartoris's dreams of a plantation oligarchy, Quentin's gyneolatry, Hightower's ancestor-worship) and his protagonists' dilemmas therefore take on an added resonance which in no way diminishes their universal relevance. As Malcolm Cowley's seminal essay on Faulkner observes:

> First of all he was writing a story, and one that affected him deeply, but he was also brooding over a social situation. More or less unconsciously, the incidents in the story came to represent the forces and elements in the social situation.[42]

If we focus upon this link between character and environment then the generalisations about tragic imbalance, and the relationship between Hardeian and Faulknerian tragedy, start to become more apparent. Faulkner's novels are, he said, primarily about 'man in conflict with himself, with his fellow man, or with his time and place, his environment';[43] Yoknapatawpha, like Wessex, assumes the status and influence of a character in its own right, displaying its own internal struggle between tradition and modernism. This environmental tension has the effect of exacerbating those forms of tragedy which spring chiefly from timeless and universal defects, such as the conflicts between ambition and selflessness embodied in the stories of Sutpen, John Sartoris or Henchard; and simultaneously giving rise to new and unprecedented crises of identity and loyalty involving the relation between character and environment, which oppress sensitive idealists like Quentin, Hightower or Horace; Grace, Angel, Jude and Sue. The problem of balancing this relationship between character and environment is succinctly defined by the philosophical voice of Lucius Priest in *The Reivers*: 'my definition of intelligence ... is the ability to cope with environment: which means to accept environment yet still retain at least something of personal liberty' (*TR*, p. 103).

This I think provides a useful touchstone for a general assessment of Faulknerian tragedy. Faulkner's tragic stories reiterate the necessity for compromise and flexibility in human affairs, and reveal the dangers of those universal forms of extremism or imbalance which were particularly prevalent in Southern society – a reliance upon rigid abstractions, ideals, and 'words'. Tragedy therefore occurs when man cannot accept his environment and reacts by some form of retreat, as do Bayard, Quentin, Darl or Isaac; or when he manages to accept his environment only at the cost of his personal 'liberty' or integrity. The latter category seems to embrace both well-meaning but inadequate characters, such as Horace, Mr Compson or Gail Hightower, and all those who succumb to pernicious abstractions, such as racism, a false respectability or religious mania, in order to reconcile themselves to a problematic social environment. Not surprisingly, these tragic imbalances of character and environment show some interesting correspondences with the tragic patterns of Hardy's fiction. Faulkner's definition of 'intelligence' is clearly equally applicable to the survivors of Hardy's tragedies, characters who are able not only to endure hardships but who can also *adapt* to changing environments – such as Gabriel and Bathsheba, Thomasin and Diggory, or Elizabeth-Jane. As in Faulkner's dictum, Hardy's tragic protagonists frequently fail to cope with their environment and retreat into a destructive idealism (Henry Knight, Clym, Angel, Sue), or are simply overwhelmed (Elfride, Eustacia, Lucetta). Some accept their social environment but thereby lose their liberty or integrity, (Ethelberta and Grace); while others, such as Sutpen, Mink or the lovers of *The Wild Palms*, continue struggling against their social environment even though it eventually helps to destroy them – Henchard, Giles, Tess, Jude. Both writers examine the dangers of over-absorption into natural environment. As a result of an altruistic but somewhat excessive idealism, Clym Yeobright and Isaac McCaslin both withdraw from society into an intimate relationship with the wilderness. This impulse toward primitivism is viewed not unsympathetically, and their revulsion from conventional society has some justification, yet both men's isolation from the compromised world of ordinary humanity appears in the final analysis to be unhealthy. Their hermetic ideals help to destroy their marriages, and each story closes with a dramatic encounter with a vital and socially extrovert young woman who pointedly contrasts with the spiritual impotence of Clym and Isaac.[44]

Mink Snopes provides another interesting example of Faulknerian imbalance. Faced with an unremittingly harsh environment of
poverty and backbreaking toil, he struggles uncomplainingly,
sustained by a desperate pride which eventually prompts him to
murder the arrogant Jack Houston. By this act Mink brings down
upon himself additional and insurmountable difficulties, variously
described in *The Hamlet*, *The Mansion*, and the short story 'The
Hound'.[45] We see him battle against isolation, fatigue, hunger, his
treacherous cousin Lump, and seemingly nature itself, by the sheer
force of a stoical detachment: 'still there was nothing in his face – no
alarm, no terror, no dread … only the cold and incorrigible, the
almost peaceful, intractability … it was as if he were standing
outside of himsel' (*TH*, pp. 205, 210). In the transition of the story
from 'The Hound' in *The Hamlet*, Faulkner deliberately increases the
sense of the huge physical difficulties which Mink faces in
concealing Houston's body. As with many of Faulkner's obsessive
protagonists, Mink's behaviour provokes mixed reactions of
grudging admiration, astonishment and unease in the reader. One
is forced to acknowledge his desperate courage and determination;
after his arrest Mink tries to strangle himself by leaping out of the
sheriff's surrey,[46] and one pities the way in which he is endlessly
thwarted, even in this. Mink's fierce pride is equally striking –
self-respect is all that makes his life tolerable, and so Jack Houston's
careless contempt ensures that the only way in which Mink can cope
with his environment is by sacrificing his liberty, through murder.
Simultaneously, we regret Mink's harshness, his inflexibility, his
tragic and pathetic inability to distinguish between the true social
and economic causes of his wretchedness, and lesser indignities like
'that-ere extry one-dollar pound fee' for which he shoots Houston.
It is characteristic of Faulkner's story-telling that Mink's tragic
imbalance even has its grimly comic features. Having arrived at the
Jefferson jail half-starved and half-strangled, he smells supper
cooking. As the black inmates scatter in panic on hearing Mink's
terrible narrative ('I could have handled that dog…. But the son of a
bitch started coming to pieces on me'), his first indignant reaction is
to wonder 'Are they going to feed them niggers before they do a
white man?' (*TH*, p. 232). As we learn in 'The Hound', Mink 'had
never known a negro himself, because of the antipathy, the
economic jealousy, between his kind and negroes' (*DM*, p. 55).
Mink's ultimate tragedy is that, trapped in the poverty and
ingrained prejudices of the poor-white caste, he cannot see that

black sharecroppers are equally human and equally oppressed, or that Jack Houston is ironically, in his grim isolation and savage pride, a man very much like Mink himself. The attitude of studied moral detachment that Faulkner adopts towards Mink expresses his almost anthropological interest in man's ability to cope with difficulties, and his belief that

> Life is not interested in good and evil. Don Quixote was constantly choosing between good and evil, but then he was choosing in his dream state.... He entered reality only when he was so busy trying to cope with people that he had not time to distinguish between good and evil. Since people exist only in life, they must devote their time simply to being alive. Life is motion.[47]

This statment helps to illuminate the erroneous nature of Quentin's and Isaac's idealistic attempts to step aside from what they see as the corruption of the 'loud world', for, by withdrawing from ordinary humanity, they have abandoned that creative motion seen at its most fructifying in the travels of V. K. Ratliff or Lena Grove. And this is to touch upon another notably ambivalent theme, which might be termed that of 'quest'. Like Keats's 'noble animal Man', the Faulknerian protagonist invariably 'has a purpose and his eyes are bright with it', bent in search of (or in flight from) some crucial experience which has the power to radically transform his or her life. One recurrent motif is that of the journey, either in pursuit of a goal or in retreat from some threat: thus, for example, the stories of Bayard III, the Bundrens, Horace Benbow, Lena Grove, Joe Christmas, the Reporter and the aviators in *Pylon*, Harry and Charlotte in *The Wild Palms*, the itinerant Ratliff and Lucius Priest, all revolve around the reader's awareness of their constant motion, whether neurotic or purposeful. This overlaps with other related paradigms, such as the hunt, or a sense of exile and estrangement.[48] Another related pair of quest-motifs feature protagonists who battle against great physical difficulties (the Bundrens, the tall convict, the slave in 'Red Leaves'), or who struggle with weighty social or psychological problems, including attempts to right injustices or solve puzzling enigmas (see, for example, the activities of Quentin and Shreve, Ratliff and Gavin Stevens, Horace Benbow, Byron Bunch, Bayard II, Isaac, Chick Mallison, Mink Snopes and Lucius Priest).

Lastly, and closely related to all these motifs, there is the theme of initiation, expressed through a testing encounter, an epiphany, or a traumatic discovery. Faulkner's stories frequently focus upon the initiation of a boy or young man into adult knowledge, though opportunities for initiation and knowledge are equally available to older characters such as Byron Bunch, Gail Hightower or Gavin Stevens. Versions of this theme seem to function with particularly impressive power in Faulkner's short stories, presumably because the genre tends to depend so centrally upon a single moment of illumination.[49]

The eccentric novel *Pylon* provides some interesting examples of Faulknerian equilibrium, quest and ways of 'coping'. The urban modernism of its setting is characterised by a florid artificiality and sordid nihilism, powerfully conveyed in Faulkner's descriptions of the airport and its patron (pp. 14–15, 17, 236–7); yet unlike the Yoknapatawpha novels, *Pylon* offers no redeeming glimpses of a more integrated rural life. Instead, the antidotes to despair adopted by its frantic protagonist, the anonymous Reporter, are two versions of quixotic quest:[50] his obsessive desire to be accepted by the aviators, and his callow literary ambition to celebrate their way of life in print. *Pylon* traces his inability to cope with these quests to that tragi-comic lack of equilibrium and self-knowledge visible in other men of excessive sensibility and impracticality, such as Quentin, Darl, Horace or Gavin. The Reporter is just as restless and isolated as the aviators, but where they exhibit a Spartan resourcefulness, he is plainly a naïve, romantic idealist beneath his cynical exterior. Faulkner evokes him as a sort of novelist manqué, whose sub-literary aspirations are all too evident to the exasperated newspaper editor.[51] The Reporter's practical attempts to help the aviators end in disaster, and the two alternative descriptions of Schumann's death and funeral ceremony that he writes for the newspaper savagely expose the equal futility of his love of words. Like that other flawed Southern journalist, the unregenerated Jack Burden of *All the King's Men*,[52] he can see life only through eyes that are wholly romantic or wholly cynical. In the novel's closing scene, an impressionable young copyboy pieces together fragments of the Reporter's first, rejected copy, believing it to be 'not only news but the beginning of literature' (p. 314). What he has discovered, however, is a hyperbolic self-indulgence,[53] like the Reporter's whole obsession with the aviators; the second version, left ready for publication beneath an empty whiskey bottle, is deliberately and

brutally cynical.[54] The Reporter's inner torment is directly related to
that felt by Quentin at the end of *Absalom, Absalom!*[55] Both of the
Reporter's versions of Schumann's fate are wildly unbalanced and
false to the tragic reality of what he has witnessed, as he himself
evidently suspects, for an attached note to the editor snarls: 'I *guess
this is what you want you bastard and now I am going down Amboise St.
and get drunk a while*' (p. 315).

So far I have said little about Faulkner's personal life and family
background. *Mississippi* voices Faulkner's ambivalence towards his
regional environment, and I have tried to show how his fiction
expresses a need to balance and cope with many contrary responses
to the land and its people. Recent biographers have pointed to
similar areas of tension and ambivalence in Faulkner's personal life.
I should like, therefore, briefly to consider some of the ways in
which the concerns of Faulkner's fiction may be related to the lack of
equilibrium evident in his familial circumstances, and to attempt
subsequently to identify some of the related patterns of behaviour
and latent causes of tragedy which Faulkner uses to express his
vision of human behaviour.

Again, parallels with Hardy's life and writings prove instructive.
Both men experienced a decisive degree of alienation from their
social and cultural peer-groups, and the 'ache of modernism' felt by
their protagonists may be traced in part to this sense of estrangement. Hardy returned to Dorset from London in 1867, restless and
full of uncertain literary ambitions; Faulkner, similarly motivated,
returned from Canada after the First World War to find himself 'at
home again in Oxford, Mississippi, yet at the same time ... not at
home'.[56] His experience closely matches Hardy's awareness of the
'lost sense of home'. The reacquaintance with the rural world of
childhood was richly stimulating to the creative imagination,
indeed central to the discovery of subject. In each case it was the
writer's third novel (*Under the Greenwood Tree, Sartoris*), focussing
sharply upon the fictionalised world of the novelist's familial and
regional background after a period of personal and artistic oscilla-
tion, that finally crystallised his literary ambitions and imaginative
resources into a powerful formative model of Wessex or Yoknapatawpha.[57] But, equally, each novel's glowing celebration of that
familiar rural world is overshadowed by disturbing suggestions of
disruption and instability, faintly in *Under the Greenwood Tree*, more
emphatically in *Sartoris*. For each writer had simultaneously
discovered his ambivalence towards his environment, that his

truest art would be one which would directly confront and use this sense of inner division. Faulkner's recognition was necessarily a painful one: 'I think that a writer is a perfect case of split personality. That he is one thing when he is a writer and he is something else while he is a denizen of the world.'[58]

Hardy's love of the Dorset countryside and its people, maintained in energetic wanderings by bicycle, train and car far into his old age, also ironically found its expression through a punishing and intensely solitary dedication to his study, immured within it for hours and days at a time.[59] Faulkner's working life followed a similar pattern of retreat into a plain and monastic study,[60] even removing the door-knob to prevent unwelcome intrusions.[61] He saw the artist as a 'creature driven by demons'[62] and his inspired periods of literary creativity were punctuated by equally intensive bouts of alcoholic introspection. A psychiatrist whom Faulkner consulted during one of his worst periods of depression concluded that the novelist, in Blotner's words,

> had an intense emotional responsiveness which was different from that of ordinary people. He had such receptiveness for others that their problems hurt him. On another level, he suffered with problems of the South which were somehow related to his own tensions. He was so sensitive ... that life must have been very painful for him.... He was a man with a strong need for affection, it appeared, one looking forward to some sort of emotional equilibrium but very uncertain of finding it. He was a man built to suffer.[63]

If a psychological approach seems irrelevant to the novels, it should be emphasised that Faulkner readily acknowledged the direct relationship between the artist's inner life and creativity, remarking in his 'Introduction' to The Sound and the Fury that 'the writer unconsciously writes into every line and phrase his violent despairs and rages and frustrations or his violent prophesies [sic] of still more violent hopes',[64] and in a letter to Malcolm Cowley that 'I am telling the same story over and over, which is myself and the world'.[65] Nor need this approach be at odds with the fact that Faulkner (while clearly closer to some than to others) cannot be identified with any single character or narrative voice in his fiction. Rather, Faulkner reacted to the 'voices' which he heard within him by creating a multiplicity of voices, characters and viewpoints,[66] all

of whom speak with a certain validity and a certain degree of
fallibility.[67]

What then were the personal pressures which contributed to
Faulkner's preoccupation with conflict and balance? Wittenberg's
Faulkner: The Transfiguration of Biography and David Minter's *William
Faulkner: His Life and Work* construct a Freudian interpretation of a
childhood overshadowed by the unhappy marriage of Faulkner's
parents and the difficult choice of loyalties thrust upon him by a
fierce, proud mother and a weak, unaffectionate father.[68] Although
the marriage of Hardy's parents seems by contrast to have been a
happy one, there are some interesting parallels with Faulkner's
familial circumstances. Both writers had very strong, dominant
mothers and less forceful fathers. Jemima Hardy was stern,
sardonic and highly ambitious for the family, seeking 'to weld it
together with an intense clannishness', and Hardy was arguably
'damaged ... by so extreme an emotional dependence on his
mother'.[69] The Faulkner brothers all 'felt their mother's strong
domination and ... feared and resented it'. Nevertheless, William
continued to seek his mother's approval, admiring her 'fierce will
and enduring pride', but resenting the tensions which arose from
his parents' antipathies.[70] These tensions were largely absent in the
Hardy family, and Thomas always felt close to his father, whereas
William and Murry never established any intimacy and were
occasionally openly hostile.[71] Both writers' mothers were well-read
and encouraged their sons' study; both were fiercely ambitious for
their sons; both Jemima Hardy and Maud Faulkner resented their
son's choice of wife (and both Thomas and William soon found
themselves, to different degrees, to be unhappily married).[72] Both
writers eventually became heads of their 'clans', taking on the
responsibilities of caring for their relatives with some deliberation,
even ceremony.

Minter and Wittenberg concur in their suggestions that the strong
mother, whom Faulkner preferred to the remote father, had in his
eyes rejected him at an early age, and that this contributed to
Faulkner's ambivalent attitudes towards women.[73] Certainly the
novels express a strong attraction to and idealisation of women,
often comprised by fear and distrust: Faulkner's women protagonists are tougher, more practical than most men, natural survivors
where the men are often made vulnerable by different forms of
idealism. For example, Faulkner's first female protagonist, the aptly

named Margaret Powers, displays a pragmatism in pointed contrast to Joe Gilligan's idealisation of her:

> My good name is your trouble, not mine, Joe.... Men are the ones who worry about our good names, because they gave them to us. But we have other things to bother about, ourselves. What you mean by a good name is like a dress that's too flimsy to wear comfortably. (*SP*, p. 87)

Equally typical of the male attitude to women are Jack Houston, with 'his inherited southern–provincial–protestant fanaticism regarding marriage and female purity, the biblical Magdalen' (*TH*, p. 189), and Henry Sutpen's 'simple and erstwhile untroubled code in which females were ladies or whores or slaves' (*AA*, p. 114).

One is forcefully reminded of Hardy's similar insights, as expressed in the relationship of Angel and Tess, or in his remark concerning Lady Constantine's illicit pregnancy, that 'Women the most delicate get used to strange moral situations. Eve probably regained her normal sweet composure about a week after the Fall' (*TOAT*, p. 247).[74]

Faulkner's relationship with his mother remained to all appearances a strong one – she would later defend his novels against his father's criticism[75] – but he seems to have felt as a child, perhaps with some justification, that he suffered unfairly from a parental favouritism which was directed towards his brothers.[76] Certainly, Murry Falkner showed signs of aversion and unkindness towards his oldest son, which no doubt colour the succession of hostile father-figures in the fiction.[77] Wittenberg therefore concluded that Faulkner's later life, and fiction, expresses a

> conflict between stability and disorder ... his inner struggle with the troubling figures and relationships of his childhood and young manhood. These often appear in the form of reiterated motifs, such as tension between father and son, fraternal hostility, and the failure of love, and in recurrent character types, like the powerless child, the absent mother, the destructive father, and the young man who is impotent or doomed.[78]

Faulkner's instinctive means of coping with these tensions in his youth was to adopt an attitude of self-effacing receptiveness and curiosity towards the world around him, with a penchant for experiments in imaginative fantasy which gradually developed into forms of artistic expression.[79] Like Hardy with his 'triple existence',[80] the young Faulkner enjoyed familiarity with a wide range of town and country folk from the many different classes and races of back-country Mississippi, and Minter's comments upon this relationship are indeed strikingly evocative of Hardy's rural upbringing:

> Since William Faulkner grew up in small villages as a member of an extended and prominent family, personal and familial experiences intensified the lessons his region inculcated.... The sense of being entangled in a great web of persons and events, centering on family but extending beyond it, is everywhere present in Faulkner's fiction, from the Sartorises to the Compsons to the McCaslins.... They come to view their lives as one perpetual instant in which the life of self, family and region mingle.[81]

Faulkner's habitual courtesy and taciturnity made him a good listener, and his fiction was later to bear the rich fruit of those hours spent listening to garrulous country sages. The imaginative and aesthetic influence upon his work of those orally transmitted 'old tales and talking' is, of course, a remarkably significant strength which he shares with Hardy, who according to Millgate's biography, was also 'to an extraordinary degree – a child of the oral tradition, and perhaps, *in England*, that tradition's last and greatest product'[82] [my emphasis].

Faulkner would strive to recreate this 'great web' in the imaginative microcosm of Yoknapatawpha, and he would impose artistic order upon its bewildering cacophony of voices by refusing to choose between them, but instead reproducing everyone's point of view in carefully orchestrated series of personae. Meanwhile, as a sensitive and impressionable boy he experimented with other means of coping with conflict, somewhat reminiscent of Joyce's strategy of silence, exile and cunning. The adolescent Faulkner began appearing on the streets of Oxford in an exaggerated dress suit, which together with his appetite for alcohol and disinclination for work earned him the nickname of 'Count No 'Count'.[83] Later defensive masks and personae would include Faulkner's appearances as bohemian artist, flamboyant drunkard, Southern gentleman, First World War veteran, backwoods hunter, simple farmer and quasi-English foxhunter.

Another means of combined self-discovery and disguise lay in Faulkner's adoption of alternative father-figures, most prominent of whom was his great-grandfather William Clark Falkner whose exploits as cotton-planter, Confederate officer, entrepreneur, duellist and writer seemed to dwarf the careers of Faulkner's grandfather and father.[84] Listening to memories and tales about the old days of Mississippi, the young Faulkner inherited a unique, puzzlingly rich variety of perspectives upon his regional past and its legacy to his own society; and as he came to study his ancestor's adventurous and violent life more closely, he was evidently disturbed by the arrogance and ruthlessness which underlay the Old Colonel's glamorous image. Similarly, the young protagonists who meditate upon the career of the 'pioneer-ancestors',[85] John Sartoris, Carothers McCaslin or Thomas Sutpen, are left confused by the contrary impressions which they receive. Wittenberg identifies this theme as the 'confrontation of a young male with a troubling and powerful father-figure,'[86] and it seems ironic that in the difficult choice of responses to the ambiguous history of his region, Faulkner perhaps recognised a painful repetition of the primal tensions between himself and his parents.

These patterns help to explain the frequency in Faulkner's work of stories told from the perspective of an impressionable child or young adult. Such a protagonist finds it difficult to distinguish between legend and reality, between the claims of the traditional but disintegrating culture of the Southern past, and the confusing demands of the more impersonal, unpredictable present. This character-type clearly bears a close resemblance to Hardy's young protagonists, equally torn between tradition and modernity, and it is apparent that one crucial common factor in this disorientation is the absence of any sympathetic and dependable parent-figures. Millgate refers to the persistence of this condition in Hardy's novels,[87] and Minter's critical biography identifies what he calls Faulkner's theme of 'betrayed children' as perhaps the most prominent pattern discernible in his narratives.[88] The children of the Compson, Sartoris, Sutpen and McCaslin families, Darl Bundren, Popeye, Lena Grove, Joe Christmas, the Reporter, Charles Bon, Eula Varner and many lesser protagonists all suffer from the neglect, absence or inadequacy of their parents, in such a way as to originate or intensify their tragic vulnerability. Minter's interest in this theme is largely in its Freudian origin and compulsive expression. My concern is rather to emphasise the way in which it automatically dramatises problems of imbalance and indecision in a time and place already characterised by chronic disorientation, and the way in which it thereby interlocks with Hardy's novels as a universal paradigm of the 'ache of modernism'. To put the matter quite simply, Faulkner's theme of 'betrayed children' tests the abilities of his young protagonists to 'cope' with different kinds of conflict as independent individuals. As such it affords some of his most powerful and moving examples of tormented consciousness, like the deranged metaphysical speculations of Darl, damaged by his mother's lack of love and his own fatal introspection:

> In a strange room you must empty yourself for sleep. And before you are emptied for sleep, what are you. And when you are emptied for sleep, you are not. And when you are filled with sleep, you never were. I don't know what I am ... if I am or not.... Yet the wagon *is*, because when the wagon is *was*, Addie Bundren will not be. And Jewel *is*, so Addie Bundren must be. And then I must be, or I could not empty myself for sleep in a strange room. And so if I am not emptied yet, I am *is*.
>
> How often have I lain beneath rain on a strange roof, thinking of home.   (*AILD*, p. 65)

Darl is a kind of poet, and his strangely eloquent voice (actually heard more frequently in the monologues of *As I Lay Dying* than any other) establishes its own kind of poetic authority. But it is a dangerous power. His intuitive knowledge of others' secret hearts arouses the enmity of Jewel and Dewey Dell, and his sheer inability to break out of words and thinking into some sort of meaningful activity which will integrate him with others and the world, dooms him to isolation, nihilism and madness. Millgate points out that the passage above has correspondences with 'Quentin's state of mind on the day of his suicide';[89] and one can discover other related passages in the novels which fuse the sound of rain on a roof with reveries of nihilistic despair,[90] suggesting that the experience evoked some powerful personal significance in Faulkner's mind, emotionally akin to Hardy's equally poetic use of certain objective correlatives.[91] Faulkner's theme of betrayed children must, of course, be viewed in the context of the atmosphere, pervasive in his novels, of wider social decline in the South. For example, the plight of the Bundren children must be related to the poverty and

fecklessness of their father's wretched form of farming, and Anse
Bundren can usefully be seen as a sort of hillbilly John Durbeyfield,
while Addie's spiritual traumas render her alternately passionately
over-possessive or remote to her different children.

The Bundrens do, however, cope after a fashion, as Faulkner
acknowledged.[92] Other, more hopeless, cases of betrayed children
are closely interrelated with a yet more deadly form of social
stagnation, as central to Faulkner's Yoknapatawpha as was the
fragmentation of that traditional rural culture centring upon the
liviers to Hardy's Wessex. This phenomenon is the moral, economic
and political decay of the traditional Southern upper class, that
quasi-aristocracy represented in the novels by the Compsons or
Sartorises. The history of Faulkner's own family seemed to typify
the eclipse of this class, his father's spasmodic and ineffectual career
offering a sorry contrast to his forebears' august pursuits of cotton
planting, law or politics.[93] In Faulkner's novels the pioneer-ancestors at least possessed qualities of energy, courage and resourcefulness, which their deracinated descendants steadily exhaust,
replacing achievement with various forms of escapism. Mr Compson retreats into whiskey and satirical poetry, while Quentin's
mother exudes a maudlin self-righteousness, sacrificing all considerations of her children or of reality to her obsessive maintenance
of vain pretensions and empty proprieties, a specialised brand of
hypocrisy which Faulkner specifically associated with the moral
bankruptcy of the Southern gentry.[94] The Compsons' various
evasions of reality cripple their children's ability to cope with the
world. Caddy, Benjy, Quentin and Jason are all lost souls, each
succumbing to a different doom – self-destructive promiscuity,
solipsism and suicide, madness, avarice and cruelty. The three
brothers are each obsessed with and dependent upon Caddy, and
help to destroy her; moreover each of them is wildly unbalanced
and hence, in separate ways, insane. Nevertheless, Faulkner's
'Appendix' of 1945 ironically describes Jason as 'the first sane
Compson since before Culloden' ('Appendix', p. 16) and it should
perhaps be taken as a sign of the novelist's somewhat mellowed
moral vision that here a few modest hints of sympathy for even this
wretched man have made their appearance: Jason, too, Faulkner
sees, is largely the victim of his upbringing.[95]

Faulkner spoke of *The Sound and the Fury* as his 'best' book, 'the
one that I love the most ... the most splendid failure',[96] and he was
obviously haunted by the vision of hollowness and futility

represented by the Compson family's progressive spiral of decline.[97] Despite the 'failure' of his ideal conception of the novel, he experienced while writing it an 'ecstasy, that eager and joyous faith and anticipation of surprise which the yet unmarred sheets beneath my hand held inviolate and unfailing', which indicates the highly personal and therapeutic nature of his imaginative discovery: it 'seemed to explode on the paper before me'.[98] The discovery was not simply one of imaginative release, important though that evidently was to Faulkner the man. Faulkner the artist had discovered his true subject, the exploration of that sense of inner conflict which seemed to fill his personal life and his environment, and he had discovered his own powerful means of confronting and reconciling those conflicting voices. He had compulsively produced drawings, poems and stories from an early age,[99] out of an instinctive drive which he later recognised as confessional.[100] In his urge to achieve a sense of harmony and equilibrium through art, Faulkner at first wrote escapist poetry, a turning away from harsh realities. But when he took up the form of the novel, he began immediately to employ contrasting masks and voices, in a tentative way: his first novel even offers the reader the internal consciousness of a mule.[101] The exploration of those jarring impulses is perceptible in the ambivalences of *Sartoris*, but was achieved directly and completely for the first time in the fragmented narrative structure of *The Sound and the Fury*: 'the book just grew that way.... I was still trying to tell one story which moved me very much and each time I failed.'[102].

As one Faulkner critic has slyly remarked, 'whenever Faulkner was tempted to confess that he had failed ... the confession tended to be made in a way that made it sound more like a boast, really, than anything else'.[103] For he had learnt that his true subjects were those qualities of internal conflict, change, paradox and incompleteness which make man's life the mystery it is, and to be looked at truly they must embody those very qualities in their own telling. Form and subject must be one. Hereafter Faulkner's deliberate exploration of internal division and variety would give his work its particular richness, fluidity and tragi-comic tension. Another critic comments, 'As almost every reader has discovered, one of the characteristics of Faulkner's work is its capacity to lend itself to an unusually large number of interpretations, almost like human experience itself.'[104]

Hardy's sense of the ceaseless fluctuations and entanglements of 'life's little ironies' finds its psychological parallel in Faulkner's insistence upon the chequered nature of experience. Consequently, the passionate romantic drama of the novels is continually undercut with irony, as in the celebrated passage which closes *Sartoris*.[105] Or this effect is achieved by the heterogenous voices which argue over the meaning of events, or characters are viewed from several different perspectives. Here, for instance, is another explanation of the doomed romanticism associated with Bayard Sartoris, a flippant but not entirely unjustified opinion advanced in a much later novel:

> Bayard Sartoris drove too fast for our country roads (the Jefferson ladies said because he was grieving so over the death in battle of his twin brother that he too was seeking death though in my opinion Bayard liked war and now that there was no more war to go to, he was faced with the horrid prospect of having to go to work).   (*TTO*, p. 125)

As so often in Faulkner's work, the face of tragedy is shown to wear a grimace of wry humour when glimpsed from a slightly different angle. This attempt to impose artistic order upon contraries, to create a 'splendid and timeless beauty' out of 'the hackneyed accidents which make up this world'[106] is especially effective in Faulkner's depictions of the mingled splendour, tawdriness and folly generated by the relations between men and women. The tall convict's disastrously hare-brained scheme to rob a train is traced back, through his avid consumption of dime novels, to the romantic yearnings which he projects upon the young country girl whom he regards as his sweetheart. She visits him once in jail, is seen 'in animated conversation with one of the guards', and months later sends him a postcard of a Birmingham hotel, one window marked by an X and inscribed, 'This is where we're honnymonning at. Your friend (Mrs) Vernon Waldrip' '*TWP*, pp. 19–20, 238–9). When Will Varner discovers his daughter's pregnancy, three young men set out 'secretly and by back roads' for Texas. One is Hoake McCarron, the baby's father; the other two are unsuccessful suitors upon whom rumour has conferred ... likewise blindly and unearned the accolade of success. By fleeing they too put in a final and despairing bid for the guilt they had not compassed, the glorious shame of the ruin they did not do' (*TH*, p. 131). Both incidents beautifully capture Faulkner's delicate balancings of judgement and his interest in man's quixotic spirit, three parts shabby to one part noble.

Faulkner's artistic urge to balance and harmonise a mass of contraries found its ultimate expression, of course, in his creation of Yoknapatawpha Country; and his discovery of this personal 'cosmos' displays very close similarities to Hardy's discovery of his 'partly real, partly dream country', Wessex. The similarity continues in their use of those microcosmic worlds. Michael Millgate, who has produced some of the finest critical studies of each man's work, suggests that Yoknapatawpha County embodies a 'pastoral' strategy, 'deriving from a perennial impulse to evaluate complex societies – in the modern period, those in the urban–industrial mainstream – in terms of the standards of simpler rural worlds'.[107] This may sound like a vague truism, but if one reflects upon Millgate's particular application of the 'pastoral' to *The Hamlet*, the concept takes on a new resonance, strongly reminiscent of Hardy's choice of title for that equally 'pastoral' novel, *Far from the Madding Crowd*. The special pastoralism of both Hardy and Faulkner consists not of a simple Arcadian perspective but of a common emphasis upon irony and ambivalence in the two novelists' examinations of the tension between rural and urban, traditional and modern, 'customary' and 'educated' life. Each constantly reminds his readers that the apparent 'simplicity' of rural life is more apparent than real. John Barrell has remarked that the tone of Hardy's narratives frequently resembles that of 'a well-written Victorian guidebook', in which the authorial consciousness becomes that of a guide positioned in the landscape, pointing out its features to that urban audience of mental 'tourists'.[108] Indeed, at the end of one example cited by Barrell, the description of Blackmore Vale in chapter 2 of *Tess*, the tourists *do* appear, in the form of Angel Clare and his brothers on a walking tour; and Angel will subsequently learn to disabuse himself of some of his 'urban' notions about 'simple' milkmaids. More often though, Hardy relies upon shifts in authorial tone to counter the 'tourist's' viewpoint with a more intimate and accurate understanding of his rural world.

Faulkner's bolder experimentation with personae and multiple viewpoints enables him to develop this version of pastoral more radically, and by direct dramatisation, as in the 'astonished interest of Gavin Stevens's friend, the college professor, in Doc Hines and his wife (*LIA*, pp. 333–4). Like James Dickey's ingenuous canoeists in *Deliverance*,[109] the 'tourists' who venture into the remote recesses of Yoknapatawpha often find themselves trapped in unforeseen difficulties. The misadventures of Horace Benbow, Gowan Stevens and Temple Drake are perhaps the most instructive examples, and that other 'tourist' who is the reader is forced to share Horace's education into the hellish version of the New South which is the world of *Sanctuary*. Like Weatherbury, Hintock or Marlott, Jefferson and Frenchman's Bend are far from idyllic communities. The fates of Fanny Robin and Marty South, or of Lucy Pate and Jack Houston, are accustomed and unremarkable elements in the patterns of these 'simple rural worlds', which, the further the reader penetrates, are seen to be not so simple or coherent: *et in Arcadia ego*. Where the sentimentalism of local-colour writing offers the urban middle-class reading public a chance safely to revel in rural exoticisms, the deliberate ambivalences which characterise the presentation of Wessex and Yoknapatawpha make the reader's choice of responses both more problematic and more exciting. In their consciousness of the 'ache of modernism', Hardy and Faulkner stand both inside and outside their regional cultures, creating unique literary microcosms characterised, like our own worlds, by intense fluctuation and uncertainty.

This, of course, does not mean that the moral values of these novels are imponderable. One of the most admirably direct and forceful commentators upon the meaning of Faulkner's Yoknapa-tawpha, the novelist and critic Robert Penn Warren, remarking upon those qualities of 'unevenness' and 'vitality', explains that Faulkner

> writes of two Souths: he reports one South and he creates another.... No land in all fiction is more painstakingly analysed from the sociological point of view.... But this achievement is not Faulkner's claim to our particular attention.... Yoknapatawpha County, its people and its history, is also a parable ... [of] the recognition of the common human bond, a profound respect for the human [and of] the difficulty of respecting the human.[110]

This 'parable' is based upon the history of the South, the inner decay of its traditional culture as represented by the decline of the Compsons and Sartorises, and the rise of 'the forces of "moder-nism", embodied in ... the Snopeses ... [and] the society of finance capitalism'. But Warren argues that, beyond this, the parable of Yoknapatawpha is ultimately of universal application 'to our modern world ... not merely a legend of the South but of a

general plight and problem. The modern world is in moral
confusion... it is a world in which self-interest, workableness,
success provides the standards of conduct... in which the individual has lost his relation to society, the world of the power state in
which man is a cipher'. Various worlds of the past, like the Old
South, 'allowed traditional man to define himself as human by
setting up codes, ideas of virtue, however mistaken; by affirming
obligations, however arbitrary; by accepting the risks of humanity'.
Faulkner balances the instinctive conservatism of this philosophical
impulse by a radical critique of the traditional world, which through
evils like slavery was '"accurst" and held the seeds of its own ruin';
and by pointing beyond the tragic experience of Yoknapatawpha, to
characters who even in the modern world embody positive values,
'the glorification of human effort and human endurance', which are
not confined to any one time.[111]

This seems to me a wholly satisfying exegesis of Faulkner's
Yoknapatawpha; and, incidentally, of Hardy's Wessex. So, granted
the universal relevance of Yoknapatawpha, upon which critical
discussion widely concurs,[112] and given the rich potential of
Faulkner's regional and pesonal worlds, what *practical* fictional
strategies does Faulkner follow in expressing the ache of modernism?

In chapter 1 I suggested that the varied dating of Hardy's formal
settings was such that it allowed him to portray, in a quite
comprehensive and consistent way, the decay of the traditional
rural community life of Wessex. If one examines the apparent dating
of the action of Faulkner's Yoknapatawpha novels in the same way,
by reference to both the novels' own internal evidence and to
Cleanth Brooks's painstaking researches, then it becomes clear that
Faulkner focussed overwhelmingly upon the experience of one
particular generation of Mississippians, that born roughly between
1890 and 1905.[113] It was, of course, his own; his protagonists' dates
of birth are grouped almost equally on either side of Faulkner's, in
1897. This generation grew up during the confusing transition
between the late nineteenth-century South, long overshadowed by
past glories and defeat, and the brash world of the 'New South'
coming of age either just before, or not long after, the equally
significant watershed of the First World War. Faulkner's interest is
typically in those whom Edmond Volpe has called 'young protagonists', shown undergoing 'one crucial experience: the transition of a
boy to manhood... variations of a single prototype [which

provides one of the unifying elements in Faulkner's work'.[114] It seems to me highly significant that Faulkner chooses to examine the consciousnesses of those Southerners who, like Hardy's liviers, were most severely tested by the need to cope with rapid and disorientating social change; especially since the exceptions to this general tendency of dating can be seen to relate to other important examples of social and cultural disruption.

Correspondingly, the majority of Faulkner's novels fall into one of two categories of dating, and both suggest his interest in the effects of violent social change. One group of stories is set roughly in the first decade of the twentieth century, and these stories portray confused children or young men. Two groups of related stories predating this category, *The Unvanquished* and *Go Down, Moses*, examine other earlier periods in which children and young men experience confusing social change (the Civil War, Reconstruction and the destruction of the wilderness).[115]

The other main category comprises stories set in the 1920s, exploring a theme of intense disorientation corresponding to that era of the New South which, in Cash's words, saw 'the collapse of old standards without the creation of adequate new ones'.[116] A few other stories continue this theme into the 1930s, looking at alienated young Southerners of the 1900 generation, aimlessly drifting.[117] The two novels which have important sections set in the 1940s, *Go Down, Moses* and *The Mansion*, significantly both study the reactions of an older generation of Southerners (Isaac born in 1867, Mink in 1883) to an abrasive modern world.[118]

In these informal chronological patterns, one may perceive the same intuitive, loosely organised[119] tendencies toward sociological emphasis and thematic repetition of the ache of modernism as in Hardy's Wessex tales. In the other main organisational feature of the two microcosms, one must make a relative distinction. Faulkner's cross-referencing of persons and places in the Yoknapa-tawpha cycle is much more deliberate and pronounced than Hardy's modest moves in the same direction. Sometimes the contrasting characterisations are arbitrary and apparently without significance, as in the very different portraits of Henry Armstid in *Light in August* and *The Hamlet*: more often they establish subtle progressions in our understanding, as in the appearances of Miss Reba in *Sanctuary* and *The Reivers*; while the wildly muddled jigsaw puzzle of Thomas Sutpen's portrayal in *Absalom, Absalom!* contains much of the novel's cryptic meaning.

Finally, it would perhaps be profitable to see how some of these ideas work in one of Faulkner's most tragic novels. *Sanctuary* shows the tentative development of Faulkner's ability to cross-reference characters in the Yoknapatawpha cycle. Horace and Narcissa Benbow previously appeared in *Sartoris*, he a romantic intellectual and his sister a cool epitome of the Southern belle. Our understanding of their characters is dramatically enlarged in *Sanctuary*, while Narcissa's hypocrisy is eventually fully exposed in the story 'There Was a Queen'. Meanwhile, other personalities newly created in *Sanctuary* will reappear in different stories.

Horace's inability to cope with the conflict between his own inner compulsions and the facts of his environment is tragic because, though sharing Quentin's obsessive idealism, he shows a good deal more energy and awareness of others' needs. Like most of Faulkner's romantics, his greatest inadequacy is that foolish idealisation of women associated with the Southern aristocratic code. So when Horace discovers the disingenuousness of his idolised step-daughter Little Belle, he walks out in disgust, forgetting with characteristic impracticality to take any money with him. We are reminded of his tendencies to forgetfulness and escapism in *Sartoris*,[120] and the way in which Horace's very first encounter with Ruby Lamar reinforces Faulkner's familiar contrast between 'words' and 'doing', when she cuts directly through Horace's drunken explanations with the question 'Why did you leave your wife?' (p. 16).

Horace's quixoticism is admirable as well as foolish, however. He genuinely desires to help Ruby[121] and the unjustly accused Lee Goodwin, seeing his lawyer's quest as 'necessary to the harmony of things' (p. 219), and he struggles courageously against corrupt social forces which prove to be insuperable. His initiation into a tragic vision of reality is twofold. Like Quentin, Joe Christmas, Isaac, and many other Faulknerian protagonists, Horace is aghast to discover that women possess a secret practicality which can adapt to, and manipulate, the baser aspects of human nature, in direct contradiction to man's fond romanticisations. This practicality is seen at its best in the character of Ruby Lamar,[122] at its worst in Temple and Narcissa. Far from feeling shame at her subjection to Popeye's bizarre sexual assault, Horace realises that Temple 'was recounting the experience with actual pride, a sort of naïve and impersonal vanity ... looking from him to Miss Reba with quick darting glances like a dog driving cattle along a lane' (p. 172). The remarkable passage describing Horace's reactions to the full implications of Temple's story throws up a stream of forceful, cinematic images and associations which, while conveying Horace's own sensitivity and despair, also echo Quentin's death-wish, Darl's confusion and Wash Jones's disillusioned soliloquy:[123]

> Better for her if she were dead tonight, Horace thought.... Removed, cauterized out of the old and tragic flank of the world. And I too, now that we're all isolated, thinking of a gentle, dark wind blowing in the long corridors of sleep, of lying beneath a low cosy roof under the long sound of the rain; the evil, the injustice, the tears.   (pp. 175–6)

Horace stares at his photograph of Little Belle and loses sight of her face among blurred suggestions of female sexuality which combine 'voluptuous' promise with a surreal vision of rape. Vomiting in the bathroom, his appalled sensibilities are overwhelmed by the nightmarish sequence of images in which he is unable to distinguish between Temple's ordeal, Belle's lubricity and his own implied liability to evil (pp. 175–6).

Horace is equally shocked by his confrontations with the wholesale corruption of the society of the New South, its crooked attorneys and senators, bigoted 'church ladies' and gleeful lynch mobs. In the face of these two traumatic discoveries, Horace's sustained attempts to cope with unexpected obstacles (his beloved sister) and unfamiliar circumstances (sleeping in the cell with the Goodwins and their baby) are not unimpressive. Despite, or perhaps because of, his sustained sense of culture-shock, especially when Ruby offers her body in payment for his fees, Horace retains a bemused respect for the Goodwins' stoicism, and he considers that he has learnt at least a little from Ruby's tough self-reliance: 'Forget it, I've been paid. You won't understand it, but my soul has served an apprenticeship that has lasted for forty-three years' (p. 223). Unfortunately, Horace's complacency is a little too premature. When the travesty of justice which Lee Goodwin predicted culminates in his lynching, Horace surrenders to numbness, and eventually to the sterility of his former domestic round.

The novel's enigmatic title is of considerable interest. Whether it originates in *Measure for Measure* or Conrad's *Chance*,[124] the 'sanctuary' which Faulkner has in mind is capable of multiple interpretations. In its broadest application, it relates to the novel's central attack upon the corruption and futility of the modernistic world, suggesting the desire for harmony and security expressed by Horace's chivalric attitudes to women, and its ironic reflection in the varieties of refuges to which the women in his life actually resort. Temple protects her virtue in the corn-crib, the brothel and the smart exile of Paris; Ruby is forced to seek shelter in the dubious refuges of Southern justice and the jail; Narcissa preserves respectability by discreet treachery and untruth. The title is also applicable to Horace's own attempts to escape inner despair through idealisation of women, perhaps including Ruby. The catalogue of meanings could doubtless be extended. The novel demonstrates that in the Yoknapatawpha of 1929 there is no 'sanctuary' in which decent human values are guaranteed respect: the fictional world which Faulkner presents is as blighted as the universe of *Jude*. A few lonely hints of affirmation other than Horace's doomed struggle may be found, but they are more insubstantial than in any other Yoknapatawpha novel.

It seems highly significant that (again as with *Jude*) there is less evidence of any 'sanctuary' in country life than in *Sartoris* or *As I Lay Dying*.[125] *Sanctuary* is not a wholly urban novel, but nature seems as richly sinister as Little Belle's photograph (consider, for example, Faulkner's description of the heaven-tree in the jail yard, p. 101), while agrarian life is in a state of stagnation comparable to that created by the eviction of the liviers and the decay of village life in Hardy's Wessex:

> The house was a gutted ruin rising gaunt and stark out of a grove of unpruned cedar trees. It was ... known as the Old Frenchman place, built before the Civil War; a plantation house set in the middle of ... cottonfields and gardens and lawns long since gone back to jungle ... surrounded by abandoned grounds and fallen outbuildings but nowhere was any sign of husbandry – plough or tool; in no direction was a planted field in sight – only a gaunt weather-stained ruin in a sombre grove through which the breeze drew with a sad sound.   (pp. 8, 35)

Popeye's use of the corn-cob to rape Temple also seems to indicate the way in which the impotent values of modernistic urban culture which he represents have perverted natural and life-giving functions;[126] just as his urban bootlegging racket has disrupted the hitherto small-scale, local and traditional moonshiners' trade. It would, however, be wrong to suggest that *Sanctuary* offers an unequivocal choice between 'natural' wholesomeness and urban, modernistic chaos, for the novel's human and natural worlds often seem equally threatening.[127]

There is no sanctuary in love in this novel either, which appears at best only as a hard and violent compulsion; as in Ruby's story of Frank, her first lover (her father shoots him), or of how she prostituted herself to get Lee out of jail (he promptly beats her up). *Sanctuary* portrays various views of sex, but none of them are attractive; it is seen as futile, in the stale atmosphere of the Memphis brothel (p. 124); impossible, in the case of Popeye; or vaguely repugnant, as in the case of Horace and Belle's marriage,[128] Little Belle's sexuality or Temple's dehumanised nymphomania.[129]

Even more emphatic is *Sanctuary*'s distaste for the morally bankrupt Southern ruling class. The role of the Southern gentleman is exposed in all its hollowness in the selfish irresponsibility of Gowan Stevens, or the theatrical arrogance of Temple's father and brothers.[130] The stereotype of the Southern belle's purity is contradicted by Temple's mindless lust and perjury, or Narcissa's obsession with maintaining the appearance of respectability regardless of truth or consequences. In all these cases, the superficial image of gentility has degenerated to an empty shell, bereft of substance.

Similarly, there is no sanctuary to be found in the social institutions which supposedly maintain 'the free Democratico-Protestant atmosphere of Yoknapatawpha County' (p. 102). The bootlegger Goodwin, once arrested, is abused from the pulpit by a fanatical Baptist minister and is eventually lynched on a vacant lot. Senator Clarence Snopes and the district attorney Eustace Graham personify a secret web of political venality which links the state government and the brothels of Memphis. *Sanctuary*'s frequently unexplained suggestions of corruption and conspiracy give the novel a mood of almost unrelieved darkness, reminiscent of Jacobean tragedy or, closer to home, the genre of *film noir* which centred, like *Sanctuary*, upon the exploration of modern criminal life. As in these films, the novel's atmosphere of intrigue and corruption is a more potent influence than any single character, forming a metaphor of modernistic despair, alienation and moral anarchy. Consider, for example, the arrest and execution of Popeye. Faulkner shows us Popeye's horrific childhood in a vivid authorial flashback (pp. 241–6) but he offers no motivation for his protagon-

ist's refusal to defend himself, while Popeye is actually innocent of
the crime for which he is hanged. Meanwhile the doomed gangster
meticulously fusses over cigarette ends and shaving lotion, and is
preoccupied on the gallows only with his awry hair-style (pp.
247–52). These images all suggest a deliberate preoccupation
with style and an anarchic chaos of content which distinguishes
both the vision of modernism in *Sanctuary* and the conventions of
1940s *film noir*, which explores

> a landscape fraught with danger, full of corruption, where moral
> and intellectual values are as ill-defined and murky as the
> streets. Nothing is what it seems, and the people who ... move
> through the landscape pursue guilty secrets and dark motives
> that would not bear scrutiny under sunlight ... the use of
> flashback is often a crucial device.... [Nevertheless] *film noir*
> protagonists are not 'explained', either by the films' narrative or
> through the actors' performances. Explanations are of little value
> in a world of shifting moralities and crumbling certainties.
> Everything is suspect.[131]

This world is sharply reflected in *Sanctuary*'s depictions of the
sordid streets of Memphis, the raucous and macabre gangland
wake, the flashback sequence of Popeye's childhood or the final
glimpse of Temple Drake in Paris (cf. pp. 113–4, 193–8, 241–6,
252–3). The effects of Faulkner's tender descriptions of malig-
nant subjects gives *Sanctuary* a peculiarly unpleasant eloquence,
unique in his work. Sometimes the lurid contrasts of tone point to
the differences between two characters, such as Ruby and Horace.
Sometimes the modulations between a hardboiled, laconic Hemingway manner and lush Faulknerian rhetoric suggest the gulf
between sordid reality and private dreams, as in the poisonous
description of Horace's trip to Oxford (pp. 133–4, 137). Such
techniques sound quite civilised in the calm setting of critical
discussion, but in fact the effect of *Sanctuary*'s prose is often highly
unnerving, as in the scene where Popeye shoots Tommy and
advances upon Temple:

> Moving, he made no sound at all; the released door yawned and
> clapped against the jamb, but it made no sound either; it was as
> though sound and silence had become inverted. She could hear
> silence in a thick rustling ... she screamed, voiding the words

like hot silent bubbles into the bright silence about them.

(p. 82)

Events here seem to have become paradoxical and almost meaning-less, like the lives of the participants. The customary Faulknerian concern with the ordering and balancing of disparate elements, both of subject-matter and style, is at work in *Sanctuary* as elsewhere, though, fittingly enough, the novel's vision of experi-ence resembles not the kaleidoscopic clarity of *As I Lay Dying* or *Absalom, Absalom!*, but the violent and paradoxical equilibrium of a shattered windscreen, threatening to collapse at any moment into brittle fragments.

It might seem from my comments so far that the 'pastoral' strategy of Faulkner's work has no place in *Sanctuary*, and that its reflection of experience bears no relation to Hardy's Victorian rural world. This is not quite true, and by identifying the marginal presence of a few features associated with the traditional rural life of Yoknapa-tawpha, the reader may obtain a sharper and more balanced perspective upon the tragic excesses of modernism which engulf them. Take, for example, Faulkner's description of Jefferson on a Saturday afternoon. Horace notices country women changing into their 'finery' after a long dusty ride,

unmistakable by the unease of their garments as well as by their methods of walking, believing that town dwellers would take them for town dwellers too, not even fooling one another.... Slow as sheep they moved, tranquil, impassable ... contemplating the fretful hurrying of those in urban shirts and collars with the large, mild inscrutability of cattle or of gods, functioning outside of time, having left time lying upon the slow and imponderable land green with corn and cotton.... The sunny air was filled with competitive radios and phonographs.... The pieces which moved them were ballads simple in melody and theme, of bereavement and retribution and repentance metallically sung, blurred, emphasised by static or needle – disembodied voices blaring from imitation wood cabinets or pebble-grain horn-mouths above the rapt faces, the gnarled slow hands long shaped to the imperious earth, lugubrious, harsh and sad.   (p. 89)

The traditional dignity of these country-folk still dominates the passage, despite the very Hardeian 'ache of modernism' expressed by their gauche fascination with the trappings of urban culture. Significantly, the music to which they listen is timeless and universal in theme. The black voices which sing outside the jail represent another reminder of the rough grace of Southern folk-culture, this time the more astringent tradition of blues and gospel, 'singing of heaven and being tired' (p. 98); again, Faulkner draws attention to the stubborn celebration of human endurance and self-respect enshrined in the traditional folk music of the South, whether white or black.[132]

Lastly, and most importantly, Ruby's 'practical wisdom' (p. 160) epitomises the uncomplaining resilience and ability to cope with misfortune which Faulkner and Hardy so admired in the rural traditions of their regions. Her scathing denunciation of Temple's attitude to men, and life, is a splendid, fiercer counterpart to Marty South's unspoken contempt for Grace Melbury's fickleness in *The Woodlanders*.[133] This philosophy of endurance and self-reliance is the only positive element in the novel, akin to Dilsey's heroic labours in *The Sound and The Fury*, or Lena's imperturbability in *Light in August*. Ruby lives in a quite different world from that inhabited by Temple and Gowan Stevens, and she bitterly resents poor little rich girls or boys with a taste for slumming it.[134] Horace is equally foreign to that world, but his sympathy affords him a startling glimpse of an outlaw code which, unlike Popeye's viciousness, is not without a certain bruised nobility, and which, like Mr Sleary's circus folk in *Hard Times*, rebukes the hypocritical deprecations of 'respectable' society. While Temple, Narcissa and Little Belle conceal their different kinds of corruption within the sanctuary of Southern gyneolatry, Ruby the whore embodies a measure of fidelity, courage and sacrifice unique in the novel.[135] But if Ruby, and perhaps some of the humble country folk of Yoknapatawpha, may be seen as frail affirmations of human integrity who do a little to balance the hopelessness of what is otherwise Faulkner's most baleful novel, their influence must not be exaggerated: Ruby, even more than Dilsey, is powerless, and Horace returns defeated to his obsession with Little Belle. The ending of *Sanctuary*, like that of *Jude*, examines the ache of modernism with a rancorous and cynical eye; and the death of traditional morality is acknowledged by Faulkner's compensatory preoccupation with a lavishly morbid style:

It had been a grey day, a grey summer, a grey year.... In the pavilion a band in the horizon blue of the army played Massenet and Scriabine, and Berlioz like a thin coating of tortured Tchaikovsky on a slice of stale bread, while the twilight dissolved in wet gleams from the branches, on to the pavilion and the sombre toadstools of umbrellas. Rich and resonant the brasses crashed and died in the thick, green twilight, rolling over them in rich, sad waves. Temple yawned behind her hand, then she took out a compact and opened it upon a face in miniature, sullen and discontented and sad.   (pp. 252–3)

4
'Novels of Character and Environment': the Sense of Place and the Folk-Historical Perspective

In spite of myself I cannot help noticing countenances and tempers in objects of scenery, e.g. trees, hills, houses

(*Life*, p. 285)

Thus Tess walks on; a figure which is part of the landscape.... Every threat of that old attire has become faded and thin under the stroke of raindrops, the burn of sunbeams, and the stress of winds

(*Tess*, p. 326)

The mild red road goes on beneath the slanting and peaceful afternoon, mounting a hill. 'Well, I can bear a hill,' he thinks. ... 'It seems like a man can just about bear anything'

(*Light in August*, p. 318)

DILSEY.
They endured

('Appendix' to *The Sound and the Fury*, p. 22)

In this chapter I want to explore some of the distinctive themes in the novels of Hardy and Faulkner that might be said to represent the genre of the 'folk-historical' novel. The strong sense of place which gives their work much of its special imaginative flavour is not merely a striving after geographical authenticity; man's awareness of his environment carries important philosophical implications in both Wessex and Yoknapatawpha, notably a concern with the mysterious relationship between man and nature, and with the continuum of past and present. The novels show a constant awareness of how land and place are shaped by history, and I use the term 'folk-historical' because it seems particularly significant that this history is made up of the lives of the ordinary, common people. And, as I have already remarked, the positive emphasis placed upon humble, stoic and 'enduring' characters like Gabriel Oak or Ruby Lamar is one of the most important antidotes to 'the ache of modernism'.

Hardy's subversive and radically un-Victorian critique of society's failings, like Faulkner's highly ambivalent view of Mississippi, is profoundly affirmative of man's most basic activities and longings: against his supposed 'pessimism' one must balance Hardy's sombre but abiding humanism. Gabriel Oak, Marty South, Giles and Tess, together with Faulkner's Dilsey or Lena Grove, express the authors' common belief in something uniquely noble in mankind, the capacity for sympathy, fidelity, simple wisdom, loving-kindness; in Faulkner's words, an 'inward-lighted quality of tranquil and calm unreason ... good stock peopling in tranquil obedience to it the good earth' (*LIA*, p. 305). In their unspoken sense of affinity with their surroundings, their work, and with nature, these characters show an acceptance of their relative insignificance in the cycles of history and nature which the reader is enabled to understand as ironic testimony to their very real human worth:

> Winterborne found delight in the work even when ... he contracted to do it on portions of the woodland in which he had no personal interest ... [his] fingers were endowed with a gentle conjurer's touch in spreading the roots of each little tree, resulting in a sort of caress under which the delicate fibres all laid themselves out in their proper directions for growth. He put most of these roots towards the south-west; for, he said, in forty years' time, when some great gale is blowing from that quarter, the trees will require the strongest holdfast on that side to stand against it and not fall.   (*TW*, p. 94)

'Winterborne found delight in the work'; the words are heavy with meaning. Hardy's novels discover a fructifying power in the activity of simple, creative agricultural work, signifying the possibility of integration between individual and landscape, spirit and body. Gabriel struggles to save Bathsheba's ricks while Troy plies the workfolk with brandy, saying 'it will not rain ... he cannot stop to talk to you about such fidgets' (*FFTMC*, p. 271). Giles appears on the hill-top as an autumnal cider-maker, 'his face being sunburnt to wheat colour, his eyes blue as corn-flowers, his sleeves and leggings dyed with fruit-stains' (p. 235), as Fitzpiers vanishes through the valley below in pursuit of his sterile obsession with Mrs Charmond. A sense of unspoken pride informs both men's labours, in marked contrast to the new forces of alien futility which have infiltrated their environment. Hardy does not naïvely romanticise agricultural work (Tess's exploitation in the swede-fields of Flintcomb-Ash is not a modern and debased rural phenomenon, but a part of the traditional life which has also produced Gabriel and Giles) but that life always contains the *potential* opportunity for meaningful work which degrades neither land nor labourer, and offers a sense of fulfilment, like Tess's soothing activities as a milkmaid in 'that green trough of sappiness and humidity, the valley of the Var or Froom' (p. 209).

Bathsheba and Grace have become estranged from an under-standing of 'delight in the work', and the function of the lovers' dedication is partly to offer them a reacquaintance with this possibility, what Douglas Brown has called a 'restoration ... clean-sing, refreshing and renewing'.[1] Part of this 'restoration' consists in a new immersion in the world of nature – 'I wish I worked in the woods like Marty South!' – and part in a surrender to sensual and 'natural' rather than 'social' instincts: 'his country dress even pleased her eye; his exterior roughness fascinated her' (*TW*, pp. 251, 249). Hardy saw this last process as symptomatic of a human tendency to seek 'delight' even in the most unremarkable events of life, another of his pointers to physical and spiritual wholeness, and one which is most abundantly personified in Tess, who feels a periodic upsurge of this 'invincible instinct for self-delight', whether responding to nature or to her lover (*Tess*, pp. 136, 140, 232, 332).

But at the same time, Hardy's ontological perspective is a tragic one which recognises 'two forces ... at work here as everywhere, the inherent will to enjoy, and the circumstantial will against enjoy-ment' (*Tess*, p. 332). Man's self-delight is everywhere clipped and blighted by the Unfulfilled Intention. Marty South's fingers 'which clasped the heavy ash haft might have skilfully guided the pencil or swept the string, had they only been set to do it in good time' (*TW*, p. 41). It is then all the more to her credit that, to the admiration of Giles, she still takes a pride in the work she must do, while maintaining a clear-eyed understanding of her inferior status. She explains to Fitzpiers that her ripping-tool, 'a horse's leg-bone fitted into a handle and filed to an edge', is no more efficient a barking-instrument than the other woodmen's, but "tis only that they've less patience with the twigs, because their time is worth more than mine' (p. 166). Not only is Marty's vocational potential cramped, but her 'inherent will to enjoy' is equally doomed by the Unfulfilled Intention. Even had we been given a 'happy ending' to *The Woodlanders*, wherein Fitzpiers had married Felice Charmond and Grace had accepted Giles, as Grammer Oliver had hoped, Marty would have still remained forlorn, her chestnut hair despoiled by one woman and her lover won by the other. In Hardy's depictions of the innate unfitness of things and in his explorations of the Darwinian struggle, it is noteworthy that women (especially poor women) usually appear to be more disadvantaged than men –

At last one pays the penalty –
The woman – women always do.[2]

It is therefore natural and fitting that so many of both novelists' protagonists who suffer and yet, in Faulkner's phrase, 'endure', are women. Giles is dead, yet Marty gladly works on with his tools and press, the inheritor of his woodland skills. Tess is 'ruined', yet revives in the spring – 'some spirit within her rose automatically as the sap in the twigs' (p. 136); is married and deserted, yet still finds some faint comfort in the tipsy company of Marian and their 'memories of green, sunny, romantic Talbothays' (p. 332). The obstinate human desire for seeking out some 'delight' from among life's gloom occurs in the most unexpected and therefore poignant of contexts: as Sue frenziedly rips up the pretty embroidered nightgown which she had bought long before to please Jude, 'the tears resounding through the house like a screech-owl', Mrs Edlin's shocked reaction is to complain that

'You med ha' give it to me! ... It do make my heart ache to see such pretty open-work as that a-burned by the flames – not that ornamental night-rails can be much use to a' ould 'ooman like I. My days for such be all past and gone!'
'It is an accursed thing – it reminds me of what I want to forget!' Sue repeated. 'It is only fit for the fire!'

'Lord, you be too strict! What do ye use such words for, and condemn to hell your dear little innocent children that's lost to 'ee! Upon my life I don't call that religion!'   (*Jude*, p. 384)

This is very reasonable: the Widow Edlin provides a touchstone of simple humanity and commonsense beside Sue's perverted religiosity. But it is also oddly touching, and typically Hardeian, that the reader is suddenly given a brief poetic glimpse of an old woman's undying relish for the pleasures of youth and love, which is quite gratuitous, and yet dramatises Sue's tragedy with great finality. This affecting contrast continues, to wonderful effect. Rebuking Phillotson for what he calls his 'judicious severity', the garrulous old lady provides a telling counter-image to the travesty of Sue's joyless remarriage:

'I suppose you won't go to church with us, then?'
'No. Be hanged if I can...I don't know what the times be coming to! Matrimony have growed to be that serious in these days that one really do feel afeard to move in it at all. In my time we took it more careless; and I don't know that we was any the worse for it! When I and my poor man were jined in it we kept up the junketing all the week, and drunk the parish dry, and had to borrow half a crown to begin housekeeping!'   (p. 387)

On the rainy night when Sue forces herself to go sacrificially to Phillotson's bed, she begs the widow to stay in the spare room, and pathetically seeks her company before at last following her 'duty':

Mrs. Edlin had by this time undressed, and was about to get into bed when she said to herself: 'Ah – perhaps I'd better go and see if the little thing is all right. How it do blow and rain!'
The widow went out on the landing, and saw that Sue had disappeared. 'Ah! Poor soul! Weddings be funerals 'a b'lieve nowadays. Fifty-five years ago, come Fall, since my man and I married! Times have changed since then!'   (p. 417)

This is the last time we see Sue. Were it not that Jude's story must be finished, the novel might find a fitting ending at this point, for it announces the equivalent of Jude's death in that by giving herself to Phillotson, Sue has effectively killed herself: 'Weddings be funerals 'a b'lieve nowadays!' Again, Mrs Edlin's troubled protest serves to throw such life-denying masochism into eloquent relief, just as the pathos and courage of Marty's humble toil was further illuminated by its contrast with Fitzpiers's indolence. While Fitzpiers and Sue represent agent and victim of the tragic processes of separation, Marty (by her work) and the Widow Edlin (by her instinctive compassion) movingly indicate the tenuous possibility of harmony between natural and social impulses. If the opposing forces of separation are emphasised by the reader's awareness of the two women's relative powerlessness – 'my days for such be all past and gone' – they remain defied by the loyalty of Marty, by the widow's memories – 'my man and I' – and by the example of their quiet, enduring acceptance of life's vicissitudes – 'How it do blow and rain!'

Another fundamental aspect of the 'folk-historical' perspective is the way in which both writers continually explore some indefinable but influential interrelation between man and place. While editing his collected works for the Wessex Edition of 1912, Hardy attempted 'classifying the novels under heads that show approximately the author's aim'.[3] The first, and evidently most important classification, was a group of seven novels and two volumes of short stories, which he called 'Novels of Character and Environment'. In these works in particular, the ability or inability to make a sensitive and intelligent response to the *genius loci* of their environment offers an index of the relative spiritual wholeness of Hardy's characters. One of the reader's first clues to Dr Fitzpiers's modernistic instability is the information that

> the loneliness of Hintock life was beginning to tell upon his impressionable nature. Winter in a solitary house in the country, without society, is tolerable, may, even enjoyable and delightful, given certain conditions; but these are not the conditions which attach to the life of a professional man who drops down into such a place by mere accident. They were present to the lives of Winterborne, Melbury, and Grace; but not to the doctor's. They are old association – an almost exhaustive biographical or historical acquaintance with every object, animate or inanimate, within the observer's horizon. He must know all about those invisible ones of the days gone by, whose feet have traversed the fields which look so grey from his windows; recall whose creaking plough has turned these sods from time to time; whose hands planted the trees that form a crest to the opposite hill; whose

horses and hounds have torn through that underwood; what birds affect that particular brake; what bygone domestic dramas of love, jealousy, revenge or disappointment have been enacted in the cottages, the mansion, the street or on the green. The spot may have beauty, grandeur, salubrity, convenience; but if it lack memories it will ultimately pall upon him who settles there without opportunity of intercourse with his kind.   (*TW*, pp. 153–4)

The result of this exclusion from a sense of communion with his surroundings and their past is Fitzpiers's dangerous susceptibility to escapist visions, primarily of an 'ideal mistress', which in his nonchalant way he then projects on to Grace. A rather similar cluster of images evoke for us the young Jude's alienation from the upland cornfield of Marygreen, bare and ugly in its harrowed uniformity:

though to every clod and stone there really attached associations enough and to spare – echoes of songs from ancient harvest-days, of spoken words, and of sturdy deed ... energy, gaiety, horse-play, bickering, weariness.... Under the hedge which divided the field from a distant plantation girls had given themselves to lovers who would not turn their heads to look at them by the next harvest; and in that ancient cornfield many a man had made love-promises to a woman at whose voice he had trembled by the next seed-time after fulfilling them in the church adjoining. But this neither Jude nor the rooks around him considered. For them it was a lonely place, possessing, in the one view, only the quality of a work-ground, and in the other that of a granary good to feed in.   (*Jude*, pp. 33–4)

The effect of this passage in its context is, however, rather different. Marygreen clearly *is* unattractive, a grim and mean-spirited little hamlet recently shorn of much of its history by philistine redevelopment, just as Jude's life has already been disorientated by familial migration, tragedy and poverty. Though Jude feels as foreign to the landscape as does Fitzpiers, he is not permitted to lose himself in romantic daydreams; rather, being Jude, he confronts life's harsh realities by bold if ingenuous gestures of radical reform, allowing rooks to feed in the field, creatures which

seemed, like himself, to be living in a world which did not want them. Why should he frighten them away? ... Jude enjoyed their appetite. A magic thread of fellow-feeling united his own life with theirs. Puny and sorry as those lives were, they much resembled his own. (p. 34)

The original title for *The Woodlanders* was 'Fitzpiers at Hintock', and its embryonic suggestion of arbitrary mismatching, of disengagement with his environment, can be seen to show itself first in the passage describing Fitzpiers's rustication. And in a very similar way the uncomfortable contrast between Jude's naïve idealism and the sudden physical brutality of Farmer Troutham foreshadows the tormented philosophical oppositions of *Jude*. These are also quietly echoed in the problematic variety of perspectives with which Hardy's detached authorial voice supplies us. Jude, the rooks, the farmer, the ghosts of the vanished harvesters, all have quite different attitudes towards and associations with that lonely cornfield: with which of these is the reader to sympathise? The relation of character and environment, even in these two brief glimpses, is thus used with subtle economy to adumbrate the dilemmas which Hardy will explore, the various futures which await the dreamy 11-year-old crow-scarer, and the careless doctor.

So these characters' common lack of meaningful roots in their environments, and their resulting instability, suggests that a feeling of interrelation between man and place is necessary for mental and spiritual health, for a sense of continuity and purpose in one's life. Such 'conditions ... were present to the lives of Winterborne, Melbury, and Grace', though in the father and daughter they are atrophied by social pressures. In Warren, the maltster of *Far from the Madding Crowd*, they remain stubbornly alive; old and crooked by the fireside, he recites his 'pedigree':

'Well, I don't mind the year I were born in, but perhaps I can reckon up the places I've lived at, and so get it that way. I bode at Upper Longpuddle across there' (nodding to the north) 'till I were eleven. I bode seven at Kingsbere' (nodding to the east) 'where I took to malting. I went therefrom to Norcombe, and malted there two-and-twenty years, and two-and-twenty years I was there turnip-hoeing and harvesting. Ah, I knowed that old place, Norcombe, years afore you were thought of, Master Oak.... Then I malted at Durnover four year, and four year turnip-hoeing; and I was fourteen times eleven months at Millpond St. Jude's' (nodding north-west-by-north). 'Old Twills wouldn't hire me for more than eleven months at a time, to keep me from being

chargeable to the parish if so be I was disabled. Then I was three
year at Mellstock, and I've been here one-and-thirty year come
Candlemas. How much is that?'
    'Hundred and seventeen', chuckled another old gentleman ....
    'Well, then, that's my age,' said the maltster emphatically.
    'O no, father!' said Jacob. 'Your turnip-hoeing were in the
summer and your malting in the winter of the same years, and ye
don't ought to count both halves, father.'
    'Chok' it all! I lived through the summers, didn't I?'   (*FFTMC*,
    pp. 99–100)

The bald deliberation, the awry logic and the company's amusement do not detract from the maltster's dignity; rather, they are
well-worn and cherished elements of the secure social microcosm of
the malthouse, like the familiar anecdotes, or the cracked, two-han-
dled 'God-forgive me' which, Warren remarks, is three years older
than he. Oak's acceptance of these established features signifies his
speedy integration into the Weatherbury community, just as
Hardy's description of the maltster, 'his frosty white hair and beard
overgrowing his gnarled figure like the grey moss and lichen upon a
leafless apple-tree' (p. 89), suggests something of the old man's
harmony with the cycles of rural life and labour.
    By intuiting the natural composure radiated by such integrated
figures, the reader is all the better enabled to appreciate the
numbness crippling the sensibilities of those of Hardy's, and
Faulkner's, characters who can no longer respond sensitively to
their environment. Tim Tangs, sullenly preparing for emigration
with an unloving wife, sets a man-trap on a village footpath for
Fitzpiers, and having heard a scream goes to sleep, 'for Hintock was
dead to him already' (*TW*, p. 379). Or consider the gangster Popeye,
who emanates a 'vicious depthless quality of stamped tin ... his tight
suit and stiff hat all angles like a modernistic lampshade' (*Sanctuary*,
pp. 5, 7) as he spits into the spring, or crouches in a paroxysm of
terror when an owl passes above him.
    So in both novelists' work, a reverential awareness of the tutelary
spirit of place provides a touchstone to the meaning of a character;
more than that, it is a resource, indeed ultimately a whole
subject-matter. Tess, travelling over the hills to the Valley of the
Great Dairies, 'had never before visited this part of the country, and
yet she felt akin to the landscape' (*Tess*, p. 139) and was moved to
chant a spontaneous, 'half-unconscious rhapsody', an instinctive

celebration of the wonder of the green world around her. It is pleasant to speculate upon whether similar, if more intellectualised, epiphanies may have inspired the decisions of Hardy and Faulkner to give substance to their novelistic ambitions through the focus of 'a partly real, partly dream country',[4] the newly mythicised landscapes of Wessex and Yoknapatawpha. In sober actuality, of course, the concept of a fictional microcosm probably germinated slowly, piecemeal in each writer's imaginative unconscious, the fruit of Dorset and Mississippi childhoods each spent absorbing impressions of a remote, unsophisticated region of countryside. What is truly striking is the rich imaginative potential of each man's realisation, and the remarkable similarity of concepts involved. No less interesting are the verbal and emotional affinities between the two writers' accounts of their discoveries:[5]

Hardy: The geographical limits of the stage here trodden were not absolutely forced upon the writer by circumstances; he forced them upon himself from judgement. I considered that our magnificent heritage from the Greeks in dramatic literature found sufficient room for a large proportion of its action in an extent of their country not much larger than the half-dozen counties here reunited under the old name of Wessex, that the domestic emotions have throbbed in Wessex nooks with as much intensity as in the palaces of Europe, and that anyhow, there was quite enough human nature in Wessex for one man's literary purpose. So far was I possessed by this idea that I kept within the frontiers when it would have been easier to overleap them and give more cosmopolitan features to the narrative.[6]

Faulkner: Beginning with *Sartoris* I discovered that my own little postage stamp of native soil was worth writing about and that I would never live long enough to exhaust it, and that by sublimating the actual into the apocryphal I would have absolute liberty to use whatever talent I might have to its absolute top. It opened up a goldmine of other people, so I created a cosmos of my own.[7]

In 1892, nearing the end of his novelistic career, Hardy explained to an interviewer that back in the late 1860s

I suppose the impression which all unconsciously I had been gathering of rural life during my youth in Dorsetshire recurred to

me, and the theme – in fiction – seemed to have absolute
freshness. So in my leisure ... I began to write 'Under the
Greenwood Tree'.[8]

But an imaginary Wessex did not immediately blossom full-blown
from *Under the Greenwood Tree*. The term first appears – once only –
in the 1874 serialisation of *Far from the Madding Crowd*;[9] and then a
second time in 1875, in the first chapter of *The Hand of Ethelberta*. It
does not recur until the opening sentence of *The Mayor of Casterbridge*
(begun in 1884), a novel which goes on to establish firmly Hardy's
concept of an imaginary Wessex as a coherent social and geographical entity. Farmer James Everdene (Bathsheba's uncle) and Farmer
Boldwood of *Far from the Madding Crowd* make brief appearances
among the commissioners examining Henchard's bankruptcy,[10]
and the names of Everdene, Shiner and Darton are mentioned as
prominent farmers in the locality[11] (Shiner featuring in *Under the
Greenwood Tree*, and Darton in the short story 'Interlopers at the
Knap'). More significantly, Hardy evokes Casterbridge, like Faulkner's Jefferson, as 'the pole, focus, or nerve-knot of the surrounding
country-life', bustling with carriers' vans 'from Mellstock, Weatherbury, the Hintocks, Sherton-Abbas, Kingsbere, Overcombe'.[12] In
the late 1880s, Hardy adopts this form of proto-Faulknerian
cross-referencing, with some modest deliberation. Brief images of
the Dewy family of Mellstock flicker throughout Hardy's later
fiction with a kind of totemic significance, remembered in *Tess* (pp.
147–8); 'The Fiddler of the Reels' and 'Absentmindedness in a Parish
Choir' (*LLI*, pp. 173, 241); 'The Waiting Supper' and 'The Grave by
the Handpost' (*ACM*, pp. 44, 131). Conjuror Trendle, of 'The
Withered Arm', and Conjuror Fall, of *The Major of Casterbridge*, are
also mentioned in *Tess* (p. 172).

Meanwhile the idea of 'Wessex' had matured into a formative
principle in the composition of Hardy's greatest novels: *The
Woodlanders* and *Tess* each stress the special insular and fast-vanish-
ing qualities of the region, and share with *Jude* a theme of cyclical
travel within its borders. This development was evidently quite
deliberate, for in or about 1888, Hardy wrote to his publisher to
suggest that the firm emphasise the 'Wessex' concept in their
advertising.[13] Accordingly, when in 1895 Hardy began a series of
extensive revisions to his texts, these included standardisation of
his fictional Wessex place-names and other geographical details, to
create a coherent uniformity for the first collected edition of the

'Wessex Novels'.[14] Hardy's 1895 'Preface' to *Far from the Madding Crowd* retrospectively rationalises the evolution of an imaginary Wessex world:

> The series of novels projected being mainly of the kind called local, they seemed to require a territorial definition of some sort to lend unity to their scene. Finding that the area of a single county did not afford a canvas large enough for the purpose, and that there were objections to an invented name, I disinterred the old one. The region designated was known but vaguely, and I was often asked even by educated people where it lay. However, the press and public were kind enough to welcome the fanciful plan, and willingly joined me in the anachronism of imagining a Wessex population living under Queen Victoria; – a modern Wessex of railways, the penny post, mowing and reaping machines, union workhouses, lucifer matches, labourers who could read and write, and National School children.... Since then [i.e. 1870s] the appellation which I had thought to reserve to the horizons and landscapes of a partly real, partly dream country, has become more and more popular as a practical provincial definition; and the dream-country has, by degrees, solidified into a utilitarian region which people can go to, take a house in, and write to the papers from. But I ask all good and idealistic readers to forget this, and to refuse steadfastly to believe that there are any inhabitants of a Victorian Wessex outside these volumes in which their lives and conversations are detailed.[15]

For all its apparent matter-of-fact tone, Hardy's statement is veiled in a series of elusive equivocations characteristic of the complex 'partly real, partly dream country' which he had created. His 'modern Wessex of railways' evidently enjoys a special, self-conscious relationship with both past and present, its saturation in ancient history making it peculiarly sensitive to modernistic change; and as Hardy recites his catalogue of these innovations his novelistic imagination is clearly kindled. A similar tension informs the status of Wessex as both an imaginary and an actual country: it is at once an 'anachronism', a 'dream country' designed for 'idealistic readers', and a careful simulation of a real but ephemeral society, as Hardy explained in his 'General Preface' to the Wessex Edition of 1912:

At the dates represented in the various narrations things were like that in Wessex: the inhabitants lived in certain ways, engaged in certain occupations, kept alive certain customs, just as they are shown doing in these pages.... I have instituted inquiries to correct tricks of memory, and striven against temptations to exaggerate, in order to preserve for my own satisfaction a fairly true record of a vanishing life.[16]

In a literary essay of 1891 Hardy defined realism as 'an artificiality distilled from the fruits of closest observation',[17] for by that time he was well aware of the workings of his own creative processes. A painstaking accuracy he valued not only in historical and social detail, but found essential also in capturing a true sense of place –

I always like to have a real place in my mind for every scene in a novel. Before writing about it I generally go and see each place; no, one can't do with a picture of it. Local colour is of such importance.[18]

It is therefore not surprising to learn that Hardy plotted the course of Tess's travels across Wessex in red pencil upon a map of Dorset. Again, a notable parallel with Faulkner intrudes: Hardy wrote upon this map, 'It is to be understood that this is an imaginative Wessex only, that the places described under the names here given are not portraits of any real places, but visionary places which may approximate to the real places more or less', and signed it 'Th.H/Inv. et Del.',[19] just as Faulkner signed the map which he had drawn of his Yoknapatawpha County, 'William Faulkner, Sole Owner and Proprietor'.[20] The same delicate balance between the processes of artistic selection and mythicisation, and of scrupulous fidelity to authenticity, are at work in both men's creations. Mere accuracy for its own sake was expendable. Andrew Enstice's study of Hardy's use of landscape has shown that the portrait of Casterbridge in *The Mayor of Casterbridge* 'manipulates the reality of Dorchester, emphasising some aspects and playing down others, in order to create a very particular imaginative view of Casterbridge'; as Hardy himself admitted.[21] Hardy's and Faulkner's manipulation of actual details are designed to afford their 'dream countries' a relevance which will be both local and, also, transcending that, universal.[22] Critical analysis of the relationship between the work of Hardy and that of the Dorset dialect poet William Barnes has established this ambition as a crucial distinction between two writers who were both deeply preoccupied with personal concepts of Wessex, for while Barnes was concerned with the uniqueness of Dorset, Hardy valued its ability to provide him with universal symbols.[23] This is mirrored in Faulkner's relationship to the 'local-colour' fiction writers of the South who had preceded him. Both novelists describe a primitive and fiercely traditional rural society wilting under the pressures of an alien modernism and innate defects, a richly pregnant subject which writers like Barnes (in poetry) or Thomas Nelson Page (in short stories and novels about the American South) had approached before them.[24] But Hardy and Faulkner differ radically from such precursors, not only in the formidable range and vitality of their work, but in their quality of sceptical detachment. Barnes's Blackmore Vale liviers and Page's Virginian planters are celebrated or mourned, with varying degrees of eloquence, as representatives of an agrarian golden age; but that age always remains a small, localised one, our response to its poignancy circumscribed by a recognition of its remoteness from our own modern sensibilities, prompted by Barnes's tone of pastoral serenity or Page's virulent sentimentalism. Similarly, the painstaking exactitude with which these minor writers offer sustained examples of their regional dialects serves to narrow the focus of our sympathies even as it earns our respect, for it is a continual reminder of the gulf between their world and ours. The special gift which the vision of both Hardy and Faulkner affords the reader is to examine this gulf as an inherent part of their subject-matter, and in so doing unfailingly to touch something of the common human perceptions shared by every reader:

> They reached the feeble light, which came from the smoky lamp of a little railway station; a poor enough terrestrial star, yet in one sense of more importance to Talbothays Dairy and mankind than the celestial ones to which it stood in such humiliating contrast....
> Then there was the hissing of a train, which drew up almost silently upon the wet rails, and the milk was rapidly swung can by can into the truck. The light of the engine flashed for a second upon Tess Durbeyfield's figure, motionless under the great holly tree. No object could have looked more foreign to the gleaming cranks and wheels than this unsophisticated girl, with the round bare arms, the rainy face and hair, the suspended attitude of a

friendly leopard at pause, the printed gown of no date or fashion, and the cotton bonnet drooping on her brow ... the few minutes of contact with the whirl of material progress lingered in her thought.

'Londoners will drink it at their breakfast tomorrow, won't they?' she asked. 'Strange people that we have never seen.... Who don't know anything of us, and where it comes from; or think how we two drove miles over the moor tonight in the rain that it might reach 'em in time?   (*Tess*, p. 228)

The individual specifics defining this passage's sense of place – the holly tree, the rain, the two miles over the moor – are deliberately balanced by an effect of habitual activities and commonplace details – of milk deliveries, railway stations, milkmaids' anonymous attire and city breakfasts. A similar balance informs the contrast drawn between the one 'poor enough terrestrial star' of the station lamp and the countless 'celestial ones', reminding the reader of several of *Tess*'s philosophical themes. Firstly, the star imagery echoes Tess's earlier vision of this world as a blighted apple, reinforcing the novel's continual tension between the ideal and the actual. Yet, secondly, as Hardy is quick to point out, the humble station is vital to the dairy, and therefore to the qualities of industry, fertility and healing associated with Tess's life at Talbothays. Thirdly, the contrast reiterates the novel's emphasis upon the uniqueness of each person's life, the wonder of one's apprehension that out yonder is a vast world blithely unaware of one's existence, yet subtly linked to it. In a moment of tender insight, Angel had realised that 'Upon her sensations the whole world depended to Tess; through her existence all her fellow-creatures existed, to her' (p. 195). In other words, we can only perceive the greater world through the lineaments of the microcosmic one in which we as individuals move, and an epiphany of this sort is perhaps the secret generating the concepts of Wessex and Yoknapatawpha. Wessex *is* the sight and smell of autumnal cider-making, or a girl's silhouette in a cottage window, just as Yoknapatawpha is Dilsey singing in the kitchen, or Thomas Sutpen brooding over his dynastic ambitions; but even whilst the firm concrete details of these regional worlds are satisfying our desire for vivid actuality, so our imaginative response is also left free to appreciate these specific details as part of a greater 'web of human doings' (*TW*, p. 52) involving men's and women's labour, passion, patience, or hopes on a universal scale.

All these ideas then, are latent in the individual consciousness of time and place conveyed by the passage; and the most notable feature of Hardy's creative control is the way in which he carefully avoids making this consciousness wholly identifiable with that of Tess. Indeed, for one remarkable moment, the reader's perspective upon the scene seems to ally itself with that of a modish passenger aboard the train, staring spellbound at a vision of picturesque rusticity picked out in the light of the engine's fire-box, 'this unsophisticated girl, with ... the suspended attitude of a friendly leopard at pause'. That *leopard* is wonderful in its unexpected aptness, and so too is the writer's assurance that it is Tess who looks 'foreign to the gleaming cranks and wheels', not vice versa; it is not the hissing locomotive which astonishes the onlooker, implies the tone, but *that remarkable girl*. And then, effortlessly, we are returned to the thoughts inside Tess's head, the equal wonder of 'the whirl of material progress' as observed from the meadows of Talbothays, this viewpoint then tempered by the affectionate amusement of Clare as the passage modulates in tone once again to pursue the progress of their courtship (*Tess*, pp. 227–8).

This fluid, unpredictable quality in Hardy's sense of place must be in part referrable to his continual oscillations between Dorset and London; it seems significant, for example, that he began his novelistic career in 1867, newly returned to Bockhampton tired and ill after five years spent working in the capital. This first work, *The Poor Man and the Lady*, examined both obscure 'West-country life' and 'the billows of London',[25] some tension between the two evidently providing the creative stimulus. In a comparable way it seems clear that some briefer acquaintance with New York, New Orleans and the atmosphere (if not actuality) of the First World War were necessary to stir the would-be romantic poet Faulkner into writing the novels *Soldiers' Pay*, *Mosquitoes* and *Sartoris*. Similarly Hardy's conscious decision to establish himself in Dorchester as a successful gentleman-author, a returned native who builds himself a spacious house, Max Gate, at the same time producing his first axiomatic 'Wessex' novel, *The Mayor of Casterbridge*, finds an uncanny parallel in Faulkner's purchase and renovation of an ante-bellum mansion, Rowan Oak, in Oxford, Mississippi, in 1930, significantly near the start of his great 1929–36 period of Yoknapatawpha novels.[26]

Hardy (here unlike Faulkner) seems never to have shaken off the lure of city life, and despite his permanent domicile in Dorchester, he habitually spent several months of each year in London until well into old age. As in his life, so in his art; the tone of his novels betrays a restless, divided consciousness eloquent of the 'ache of modernism'. I have already discussed some of the reasons for, and creative consequences of, these circumstances of Hardy's life and art; I should like now to examine one further instinctive creative strategem fundamental to the character of Hardy's writing, which seems highly relevant at this point. I would suggest that one of the most characteristic modulations of Hardy's prose is that when his tone, his control of his material flounders into mediocrity – as when, for example, he introduces portentous cultural references – it is Hardy's intuitive reliance upon a sense of place which invariably comes to the rescue of his text: an ability to distil the atmosphere of a landscape, a building, a vignette of a specific time and place, into images of uncannily persuasive weight and suggestivity. For example, when Mrs Yeobright rests, anxious and exhausted, upon the knoll called the Devil's Bellows overlooking Clym and Eustacia's cottage, she sees a man approach the gate. Before entering, he

> surveyed the house with interest, and then walked round and scanned the outer boundary of the garden, as one might have done had it been the birthplace of Shakespeare, the prison of Mary Stuart, or the Chateau of Hougomont.   (*TROTN*, p. 299)

Such abstruse comparisons are unlikely to have occurred to the distraught Mrs Yeobright, preoccupied by the problems of estrangement from her son and daughter-in-law. Not only do the similes fail to illuminate her state of mind, but they likewise fall short of a useful identification with the consciousness of either the reader, or an envisaged anonymous onlooker (as the 'friendly leopard' passage in *Tess* managed so brilliantly). In a word, the historical references are redundant.

Mrs Yeobright descends the hill, prepares to knock upon the door, and the chapter ends; but not before she surveys the front garden, bathed in a sultry heat. Beneath a small apple tree, she notices that

> among the fallen apples on the ground beneath were wasps rolling drunk with the juice, or creeping about the little caves in each fruit which they had eaten out before stupefied by its sweetness. By the door lay Clym's furze-hook and the last handful of faggot-bonds she had seen him gather; they had

plainly been thrown down there as he entered the house.

(p. 299)

To the attentive reader, the humble image of the wasps immediately quivers with significance. Only two pages earlier, Mrs Yeobright has paused in her walk to study 'independent worlds of ephemerons', short-lived summer insects

> in mad carousal ... heaving and wallowing with enjoyment. Being a woman not disinclined to philosophise she sometimes sat down under her umbrella to rest and watch their happiness, for a certain hopefulness as to the result of her visit gave ease to her mind, and between important thoughts left it free to dwell on any infinitesimal matter which caught her eyes.   (p. 297)

Here then is another 'infinitesimal ... independent world' of creatures; and if Mrs Yeobright remains in philosophical mood she might (along with the reader) find in the glimpse of the drunken wasps, 'stupified by ... sweetness', an apt natural corollary for the lovesick self-indulgence with which Eustacia infects young men. The first is her son, who only a few weeks earlier had spent his honeymoon in that same cottage, 'enclosed in a sort of luminous mist' (p. 261) shutting him off from his mother, and the second is Wildeve, whose furtive presence there now is the direct reason for the unopened door confronting her.

This, of course, is not pedantically to insist that Mrs Yeobright *does* reflect upon these analogies in this way: the actual moments when she knocks upon the door and wanders away desolated are left unreported by Hardy. Yet she has been introduced to us as a singularly intuitive, reflective woman,[27] and it is peculiarly satisfying – as the references to Mary Stuart *et al.* are plainly not – that the minute image of the wasps is made available to the reader as a possible analogue to the ambience of those moments, just as her son's abandoned furze-hook and faggot-bonds are suggestive of Clym's inability either to free himself from the heath (another cause of his mother's grief) or to tame its wildness.

As has often been remarked, Hardy's ability to seize upon these atmospherics of place is curiously reminiscent of a film-director's selection of sensuous particulars both visual and auditory, of the camera surveying from afar, zooming in to close range, cutting to and fro, establishing visual and behavioural affinities, and constantly relating character to, and defining it by, its environment. Just as Hardy's overall fictional strategy is to seek 'the four quarters of the globe' among 'Wessex nooks',[28] so on a smaller scale his characteristic technique is to embody the myriad poetic 'impressions' of his text in an imagery featuring very specific physical objects and landscapes. Hardy noted in his journal that 'My art is to intensify the expression of things ... so that the heart and inner meaning is made vividly visible'[29] and this process of intensification habitually takes the form of interrelating the characteristics of human nature with those of the physical world around us: 'In spite of myself I cannot help noticing countenances and tempers in objects of scenery, e.g. trees, hills, houses'.[30] Hence the inside of Tess's mouth shows red like a snake's, woodsmoke curls and droops like a blue feather in a lady's hat, blown leaves scratch floors like the skirts of timid visitors, a man's stifled passions show old floodmarks faintly visible. Hardy's proliferation of such similes and metaphors is distinguished chiefly by its startling felicity; but his poetic method also extends to the sustained use of a more imponderable imagery; in his own words, 'those familiar conjunctions of things wherewith the inanimate world baits the mind of man when he pauses in moments of suspense' (*APOBE*, p. 240), quite unique in its lavish mingling of the properties of men and things. Hardy uses this anthropomorphic technique both as an imagistic framework underlying the story, as in the tree symbolism of *The Woodlanders* or in the deliberately variegated landscapes of *Tess*, and as an intermittent, spontaneous freshet of poetic insight, responsible for many of the most impressive and disturbing moments of the novels.[31] Again, it is a characteristic amply shared by Faulkner's novels:

> It seemed to Quentin that he could actually see them facing one another at the gate. Inside the gate what was once a park now spread, unkempt, in shaggy desolation, with an air dreamy, remote and aghast like the unshaven face of a man just waking from ether, up to a huge house where a young girl waited in a wedding dress made from stolen scraps, the house partaking too of that air of scaling desolation. (*AA*, p. 132)

The 'aghast' face of the ruined park inevitably suggests the traumas of Henry Sutpen (and his alter ego, Quentin Compson), 'just waking' up to the full horror of Southern history, and its personal dilemmas of incest and miscegenation; as a more general symbol, it evokes for us the grim aftermath of the nightmarish Civil War; and of course it seems to anticipate the tragic, deadly face of Henry as an old man which Quentin will see when he finally visits the plantation. But the most forceful impact of the passage is simply that we see and feel this dream-landscape unfolding like a film inside Quentin's head: we momentarily become Quentin.

It may at first seem difficult to reach any general conclusions about the intentions informing Hardy's outbursts of this intuitive imagery, other than that, firstly, they are always prompted by a powerful sense of interplay between a specific character's sensibility and a specific sense of place and time, and secondly, that they invariably signify some quickening of the novelist's philosophical 'impressions'. Since the 'conjunctions' usually (though not always) conjoin man and nature, and since Hardy's attitude to nature is never constant, even within a single novel, these impressions remain, as ever in Hardy's work, a 'confused heap' that the reader must approach without preconception, as something forever new and unexpected. It is perhaps this unpredictable and imponderable quality in the nuances of Hardy's writing which so irritated T. S. Eliot and led him to speak of it as existing solely 'for the sake of self-expression'.[32] I have been concerned constantly to stress ambivalence, fluctuation, instability as dictating not only the subject but also the very form of Hardy's work; and with the advantage of hindsight it is possible, *pace* Eliot, to recognise in the mercurial fluctuations of Hardy's imagistic technique one of many late nineteenth-century attempts to break out of the confines of the Naturalist tradition, to 'intensify the expression of things':

> After looking at the landscape ascribed to Bonington in our drawing-room I feel that Nature is played out as a Beauty, but not as a Mystery. I don't want to see landscapes i.e., scenic paintings of them, because I don't want to see the original realities – as optical effects, that is. I want to see the deeper reality underlying the scenic, the expression of what are sometimes called abstract imaginings.
>
> The 'simply natural' is interesting no longer. The much decried mad, late-Turner rendering is now necessary to create my interest. The exact truth as to material fact ... does not bring anything to the object that coalesces with and translates the

qualities that are already there, – half hidden it may be – and the
two united are depicted as the All.[33]

It is significant that this entry in Hardy's notebook was provoked
by a consideration of two painters and their visual responses to
landscape, for Hardy's 'abstract imaginings' always thrust outwards from the basis of concrete particulars of place and object.
Accordingly, to the habitual reader of Hardy, one of the most
familiar progressions of imagery begins with a character, crisply
evoked in a specific setting, drifting into a state of reverie; the prose
then quickens, assuming a trembling, quicksilver quality of
impressionistic poetry which suddenly seizes upon the physical
details of time and place in a kind of fierce lust for metaphysical
fulfilment. Consider, for example, the technique by which Elizabeth-Jane's nightly vigils over her dying mother are recorded:

> To learn to take the universe seriously there is no quicker way
> than to watch – to be a 'waker', as the country-people call it.
> Between the hours at which the last toss-pot went by and the first
> sparrow shook himself, the silence in Casterbridge – barring the
> rare sound of the watchman – was broken in Elizabeth's ear only
> by the time-piece in her bedroom ticking frantically against the
> clock on the stairs; ticking harder till it seemed to clang like a gong;
> and all this while the subtle-souled girl asking herself why she
> was born, why sitting in a room, and blinking at the candle; why
> things around her had taken the shape they were in preference to
> every other possible shape. Why they stared at her so helplessly,
> as if waiting for the touch of some wand that should release them
> from terrestrial constraint; what that chaos called consciousness,
> which spun in her at this moment like a top, tended to, and began
> in. Her eyes fell together; she was awake, yet she was
> asleep. (*TMOC*, p. 147)

Hardy's prose rapidly accelerates from firm particulars into 'abstract
imaginings' which we seem to feel pulsating inside Elizabeth-Jane's
mind. The unexpected movement between the calm, indeed
sometimes drab, surface of Hardy's more workaday prose and these
interjections of poetry, now in the ascendant, now in minor key,
often absent altogether for long periods, is a constant element of his
writing,[34] as is the progression between outer and inner mental
landscapes; but, as I have said, each of these 'conjunctions of things

is otherwise quite unique and autonomous. Sometimes these poetic images manifest themselves as fully-rounded objective correlatives in the formal sense of Eliot's definition,[35] as when Giles and Grace feel the upsurge of a mutual but unspoken, taboo passion:

> With their mind on these things they passed so far round the hill that the whole west sky was revealed. Between the broken clouds they could see far into the recesses of heaven as they mused and walked, the eye journeying on under a species of golden arcades, and past fiery obstructions, fancied cairns, logan-stones, stalactites and stalagmites of topaz. Deeper than this their gaze passed thin flakes of incandescence, till it plunged into a bottomless medium of soft green fire.   (*TW*, p. 236)

The majesty of the sunset sky offers a richly appropriate correlative for Giles and Grace's unattainable yearnings. Its remarkable power springs partly from the visual splendour of the imagery, with its irresistible chains of association between sacred otherworlds ('heaven', golden arcades, cairns and logan-stones) and longed-for sensual fulfilment (a dream-landscape with the buried erotic connotations of recesses and stalagmites, a continual 'plunging' motion 'deeper' into 'bottomless ... soft green fire'). The context of the passage, startlingly rearing up in the midst of the lovers' shy and stilted conversation, also helps amplify its effects. Yet in terms of literary technique, Hardy's objective correlative of sunset for human passion is a simple and straightforward poetic conception: indeed, that is part of its strength.

Elsewhere Hardy's imagination frequently throws off these 'conjunctions of things' in a more complex gratuitous profusion, seemingly only semi-consciously, like an imagistic shorthand noted down by a mind too impatient to render a full transcription. Frequently, the effect suggests a teasing revelation of some esoteric mystery, a trembling upon the brink of some anthropomorphic knowledge. A striking illustration of this Hardeian technique of understated or half-submerged 'conjunctions' is provided by the descriptions of Mrs Yeobright's experiences on the afternoon of the day she dies, which I touched upon earlier. Unfortunately, adequate quotation is difficult, for her journeys over the heath occupy most of two chapters.[36] As briefly as possible, then, Mrs Yeobright sets out 'to do her best in getting reconciled with [Clym] and Eustacia', and on her walk to and from their cottage she engages in a series of contemplations over 'independent worlds' comprising other, humbler creatures (pp. 296, 297). We muse with her over the maggots in a dried pool, 'heaving and wallowing with enjoyment'; a furze-cutter who seems 'a mere parasite of the heath'; the trees on the Devil's Bellows, as 'storm-broken and exhausted' as she feels by then; the natural life of the garden at Alderworth, including the drunken wasps remarked earlier; the little Johnny Nonsuch; a colony of ants; and a heron. There is a crucial distinction to be observed between Mrs Yeobright's own perspective upon these conjunctions of things, and that given by Hardy to the reader. Mrs Yeobright's 'philosophises' upon these 'independent worlds', establishing a number of latent comparisons between natural and human life: the furze-cutter is like an insect, hollyhocks hang like half-closed umbrellas, the ants' pathway is like a city street. It is clearly her varying moods which are responsible for the subjective selection and description of these worlds: she watches the maggots blithely when she is optimistic, sees the trees as 'storm-beaten and exhausted' when she is weary, fails to communicate with Johnny Nonsuch when she feels rejected. As Hardy wrote of Knight on the cliff, 'we colour according to our moods the objects we survey'. What the reader therefore learns from this imagery is not what nature is really like – indeed Hardy constantly reminds us that, despite Mrs Yeobright's comparisons, the 'independent worlds' remain inscrutable, quite heedless of man – but what the old lady is feeling. These 'conjunctions' therefore provide for the reader a series of oblique analogues for Mrs Yeobright's varying states of mind. Some function fairly straightfor- wardly as objective correlatives, such as the blasted fir-trees; others, like the drunken wasps, are more subliminal in their effects. The reader is enabled to perceive that the one common feature shared by each of these 'independent worlds' is, precisely, their independ- ence from man, and lack of concern for his activities, despite superficial resemblances.

It is unclear whether Mrs Yeobright shares this perception, but one suspects that it is unlikely, a suspicion which serves to increase the pathos of her experiences. The fourth book, from which these two chapters are drawn, is ominously entitled 'The Closed Door', and Eustacia's refusal to answer that door is merely one of a melancholy succession of symbolic reminders in *The Return of the Native* of the human inability to communicate adequately with others, like the images of exclusion, loneliness and fear which fracture the conversation between Mrs Yeobright and Johnny Nonsuch. Her attempt at reconciliation comes to naught, while each of her other encounters suggests the same sense of insurmountable isolation between human and natural worlds. While this is perhaps partly due to Mrs Yeobright's own rather dour aura, there are more important implications that this sense of exclusion and estrangement is a part of the general human condition. Mrs Yeobright's journey is only one minute element in a colossal pattern of other creatures' activities and desires, as is made clear by the sweeping cinematic technique of Hardy's narrative, and by its detached tone. Thus 'Thursday, the thirty-first of August' is to prove a momentous day for the Yeobrights; but to most creatures on Egdon it is merely 'one of a series of days during which snug houses were stifling' (p. 296), part of an impersonal continuum of time and space. Her contemplations succeed only in illuminating the paradoxical human predicament of being closely interrelated with creatures and places and processes which will always remain ultimately unknowable:

> The sun had now got far to the west of south and stood directly in her face, like some merciless incendiary, brand in hand, waiting to consume her. With the departure of the boy all visible animation disappeared from the landscape, though the intermittent husky notes of the male grasshoppers from every tuft of furze were enough to show that amid the prostration of the larger animal species an unseen insect world was busy in all the fullness of life.
> ... In front of her a colony of ants had established a thoroughfare across the way, where they toiled a never-ending and heavy-laden throng. To look down upon them was like observing a city street from the top of a tower. She remembered that this bustle of ants had been in progress for years at the same spot – doubtless those of the old times were the ancestors of those which walked there now. She leant back to obtain more thorough rest, and the soft eastern portion of the sky was as great a relief to her eyes as the thyme was to her head. While she looked a heron arose on that side of the sky and flew on with his face towards the sun. He had come dripping wet from some pool in the valleys, and as he flew the edges and linings of his wings, his thighs, and his breast were so caught by the bright sunbeams that he appeared as if formed of burnished silver. Up in the zenith where he was seemed a free and happy place, away from all contact with

the earthly ball to which she was pinioned; and she wished that she
could arise uncrushed from its surface and fly as he flew then.

But, being a mother, it was inevitable that she should soon cease
to ruminate upon her own condition. Had the track of her next
thought had been marked by a streak in the air, like the path of a
meteor, it would have shown a direction contrary to the heron's,
and have descended to the eastward upon the roof of Clym's
house.   (pp. 308–9)

The images continue to echo Mrs Yeobright's subjective emotions –
the sun appears as a personification of cosmic malevolence, the
grasshoppers testify to nature's unconcern at her lonely plight. The
ants introduce a gentle intimation of mortality, of the individual's
relative insignificance ('doubtless those of old times were the
ancestors of these which walked there now') that, aided by the
indolent rhythms of the language, seems to lull Mrs Yeobright into a
state of soothing tranquillity (the 'perfumed mat' of thyme, the 'soft
eastern portion' of sky). Suddenly this mood of Keatsian reverie is
transfigured by the sublime image of the heron, his radiance
emblematic of a last farewell to the transient beauties of the physical
world which the old lady (unbeknownst to her) is soon to quit. In her
mind he represents a dream image of the freedom which has been
denied her, 'pinioned' to this 'earthly ball', and he brings a sudden,
poignant moment of spiritual relief. But immediately we are
reminded of the minimal contact between human and natural worlds
– the heron flies on westwards, while Mrs Yeobright's thoughts
return to the problematic human world, eastwards. And yet... if
nature remains unknowable, it can at least often provide physical
phenomena which inspire and enrich the human spirit, even if
momentarily, seemingly accidentally. The cadences of the language
describing the heron approach the grace of blank verse, while the last
paragraph lapses, fittingly enough, into flatness as the moment of
vision fades away and the dull ache of human dilemma floods back.

These remarks all seem pertinent, and yet they fail to do justice to
the imaginative power exerted by Hardy in his chronicling of Mrs
Yeobright's last journey, for the sum of its poetic meanings is greater
than that of its parts, and a residue of elusive meaning continues to
defy analysis in each 'conjunction of things'.

As I have endeavoured to show by my quotations from his
notebooks, Hardy was well aware of this residual poetry, and
constantly sought to capture it. I suggested above that his attempts

may be seen retrospectively as an early modernistic attempt to transcend the naturalistic mode of the novel, though Hardy did not, however, claim for himself the role of an avant-garde experimenter in rendering consciousness. Rather, he identified his creative quest with a wild and undisciplined vein of poetic insight less the province of the educated Victorian man of letters than of the untutored spirit of traditional, agrarian mankind:

> Mr. E. Clodd this morning gives an excellently neat answer to my question why the superstitions of a remote Asiatic and Dorset labourer are the same: 'The attitude of man', he says, 'at corresponding levels of culture, before like phenomena, is pretty much the same, your Dorset peasants representing the persistence of the barbaric idea which confuses persons and things, and founds wide generalisations on the slenderest analogies.'
>
> (This 'barbaric idea which confuses persons and things' is, by the way, also common to the highest imaginative genius – that of the poet.)[37]

Virginia Woolf's fine essay on Hardy distinguishes between 'conscious' writers – Henry James, Flaubert – who 'control their genius in the act of creation; they are aware of all the possibilities of every situation, and are never taken by surprise'; and 'unconscious' writers, among whom are numbered Dickens, Scott and Hardy:

> The unconscious writers ... seem suddenly and without their own consent to be lifted up and swept onwards. The wave sinks and they cannot say what has happened and why.... [Hardy's] own word, 'moments of vision', exactly describes those passages of astonishing beauty and force which are to be found in every book that he wrote. With a sudden quickening of power which we cannot foretell, nor he, it seems, control, a single scene breaks off from the rest.... But the power goes as it comes. The moment of vision is succeeded by long stretches of plain daylight.... The novels therefore are full of inequalities; they are lumpish and dull and inexpressive; but they are never arid; there is always about them a little blur of unconsciousness, that halo of freshness and margin of the unexpressed which often produce the most profound sense of satisfaction. It is as if Hardy himself was not quite aware of what he did, as if his

consciousness held more than he could produce, and he left it for his readers to make out his full meaning and to supplement it from their own experience.[38]

This, I think, offers a profoundly sensitive and valuable interpretation of Hardy's creative process, precisely identifying those nebulous qualities in his writing to which so many readers are attracted without quite knowing why. Moments such as Elizabeth-Jane's nocturnal reverie, Giles and Grace's sunset fantasies, Tess's mingling with the properties of the garden and the harp-music, or Mrs Yeobright's vision of the heron, aspire to a rapt, imponderable expansion of sensibility. At such moments it seems to me that Hardy's prose is straining in its own unvarnished and idiosyncratic way to capture the full elusive flux of a human consciousness mode later developed rather differently and at length in Joyce's journeys to the heart of the Hibernian metropolis, or Faulkner's labyrinthine, looping endeavours to circumscribe the multiplicity of human experience in Yoknapatawpha. Hardy is trying, in other words, to express the complex blur of human associations and impressions which accrue around *things* – a hill, a tree, a house or a cracked mug – and through this focus to contain something of the myriad density of impressions that is each individual's perspective on to the world. However I describe it, this must sound like an arcane cerebral process; rather, as one discovers these glades amid the thickets of Hardy's prose, the effect is usually one of transcendent and joyful clarity. By instinctively correlating his apprehensions of character and environment, Hardy lends an extra dimension of meaning to his writing, which is both teasingly symbolic and reassuringly solid; the aura of poetic eloquence surrounding an image like that of the heron continues to haunt the reader's mind, fading yet almost palpable, beyond recollection of its dramatic context.

One of the very few critics whom I have come across to have commented upon the astonishing empathy of Hardy and Faulkner's work is Walter Allen, and I cannot better his description of the impact of their sense of place upon the reader. Grouping them together with Mrs Radcliffe's Gothic tales, Dickens's *Great Expectations* and the fiction of Elizabeth Bowen, Allen suggests that,

These novels are characterised by a peculiarly intense relationship between the characters and their immediate environments.

Character and environment are impregnated each with the other. To some extent environment is, as it were, humanised, and the character himself is as he is because of the environment and cannot be detached from it; it is a necessary element for his existence, a special kind of air. The immediate environment exists, even, in a symbolic relation to the character; this is plain if one thinks of the decaying mansions in Faulkner's novels. In other words, in such novels the ambience in which the characters move is as important as the characters themselves.[39]

With this achievement in mind, it is interesting to reflect upon Hardy's remark, made two months before he died, 'that if he had his life over again he would prefer to be a small architect in a country town, like Mr Hicks at Dorchester, to whom he was articled'.[40] For an important characteristic of Hardy's attitude to the world, one which he fully shared with Faulkner, was that although a great writer he harboured somewhere within him a profound distrust of *words*, of intellectual thought, study and self-expression. Part of him, then, evidently always yearned to create solid physical structures instead of words; even as a writer he evinces a continual reliance upon *things*, especially landscapes, buildings and natural phenomena. Hence the face of an intellectual, Clym Yeobright, shows 'that thought is a disease of flesh' (*TROTN*, p. 162), and Clym falls back upon work which brings him into direct contact with the primitive natural life of Egdon; while a traditional countryman, such as Gabriel Oak, 'would have soon have thought of carrying an odour in a net as of attempting to convey the intangibilities of his feeling in the coarse meshes of language' (*FFTMC*, p. 58). In later life Faulkner was fond of playing down his writer's vocation and posing as a farmer, while his Addie Bundren muses,

> I would think how words go straight up in a thin line, quick and harmless, and how terribly doing goes along the earth, clinging to it, so that after a while the two lines are too far apart for the same person to straddle from one to the other; and that sin and love and fear are just sounds that people who have never sinned nor loved nor feared have for what they never had and cannot have until they forget the words.[41]

A common combination of several disparate factors – cultural and temperamental ambivalence, a fascination with social change and an ability to mythicise the life of their regions – encouraged Hardy and Faulkner each to explore in his own way this gulf between 'words' and 'doing': it seemed a telling symptom of the sickness of their age. Their common preoccupation with an intimate sense of place indicates a desire to 'forget the words', to engage instead with more fundamental, palpable realities of life – the land, the seasons, physical labour and instincts, traditional agrarian mores, folk-history – which define man's identity largely through his relationship with his environment.

In my discussion of individual passages I have chosen to dwell at some length upon the imponderable quality emanating from this concern with a sense of place, for I think that, without an appreciation of Hardy's tendencies to unconscious or intuitive composition, exploiting all the 'associations' of things, much of his work's special eloquence is lost. In Faulknerian terms, Hardy's struggle to 'forget the words' within which our experience is usually circumscribed consists largely of a grappling with *things*, in a bid to capture some slippery and elusive essence of life. Hardy remarks in *The Woodlanders* that

> The countryman who is obliged to judge the time of day from changes in external nature sees a thousand successive tints and traits in the landscape which are never discerned by him who hears the regular chime of a clock, because they are never in request.   (*TW*, p. 138)

It is perhaps the reader's awareness that Hardy's novels place similar demands upon his sensibility which lures him into reading them again and again, with a recurrent shock of recognition each time he or she discovers fresh significance in their imagery. Part of the special pleasure of this process lies in the fact that Hardy himself so often evinces a similar absorption and bafflement at what he finds. It is part of his inherent poetry, and peculiar modernity.

Character and environment are equally interrelated, intimately yet mysteriously, in Faulkner's novels. The relationship between man and nature is continually viewed as a problematic one, largely due to one historical factor which distinguishes Yoknapatawpha from Wessex: the recent occupation of the wilderness by white colonists. The Southern settlers discovered a natural paradise, yet – in Faulkner's opinion – abused and corrupted it. Consequently, Faulkner's attitude to nature in general, and to the settlement of the wilderness in particular, is ultimately that of a moral philosopher, with a strong ecological inclination. Man in his stories has a chance to discover aspects of his truest, inner self in encountering the wilderness, but the experience is approached with all of Faulkner's customary ambivalence. As with Hardy's protagonists, the few who do succeed in developing their 'natural' selves often tragically fail to achieve meaningful integration into everyday society.

This may be simply society's fault: Sam Fathers, for example, thinks of himself as an Indian – his father was a Chickasaw chief, his mother a quadroon. Though only one-eighth black, the racial conventions of the South automatically categorise and segregate him as a Negro, though he seems little perturbed by social restrictions. The case of his protégé, Isaac McCaslin, is more complex. He learns the secrets of the wilderness from Sam, including, it seems, an ability to intuit falsehoods, as Mink Snopes realises:

> Hit won't do no good. He has done spent too much time in the woods with deer and bears and panthers that either are or they ain't right quick and now and not shades between. He won't know how to believe no lie even if I could tell him one. (*TM*, p. 34)

Unfortunately, we also learn in *Go Down, Moses*, that Isaac's time in the woods has not succeeded in reconciling him to the inevitable compromises and dilemmas of life in human society, and this social inadequacy must, along with that of a character like Giles Winterborne, be weighed against the two men's arcane wisdom and renunciatory virtues.

Other admirable 'primitives' who live close to the secrets of nature, such as Sam Fathers or Uncle Dick Bolivar, may remind us of the Conjurors Fall and Trendle, with their very real mystical powers. Such figures offer a salutary reminder that the violent social transitions of modernistic development frequently destroy valuable human gifts in a frantic pursuit of wealth and delusory 'Progress'. For beneath the superficial gloss of his civilisation, man's human nature is in both writers' work seen to be subtly akin to the character of the wilderness,

> neither ghastly, hateful, nor ugly: neither commonplace, unmeaning, nor tame; but, like man, slighted and enduring ... co-

lossal and mysterious in its swarthy monotony. As with some persons who have long lived apart, solitude seemed to look out of its countenance. It had a lonely face, suggesting tragical possibilities.   (*TROTN*, p. 35)

Hardy's enthusiasm for the 'vast tract of unenclosed wild known as Egdon Heath … obscure, obsolete, superseded country' (*TROTN*, pp. 33, 35) seems totally of a piece with Faulkner's love of the 'big woods' of the Tallahatchie River, 'the tremendous gums and cypresses and oaks where no axe save that of the hunter ever sounded, between the impenetrable walls of cane and brier' (*GDM*, p. 136). The Mississippi wilderness was, of course, far more huge and savage than anything Dorset could offer, but the emotional unity of the writers' attitudes is clear. During their lifetimes, both novelists saw the gradual penetration of remote countrysides by commerce and communications, accepted yet regretted the process, and celebrated the untameable and enduring qualities of wilderness with a fierce delight which, especially in Faulkner's case, approaches pantheism. Living through and describing eras of disorientating social change, Hardy and Faulkner found a common philosophical comfort in the timeless and inscrutable face that wild nature presented to man:

> To recline on a stump of thorn in the central valley of Egdon, between afternoon and night, as now, where the eye could reach nothing of the world outside the summits and shoulders of heathland which filled the whole circumference of its glance, and to know that everything around and underneath had been from prehistoric times as unaltered as the stars overhead, gave ballast to the mind adrift on change, and harrassed by the irrepressible New…. The sea changed, the fields changed, the rivers, the villages, and the people changed, yet Egdon remained.
>
> (*TROTN*, p. 36)

he stood against a little bayou whose black still water crept without motion out of a canebrake, across a small clearing and into the cane again, where, invisible, a bird, the big woodpecker called Lord-to-God by negroes, clattered at a dead trunk. It was a stand like any other stand … the same solitude, the same loneliness through which frail and timorous man had merely passed without altering it, leaving no mark nor scar, which looked exactly as it must have looked when the first ancestor of Sam Fathers's Chickasaw predecessors crept into it and looked about him, club or stone axe or bone arrow drawn and ready. (*GDM*, pp. 153–4)

Yet while their novels affirm the existence of a mysterious relationship between nature and human character, this relationship cannot be logically controlled or explained; it certainly does not reside in any Rousseauesque theory of the noble savage or nature's innate goodness, for nature in both writers' work can be terrible, even malicious: one remembers the unnerving perversity of the Cliff without a Name, or of the 'Old Man', the Mississippi River, whose power Faulkner evokes so magnificently. Even as Isaac experiences an ecstatic epiphany of immortality and harmony with nature through death's interrelation in 'earth',[42] he narrowly avoids stepping on a rattlesnake,

> more than six feet of it ... old, the once-bright markings of its youth dulled now to a monotone concordant too with the wilderness it crawled and lurked: the old one, the ancient and accursed about the earth, fatal and solitary and he could smell it now: the thin sick smell of rotting cucumbers and something else which had no name, evocative of all knowledge and an old weariness and of pariah-hood and of death.   (*GDM*, p. 251)

The biblical echoes of Eden are clear, and one is reminded too of the 'Young Platonist' at the masthead in *Moby Dick*, whose 'identity comes back in horror', though Isaac is sufficiently attuned to the character of the wilderness that he can hail the snake in the Chickasaw tongue as 'Chief ... Grandfather'.[43] Faulkner and Hardy both seem to suggest that a meaningful relationship with nature is only possible for those who accept conditions of considerable hardship and austerity. The strange interlude of the tall convict's partnership with the Cajun hunting alligators in the swamps is both awesomely harsh and idyllic in its primitive isolation, like Clym's time cutting furze-faggots on Egdon: bare subsistence living is seen in each case to possess a certain satisfying dignity. An acceptance of nature's cruelty is also part of the price for integration into its patterns. For example, Hardy and Faulkner differed sharply in their attitudes to hunting, yet it is perhaps possible to recognise an essential emotional harmony between the sensibility which could evoke the terrible beauty of Tess's hardships and that which conceived the code of the hunter which Sam Fathers teaches to Isaac, for each places a high value upon stoical acceptance of suffering and responsibility: 'I slew you: my bearing must not shame your quitting life. My conduct for ever onward must become your death' (*GDM*, p. 265). Another relevant example is the unspoken sense of honour and pride which links the Indian Three-Basket and the anonymous black slave as they prepare for sacrifice.[44] Though nature's face may suggest these 'tragical possibilities', the fate of Tess and the runaway slave are, of course, not purely 'natural' occurrences, but the result of the interaction of social pressures with natural forces. An awareness of this awkward relationship between nature and society is especially prominent in Faulkner's short stories of Mississippi frontier life, which nimbly explore the complex and ironic relationship between white, red and black men in a violent and insecure new world. His approach is partly that of the detached psychologist, assessing the strangeness of each race to the other; hence to the Chickasaw Indians, their newly acquired black slaves seem

> remote, inscrutable. They were like a single octopus. They were like the roots of a huge tree uncovered, the earth broken momentarily upon the writhen, thick, fetid tangle of its lightless and outraged life.   ('Red Leaves', *TT*, p. 79)

This intensely poetic conceit does not seem out of the place, for its imagery exactly reflects the sense of violently disturbed natural forces which characterise this era of exploration, enslavement and conquest. The reader is continually reminded of the messy cultural confusion of frontier life, where the significance of man's trophies and social status has become blurred, unpredictable and faintly ominous. The escaped slave, for instance, wears

> a pair of dungaree pants bought by Indians from white men, and an amulet slung on a thong about his hips. The amulet consisted of one half of a mother-of-pearl lorgnon which Issetibbeha had brought back from Paris, and the skull of a cottonmouth moccasin. He had killed the snake himself and eaten it, save the poison head.   (p. 94)

The Chickasaw chief owns 'ten thousand acres of matchless parklike forest where deer grazed like domestic cattle', a 'herd of

blacks for which he had no use at all', and lives in the rotting shell of
a river steamboat which slaves had hauled 12 miles overland,

> the polished mahogany, the carving glinting momentarily and
> fading through the mold in figures cabalistic and profound; the
> gutted windows were like cataracted eyes…three scrawny
> gamecocks moved in the dust and the place was pocked and
> marked with their droppings.   ('Red Leaves', *TT*, pp. 82, 88)

It would be hard to imagine anything further removed from the
complacent and sanitised stereotypes of how-the-West-was-won
epics. To all the Indians except their decadent chief, the white man is
merely a distant, enigmatic presence, the source of trinkets, whiskey
and peculiar new customs like the ownership of black slaves, which
the Chickasaws acquire without much deliberation or desire. The
Negroes meanwhile try simply to survive by any means available,
showing great courage, resolution and shrewdness. The anonymous
escaped slave, we learn, had once eaten a rat as a boy – he caught it
easily, since it was 'civilized, by association with man reft of its
inherent cunning of limb and eye' (p. 94). The Chickasaws have come
to resemble the rat, the vitality and integrity of their traditional way of
life invisibly sapped by cultural dislocation. They have virtually
abandoned hunting in order to trade and to grow crops, encouraged
by the white man's concepts of ownership of land and slaves.

The mystic and epic qualities found in Faulkner's descriptions of the
wilderness and its destruction might seem to link this aspect of his work
more closely to James Fenimore Cooper's Leatherstocking tales than to
Hardy's Wessex novels, and Cooper and Faulkner are equally alike in
taking a gloomy view of the impact of 'civilisation' upon nature. There
are strong imaginative affinities between the Adamic figures of Natty
Bumppo and Isaac McCaslin, as R. W. B. Lewis remarks.[45] But Cooper's
tales show no awareness of evil or 'tragical possibilities' in the world of
nature, and his Indians always seem rather unconvincing, either noble
savages or bloodthirsty beasts. Cooper's wilderness is, in short, a
romantic and mythic other-world, lacking the solidity of sensuous detail
which gives Faulkner's big woods their authentic texture. The brooding
ambiguity with which Faulkner characterises nature, and puny man's
relationship to it, brings the wilderness of the Mississippi Delta
unexpectedly close to the wastes of Egdon or the woods of Hintock – in
mood, tone and even details of natural observation individual descriptions are sometimes uncannily similar[46] – while Clym and Giles are, in
their different ways, as potentially Adamic as Isaac, and like him are
gently flawed.

Faulkner portrays the land or 'earth' as a slumbering but all-powerful source of energy, repaying its desecrators with malevolent ill-fortune, and rewarding its few faithful students with intimations of a pantheistic immortality, like the huge buck which Isaac McCaslin glimpses in the November woods, or the ineffable beauty of Isaac Snopes's beloved cow. A few unusually gifted 'primitives', such as Uncle Dick Bolivar or Sam Fathers, seem to approach the arcane mysteries of nature's secrets. To most of its inhabitants, however, the earth of Mississippi is simply careless, indifferent, 'implacable': Faulknerian man, like that of Hardy, is very tiny, and the earth upon which he moves is often terrible in its vastness, beauty and cruelty. Pondering upon his fate amongst 'the sunny loneliness of the enormous land' (*LIA*, p. 23), man naturally tends to take his imagery, moods and eventually his patterns of behaviour from its features. We learn for instance that the victims of the vengeful Mink Snopes get themselves killed because they have not paid such an unobtrusive creature any attention: 'He had not hurried ... not hiding, not looking: just unseen, unheard and irrevocably alien like a coyote or a small wolf' (*TM*, p. 376). Not surprisingly, it is easy to find Mink's counterparts in Hardy's novels. Amos Fry, for example, appears

> in the midst of the field, a dark spot on an area of brown ... whom it was as difficult to distinguish from the earth he trod as the caterpillar from its leaf, by reason of the excellent match between his clothes and the clods. He was one of a dying-out generation who retained the principle, nearly unlearnt now, that a man's habiliments should be in harmony with his environment.
> (*TOAT*, p. 39)

Character and environment are continually evoked as interrelated entities in both writers' work: thus the dogged nobility of Dilsey is reflected in the description of her doorway, as her 'myriad and sunken face' peers out: 'The earth immediately about the door was bare. It had a patina, as though from the soles of bare feet in generations, like old silver or the walls of Mexican houses which have been plastered by hand' (*TSATF*, pp. 236–7); and one is irresistibly reminded of Hardy's journal entry, 'An object or mark raised or made by man on a scene is worth ten times any such formed by unconscious Nature. Hence clouds, mists, and mountains are unimportant beside the wear on a threshold, or the print of a hand.'[47]

Faulkner's fascination with this interrelation, probably best exemplified by the extended history of the old jail in *Requiem for a Nun*, demonstrates how the Southern consciousness remained outside the general preoccupations of American literature, which as C. Vann Woodward has remarked, frequently sees man as an isolated individual who does not 'belong' anywhere, whereas the Southern writer sees man as a social and historical creature, 'an inextricable part of a living history and community, attached and determined in a thousand ways by other wills and destinies'.[48]

Given this common concern with a sense of place, it is not surprising that Faulkner fully shares Hardy's gift, discussed earlier, for realising psychological states through the use of physical particulars drawn from his regional, rural world. The superb description in *Sartoris* of a spring evening's drinking session allows an awareness of the serenity and kindliness of V. K. Suratt to filter gradually into the reader's mind. It would be crude to claim that the environmental details are only there to suggest his special grace, or equally that the latter is simply a response to the tranquillity of the natural mood. Rather, the long description, hard to illustrate by quotation, gathers together a number of specifically Mississippian features, some quite un-idyllic. We see the ragged hill-country, full of 'ill-tended' cotton and corn and patchy woodland; a dilapidated small farm of broken barns and rusty machinery; the men's ability carelessly to abandon work for unhurried pleasure; the mood of timelessness, and Suratt's delight in talking; and the almost wanton luxuriance of natural life. Slowly, the reader's impressions of Suratt and of the *genius loci* become indistinguishable, encouraged perhaps by an imaginative acquiescence in the passage's sense of growing intoxication, and by Suratt's association with the regenerative powers of water, earth, sunlight and homemade whiskey:

Behind the barn the ground descended into shadow, toward a junglish growth of willow and elder, against which a huge beech and a clump of saplings stood like mottled ghosts and from which a cool dankness rose like a breath to meet them. The spring welled from the roots of the beech, into a wooden frame sunk to its top in white sand that quivered ceaselessly and delicately beneath the water's limpid unrest, and went on into the willow and elder growth ....

... The rising slope of ground behind them hid the barn and the house, and the three of them squatted in a small bowl of

peacefulness remote from the world and time, and filled with the
cool and limpid breathing of the spring and a seeping of sunlight
among the elders and willows like a thinly diffused wine. On the
surface of the spring the sky lay reflected, stippled over with
windless beech leaves. Hub squatted leanly, his brown forearms
clasped about his knees, smoking a cigarette beneath the tilt of his
hat. Suratt was across the spring from him. He wore a faded blue
shirt, and in contrast to it his hands and face were a rich, even
brown, like mahogany. The jug sat rotund and benignant
between them.

'Yes, sir,' Suratt repeated. 'I always find the best cure for a
wound is plenty of whiskey.....'

Suratt poised the jug and guffawed, then he lipped it and his
Adam's apple pumped again, in relief against the wall of elder
and willow. The elder would soon flower, with pale clumps of
tiny bloom.... Suratt's slow, plausible voice went on steadily, but
without any irritant quality. It seemed to fit easily into the still
scene, speaking of earthy things.... The gnats danced and
whirled more madly yet in the sun, above the secret places of the
stream, and the sun's light was taking on a rich copper tinge....
They drank again. The sun was almost gone, and from the secret
marshy places of the stream came a fairylike piping of young
frogs.   (*Sartoris*, pp. 101–5)

The tutelary spirit of place, and Suratt's personification of those
Southern qualities of unhurried charm, kindliness and individualism, also provide an important contrast to the jagged confusion of
the protagonist's consciousness. Unlike Bayard, Suratt is unselfcon-
sciously integrated with his rural environment, greeting every
passing wagon on the road with 'a grave gesture of his brown hand',
and stopping the car by a stream to fill its radiator from a bucket,
while 'water chuckled and murmured beneath the bridge, invisible
in the twilight, its murmur burdened with the voice of cricket and
frog ... bull bats appeared from nowhere in long swoops' (*Sartoris*,
pp. 105–6). In Faulkner's novels, automobiles are often associated
with an encroaching and standardised modernism, and are seldom
regarded with enthusiasm.[49] Faulkner's emphasis upon the harmony which Suratt has established between his eccentric vehicle
and his environment is therefore highly significant, especially since
it counterpoints the violent and destructive modernity represented
by Bayard's frantic car journeys around the countryside, culminat-

ing in the crash which kills his grandfather. As in Hardy's novels, one's relationship to the natural environment is a vital indication of character; Cleanth Brooks remarks upon how 'The characters with whom Faulkner expects his reader to be sympathetic are usually men who love nature and live in some kind of close rapport with it. On the other hand, nearly all of Faulkner's villains are men who are guilty of violating it.'[50]

Brooks compares Faulkner's attitude to nature to Wordsworth's 'stoical primitivism', and even tentatively relates life in North Mississippi to that of Wordsworth's Cumberland and Westmorland, as examples of a common agrarianism.[51] Given this premise, it seems worth pointing out that Hardy's Dorset and Faulkner's Mississippi did share some interesting natural as well as social characteristics. Each region contained a surprising variety of types of landscape, having important social repercussions. Due to its geological complexity, Dorset claims to contain one of the most varied landscapes of any English county, and its resulting broken, fragmented geography served to increase the remoteness of many areas and to diversify occupations, a characteristic dramatised by Tess's wanderings in *Tess of the d'Urbervilles*.[52] This sense of the remoteness, individualism and variety of life in Wessex also finds a counterpart in the important but often overlooked sectional variety of Mississippi, originating like that of Dorset in topography. The very beginning of Faulkner's *Mississippi* essay points out that the state

> might almost be said to have only those two directions, north and south, since until a few years ago it was impossible to travel east or west in it unless you walked or rode one of the horses or mules; even in the boy's early manhood, to reach by rail either of the adjacent county towns thirty miles away to the east or west, you had to travel ninety miles in three different directions on three different railroads. (*Miss*, p. 11)

Mississippi's main feature was therefore a strong contrast between the flat, fecund cotton lands of the west, and the poorer, remote red-clay hills nd pine barrens of the east of the state. Again this diversity would be faithfully explored in Faulkner's novels, especially as his Yoknapatawpha County is located in the exact centre of North Mississippi, 'a geographical and cultural heart' or 'microcosm' of the state[53] which reflects both features of its sectionalism, with cotton planters in the rich bottom lands and small farmers in the hills.

I quoted earlier Hardy's dictum that 'We colour according to our moods the objects we survey'. Most readers of his novels would probably agree, however, that the relationship between character and environment is by no means exclusively one-way: Herman Lea, for example, noted in 1913 'the strange manner in which the scenery adapts itself to, and identifies itself with, the characters themselves. We have a striking instance of this in the life-history of Tess'.[54] Correspondingly, Cleanth Brooks has pointed out how, in Faulkner's novels, 'nature is often more than mere background.... Nature frequently reflects, and may even generate, a mood in man'.[55] Indeed, Faulkner probably inherited a ready-made set of assumptions about the imponderable relationship between Southern character and environment as part of his regional consciousness, since it had long been a commonplace dictum that the vagaries of the Southern temperament owed much to the extremities and unpredictabilities of the region's climate. W. J. Cash, for example, suggests a possible relationship between the Southern tendencies to violence and romanticism, and the 'Southern physical world – itself a sort of cosmic conspiracy against reality', with its extravagant colours, fertility, perpetual heat-haze and a prevailing mood of 'drunken reverie', disrupted by violent thunderstorms.[56] This would be difficult to prove, but certainly Cash's long description (itself rather romanticised) immediately evokes the reader's Yoknapatawpha, and the crucial role which the physical world of Mississippi plays in stories like 'The Bear' or 'Dry September'. The latter story remains characteristically ambiguous as to whether the lynching is in some way the direct circumstantial result of 'sixty-two rainless days', or whether Faulkner's interest in the harsh climatic conditions of Mississippi ('he stood panting. There was no movement, no sound, not even an insect') is simply an expressionistic counterpart to man's capacity for violence ('Dry September', *TT*, pp. 39, 53). Similarly, Brooks remarks upon how Addie Bundren's lonely and tormented voice in *As I Lay Dying* 'is clearly projecting her own feelings upon the landscape, but Dr. Peabody suggests that it is the land which creates such feelings within the human beings'.[57] Peabody reflects, 'That's the one trouble with this country: everything, weather, all, hangs on too long. Like our rivers, our land: opaque, slow, violent; shaping and creating the life of man in its implacable and brooding image' (*AILD*, p. 38).

There is no absolute answer to this enigma, for, as the tentative phrasing of Brooks's remark suggests, Faulkner's attitudes to man and nature are ambiguous and elusive. The most meaningful response to this problem is to recognise simply that, like Hardy, Faulkner saw the forces of nature and the actions of man as conjoined in one mysterious entity, a relationship beyond man's full comprehension but revealing itself in sudden incidents or epiphanies. Many examples would repay a detailed examination, but this passage from *The Hamlet* is perhaps one of the most attractive. Flem Snopes has sold his wild Texas ponies to the gullible yeomen of Frenchman's Bend. As the untameable beasts scatter in all directions, causing havoc, Ratliff and his companions fetch Will Varner to aid the injured Henry Armstid:

> They went up the road in a body, treading the moon-blanched dust in the tremulous April night murmurous with the moving of sap and the wet bursting of burgeoning leaf and bud and constant with the thin and urgent cries and the brief and fading bursts of galloping hooves.... The moon was now high overhead, a pearled and mazy yawn in the soft sky, the ultimate ends of which rolled onward, whorl on whorl, beyond the pale stars and by pale stars surrounded ....
> ... Then the pear tree came in sight. It rose in mazed and silver immobility like exploding snow; the mockingbirds still sang in it. 'Look at that tree,' Varner said. 'It ought to make this year, sho.'
> 'Corn'll make this year too,' one said.
> 'A moon like this is good for every growing thing outen earth,' Varner said.... [T]here was an old woman told my mammy once that if a woman showed her belly to the full moon after she had done caught, it would be a gal. So Mrs. Varner taken and laid every night with the moon on her nekid belly, until it fulled and after. I could lay my ear to her belly and hear Eula kicking and scrounging like all get-out, feeling the moon.'
> 'You mean it actually worked sho enough, Uncle Will?' the other said.
> 'Hah,' Varner said. 'You might try it. You get enough women showing their nekid bellies to the moon or the sun either ... and more than likely after a while there will be something you can lay your ear and listen to.'

again there was a brief rapid thunder of hooves on wooden planking.

'There's another one on the creek bridge,' one said.

'They are going to come out even on them things, after all,' Varner said. 'You take a man that ain't got no other relaxation all year long except dodging mule-dung up and down a field furrow ... a night like this ... is good for him. It'll make him sleep tomorrow night anyhow, provided he gets back home by then.' (*TH*, pp. 275–8)

At first the men's conversation and activities may seem to be in awkward contrast with the splendour of nature. But as Millgate remarks, their practical comments upon its fecundity suggest that, despite their remoteness from the heavily poetic language of Faulkner's description, they 'are not unaffected by the beauty of what they see'.[58] Varner's folk-wisdom, reminiscent of the village talk in *Under the Greenwood Tree* or *Far from the Madding Crowd*, is itself a natural and integrated phenomenon. The bawdy humour of his anecdote does not detract from our sense of his real reverence for the powers of nature; rather, like the contrast in tone between the simple 'corn'll make this year too' and the extravagance of 'a pearled and mazy yawn', Varner's wry remarks and the lushness of the spring night merge into a provocative harmony of opposites. He seems shrewdly aware that the anarchic energy of the 'almost musical' cries and hoof-beats is somehow in keeping with the 'tremulous April night murmurous with the moving of sap'. The rueful pursuers of the wild ponies will at least have an adventure worthy of discussion for years to come. And the reader may intuit too the underlying relation between the fecundity of nature, represented by the spring night, the ponies, and the story of Eula's conception, and the ravishing sexuality of the same Eula's appearance, like Fancy Day, at a bedroom window (p. 276). Yet, simultaneously, Faulkner encourages us to feel that the beauty of each interrelated element is untameable, beyond man's blundering control, else such a gorgeous creature would never have been wasted upon the soulless Flem Snopes: and nature remains unknowable.

Hardy's attitude to nature is equally complex and equivocal, and it seems appropriate at this point to look in some detail at its expression in a single work. The problematic relationship between nature and society is examined as a clash between natural, instinctive impulses and the abstractions of thought and action sanctioned by society. We are told, for example, that Tess's bitter self-reproach after the birth of Sorrow was

> a sorry and mistaken creation of Tess's fancy – a cloud of moral hobgoblins by which she was terrified without reason. It was they that were out of harmony with the actual world, not she.... She had been made to break an accepted social law, but no law known to the environment in which she fancied herself such an anomaly. (pp. 120–1)

But I hope that it will have already emerged from my discussion so far that Hardy does not always praise 'natural' impulses at the expense of 'social' considerations, in a simplistic pre-Lawrentian pattern. Indeed, examples of 'natural' folly are everywhere in his pages. Both the rural fatalism and the Darwinian world-picture from which Hardy drew his 'heap of impressions' taught him, firstly, that nature is no smiling, benign mother, but operates as an inscrutable and morally neutral 'First Cause' or 'Immanent Will'.[59] Hardy's reverence for nature is a sombre one, and he is, in Cockshutt's useful phrase, a 'pessimistic pantheist'.[60] Hardy's descriptions of nature are often no more idyllic than his view of modern competitive society:

> They went noiselessly over mats of starry moss, rustled through interspersed tracts of leaves, skirted trunks with spreading roots whose mossed rinds made them like hands wearing green gloves; elbowed old elms and ashes with great forks, in which stood pools of water that overflowed on rainy days and ran down their stems in green cascades. On older trees still than these huge lobes of fungi grew like lungs. Here, as everywhere, the Unfulfilled Intention, which makes life what it is, was as obvious as it could be among the depraved crowds of a city slum. The leaf was deformed, the curve was crippled, the taper was interrupted: the lichen ate the vigour of the stalk, and the ivy slowly strangled to death the promising sapling.
>
> (TW, p. 83)

Hardy's metaphysical anguish is given an exceptionally highly developed dramatic and aesthetic patterning in *The Woodlanders*, which substitutes, for the universal displacement and anomie of

Jude, a 'wondrous world of sap and leaves', remote and enclosed. Yet even in the Hintock woods, nature's accustomed state is one of mutual frustration, where 'the leaf was deformed' and a protagonist wonders 'if there were one world in the universe where the fruit had no worm, and marriage no sorrow' (*TW*, p. 234). The novel's astonishing splendour of form and texture stems from Hardy's ability to relate the lives of the Hintock folk to the mingled beauty and cruelty of the natural life of the woods, in a series of apprehensions which, while forming memorably poetic autonomous images, seem to the reader to be growing quite naturally out of and feeding back into the material of the story, to magical effect. When Grace, in a sharp rush of sensual perception, recognises in Giles the true lord of the autumn woods, Hardy comments that 'Her heart rose from its late sadness like a released bough; her senses revelled in the sudden lapse back to Nature unadorned' (pp. 235–6). Here form and content are one; and the novel is full of equally satisfying moments, when the meaning of the images seems to extend far beyond the horizons of their immediate context. As Grace flees from Fitzpiers through the twilight woods to seek refuge in Giles's hut, Hardy provides an expressionistic translation (inspired by and dextrously adapted from a notebook entry of two years earlier),[61] which conveys not only something of Grace's unarticulated traumas but also a faint intimation of her autumn-god's mortality:

> The leaves overhead were now in their latter green – so opaque, that it was darker at some of the densest spots than in winter time, scarce a crevice existing by which a ray could get down to the ground. But in open places she could see well enough. Summer was ending: in the daytime singing insects hung in every sunbeam: vegetation was heavy nightly with globes of dew; and after showers creeping damps and twilight chills came up from the hollows.
> The plantations were always weird at this hour of eve – more spectral far than in the leafless season, when there were fewer masses and more minute lineality. The smooth surfaces of glossy plants came out like weak, lidless eyes: there were strange faces and figures from expiring lights that had somehow wandered into the canopied obscurity; while now and then low peeps of the sky between the trunks were like sheeted shapes, and on the tips of boughs sat faint cloven tongues.[62]

The philosophical implications underlying this system of intensive poetic patterning are several and complex. Firstly, as in *Jude*, Hardy is demonstrating that since man is a part of nature, he will obviously suffer if he codifies and restricts too many of his 'natural' urges. But venturing beyond this premise, Hardy's further disturbing inference is that, in strict Darwinian terms, society itself must logically be recognised as a 'natural' part of man's evolution. In *The Woodlanders*, social processes are seen to encourage rivalries and struggles for mastery which are no more and no less ugly and intractable than those of the woods, where trees are found

> wrestling for existence, their branches disfigured with wounds resulting from their mutual rubbings and blows.... Beneath them were the rotting stumps of those of the group that had been vanquished long ago, rising from their mossy setting like black teeth from green gums.   (p. 339)

That this relationship was 'natural' was the assumption upon which 'Social Darwinism' built its Victorian ideology of gleefully ruthless competition, and all of Hardy's writing (but in particular *The Woodlanders*) is permeated by his characteristically ambivalent reactions to this perspective upon human life. As in the description of Knight on the cliff quoted earlier, *The Woodlanders* gains a remarkable ease and flexibility from Hardy's synthesis of a countryman's 'natural' gift of observation and an educated Victorian's 'modern' insights:

> presently the bleared white visage of a sunless winter day emerged like a dead-born child. The woodlanders everywhere had already bestirred themselves.... It had been above an hour earlier, before a single bird had untucked his head, that twenty lights were struck in as many bedrooms....
> Owls that had been catching mice in the outhouses, rabbits that had been eating the winter-greens in the garden, and stoats that had been sucking the blood of the rabbits, discerning that their human neighbours were on the move, discreetly withdrew.

Here [in Melbury's yard] Winterborne had remained after the girl's departure, to see that the loads were properly made up. Winterborne was connected with the Melbury family in various ways. In addition to the sentimental relationship which arose from his father having been the first Mrs. Melbury's lover, Winterborne's aunt had married and emigrated with the brother of the timber merchant many years before – an alliance that was sufficient to place Winterborne, though the poorer, on a footing of social intimacy with the Melburys. As in most villages so secluded as this, intermarriages were of Hapsburgian frequency among the inhabitants, and there were hardly two houses in Little Hintock unrelated by some matrimonial tie or other.

For this reason, a curious kind of partnership existed between Melbury and the younger man – a partnership based upon an unwritten code, by which each acted in the way he thought fair toward the other, on a give-and-take principle. Melbury, with his timber and copse-ware business, found that the weight of his labour came in winter and spring. Winterborne was in the apple and cider trade, and his requirements in cartage and other work came in the autumn of each year. Hence horses, waggons and in some degree men, were handed over to him when the apples began to fall; he, in return, lending his assistance to Melbury in the busiest wood-cutting season, as now.   (pp. 54–6)

The Hintock world is clearly a cohesive one, but the reader's impressions are necessarily tinged with unease. Life is unremittingly harsh – Marty South has been up all night cutting thatching spars, to fend off poverty, and the villagers must all rise before dawn to begin work. The narrative voice supplies associations which are far from Arcadian: the sustaining cycle of natural life includes the continual bloodshed of animals, and Hardy establishes a covert but potent analogy between these creatures and 'their human neighbours', who, like the owls and mice, act en masse – 'twenty lights were struck in as many bedrooms'. The tone is detached, suggestive of the scrupulous objectivity of a naturalist observing an interesting new species of 'woodlander'. Just as the stoats prey upon the rabbits, so Mrs Charmond and Barber Percombe conspire to gain Marty's hair, by threats and guineas as surely as by violence, while the woodlanders and woods engage in a never-ending struggle for mastery. Within this grim context, the woodlanders' distinguishing and ennobling characteristic appears to be their ability to evolve 'an unwritten code' of 'give-and-take', with interdependent levels of respect, loyalty and partnership upheld between man and nature and between themselves.[63] Indeed, universal interrelationship is a principle informing both the structure and the meaning of *The Woodlanders*, Hardy noting in his journal while at work on the novel, 'The human race to be shown as one great network or tissue which quivers in every part when one point is shaken, like a spider's web if touched',[64] and referring in the novel to a 'pattern' of 'a great web of human doings then weaving in both hemispheres from the White Sea to Cape Horn'.[65] Therefore, another important aspect of the story reveals how the viability of the Hintock community is ensured only whilst its inhabitants can sustain their mutual interdependence, as represented by Melbury and Giles's co-operation with each other, and with nature, in their seasonal occupations. This traditional relationship is mirrored in the extended bonds of marriage and kinship, the unexpectedly exotic adjective 'Hapsburgian' deftly underscoring the invisible 'web of human doings' which links this tiny settlement, 'outside the gates of the world', with the more illustrious centres of civilisation.

But the novel sombrely records how the community's maintenance of this essential equilibrium is gradually lost. Giles's and Marty's almost mystical affinity for 'intelligent intercourse with Nature' inevitably suggests a close correspondence with Faulkner's vision of Isaac McCaslin's and Sam Fathers's pantheism in *Go Down, Moses*; and indeed both novels combine a moving lament for the passing of such arcane knowledge with a withering critique of those responsible for squandering this precious inheritance. The wretched George Melbury, corrupted by shallow notions of vicarious social success to such an extent that he can view his daughter as an investment which will 'yield a better return' than his timber business, is close kin to the demented Boon, whom Ike finds laying claim to a tree full of squirrels, hammering on a broken gun and screaming, 'Get out of here ... Don't touch a one of them! They're mine!'[66] In each novel, patterns of divergence both psychological and socio-economic inexorably replace the former cohesion: as Melbury plans for Grace to 'marry well', so Giles's fortunes dwindle, and the traditional partnership between the men shrivels away. Giles's doomed courtship of Grace struggles against constant reminders of their separation. She rejects him while he is far above her head in South's elm, 'cutting himself off more and more from all intercourse with the sublunary world'; she patronises him when he is below her in the yard of the 'Earl of Wessex', a homeless migratory worker; and, until it is too late, Grace cannot bring herself to defy propriety by calling him back into his hut in King's Hintock wood, out of the autumn rains (pp. 125, 297, 334–6).

To return therefore to the relationship between the novel and the
theory of Social Darwinism, we may ask why the traditional Hintock
life succumbs to the inroads of modern change and separation. For it
is noteworthy that, although Fitzpiers and Felice Charmond may
represent the most obvious agents of this process, Hardy's portrait
of the Hintock community does itself suggest internal flaws
contributing to its decline. The ambivalent attitudes to rural change
found in *The Dorsetshire Labourer* help to give the later novels too
their special density of meaning, and consequently one critic
recognises in these works

> a gathering realisation that the earlier way [of traditional life]
> did not possess the inner resources upon which to fight for its
> existence. The old order was not just a less powerful mode of life
> than the new, but ultimately helpless before it through inner
> defect.[67]

Holloway cites, as examples of this, the villagers' abandonment of
their 'birthright' – Giles handing his tree to a bystander in the
market-place, or leaving Marty to finish the planting alone; John
Smith allowing his tree to be cut down; and the Melbury's
disruptive ideals.[68] One might also point to the images of
listlessness and decay associated with the otherwise charming
opening description of Little Hintock.

But it is Giles himself who can provide the clearest illustration of
Hardy's use of the Social Darwinist theory. One of Hardy's most
interesting livier-heroes, Giles is unlike most of his counterparts in
that he apparently has no experience of modern urban or educated
life – he is a wholly 'customary' character, seemingly educated more
by the woods than by society. His close attuning to the rhythms of
the woodlands seems to have implanted within his personality
some of nature's dourly unfulfilled intentions, for in his dealings
with others Giles shows 'a taciturn hesitancy taught by life as he
knew it' characterised by 'ruminating silences' (pp. 68, 300).
Significantly, we see him first at daybreak in the long passage
quoted earlier, when 'the bleared white visage of a sunless winter
day emerged like a dead-born child', for Giles's surname seems to
offer clues to his self-repressed nature (as if 'born' of winter) and
bleak fate (having stoically 'borne' the winter of Grace's vicissitudes).[69] Dimly aware of his lack of the social graces which Grace
(again, aptly named) desires, Giles veers disastrously between an

absent-minded reticence, and an ill-considered outspokenness. Hardy suggests that Giles loses Grace partly through his own lack of self-assertion and perseverance:

> Grace heaved a divided sigh with a tense pause between, and moved onward, her heart feeling uncomfortably big and heavy, and her eyes wet. Had Giles, instead of remaining still, immediately come down from the tree to her, would she have continued in that filial, acquiescent frame of mind which she had announced to him as final? ... But he continued motionless and silent in that gloomy Niflheim or fogland which involved him, and she proceeded on her way.   (p. 126)

Similarly, the loss of his cottage is in one way the direct consequence of Giles's tendency to 'a certain dilatoriness', which causes him to needlessly delay paying the fine which would have renewed his leases (p. 122), alternating with a blunt tactlessness which offends both Mrs Charmond and his prospective clients.[70]

To this extent, therefore, Giles – and, by extension, the rest of the obstinately old-fashioned woodlanders – are responsible for their own downward momentum towards extinction. Hardy shows Giles's roughness as a suitor to be a foolish failure to adapt to romantic circumstances, in pointed Darwinian contrast to the 'handsome, coercive, irresistible Fitzpiers', who can charm a Suke Damson or a Felice Charmond with equal ease:

> It had sometimes dimly occurred to him ... that external phenomena – such as the lowness or height or colour of a hat, the fold of a coat, the make of a boot, or the chance attitude of a limb at the instant of view – may have a great influence upon feminine opinion of a man's worth, so frequently founded upon non-essentials; but a certain causticity of mental tone towards himself and the world in general had prevented today, as always, any enthusiastic action on the strength of that reflection; and her momentary instinct of reserve at first sight of him was the penalty he paid for his laxness.   (p. 68)

Hardy is careful also to include in this undercurrent of Darwinist comparison some tribute to Fitzpiers's potential skill as a doctor, bringing modern expertise to a backward community which distrusts his knowledge.[71] Yet the balance of these considerations is, of course, finally decided by the obvious superiority of Giles's 'watchful loving-kindness' towards Grace over Fitzpiers's kind of love, one not of 'sympathetic interdependence', but 'of such quality as to bear division and transference ... his differed from the highest affection as the lower orders of the animal world differ from advanced organisms, partition causing not death but a multiplied existence ... double and treble-barrelled hearts' (pp. 233, 239).

The theme of modernistic separation so powerfully present throughout *The Woodlanders* is therefore evident even in Fitzpiers's erotic responses; and the novel's formal principle of interrelationship eventually reveals how Giles's shortcoming of a stubborn self-repression is turned into the self-abnegatory virtue of a 'stoical pride' and 'tender deference' when he turns over his hut to Grace (pp. 331, 333). The exquisitely-wrought interrelations of this final tragic episode with the earlier events seem to have been left unremarked by critics,[72] some of whom find Giles's sacrifice implausible or ridiculous.[73] This seems an insensitive response to the novel's very deliberate social themes. Giles is a simple and honest man, in love with a socially superior 'lady' and feeling himself outmanoeuvred by other more sophisticated forces – Fitzpiers's romantic deviousness, the lady of the manor's rights of property, changes in divorce laws. Upon each social occasion when Giles has sought to pay formal court to Grace, he has been left writhing in embarrassment and regret at a sense of his gaucherie. In particular, Hardy uses the motif of the shared meals of Giles and Grace as a traditional (and very English) index of 'table manners' and social status. Giles has found himself clutching an apple-tree as he greets Grace in the market-place, or giving her cabbage with a slug in it at his Christmas party, or buying her dinner in the unsuitably plebeian inn at Sherton. Since he considers himself to have lost this genteel and fastidious creature through his inability to 'have surrounded her with the refinements she looked for', he now takes the opportunity of paying painstaking regard to the proprieties accompanying her acceptance of his poor accommodation, and of their shared meal (this time a burnt rabbit). Giles's determination to do the right thing is fed by his unaccustomed sense of 'treachery' at having passionately kissed Grace while he knew full well (and she did not) that she was irrevocably wedded to another: 'in the intensity of his contrition for that tender wrong he determined to deserve her faith now at least' (p. 328).

Throughout chapter 41 the reader therefore sees Giles adopting what he conceives to be the proper attitude of a chivalrous Victorian gentleman towards a defenceless lady. Hardy comments upon the 'strictly business manner which belied him', his deliberate and matter-of-fact tone, 'scrupulousness' and 'stoical pride'. These are all exactly the qualities which we might expect of the self-constraining Winterborne; and the irony that that actual Victorian gentleman Edred Fitzpiers would have behaved quite differently merely increases rather than dissipates our sense of the tragical unfitness of things, as we watch Giles struggling to emulate a chimerical ethic of social refinement which has already condemned his love-suit, and his way of life:

> She again entreated his forgiveness for so selfishly appropriating the cottage. But it would only be for a day or two more, she thought, since go she must.
> He yearningly replied: 'I – I don't like you to go away!'
> 'O Giles,' said she, 'I know – I know! But – I am a woman, and you are a man. I cannot speak more plainly. I yearn to let you in, but – you know what is in my mind, because you know me so well.'
> 'Yes, Gracie, yes. I do not at all mean that the question between us has not been settled by your marriage turning out hopelessly unalterable. I merely meant – well, a feeling – no more.' (p. 334)

Set within the context of Grace's growing doubts over her 'selfishly correct' behaviour as she watches small animal 'neighbours who knew neither law nor sin', Giles's struggle to repress his feelings embodies perhaps one of the most painful 'separations' in the novel: one which returns us to that perennial Hardeian conflict between human love and the 'social law' that has forbidden 'their opening paradise' of that 'fair green afternoon in June' only a few weeks before, when Giles for once held in his arms 'her he had watched over and loved so long' (pp. 315, 319, 331).

In *The Woodlanders*, then, one finds Hardy skilfully *using* the concept of Social Darwinism for his own special purposes, without endorsing its conclusions. This confident control over his material is perhaps best demonstrated by that typically Hardeian modulation of the novel, away from the tragic and elegiac aura surrounding Giles's death, and into the worldly-wise, ironic tone which describes Grace's drift back into the arms of Fitzpiers. David

Lodge's introduction to the New Wessex Edition provides a sensitive summary of Hardy's multiple implications:

> Hardy was capable of appreciating the old agricultural order without idealising it, and did not suppose that its passing was something that could be arrested or reversed. Like many thoughtful late-Victorians, he was both an evolutionary and a pessimistic thinker: he believed in the inevitability of change without assuming that it would necessarily be changed for the better. Fitzpiers survives because he is fitter, not better than Giles – fitter to survive in a 'modern' age. That is the real significance of the doubtfully 'happy ending': Grace chooses life over death, a man with the future in his bones over a man whose individual death symbolises an old order passing. But the 'life', the 'future', that awaits her is only bourgeois prosperity and respectability, eaten away by the worm of sexual distrust.[74]

Nor is this quite all: the poetic and elegiac vein of the novel has the last word, as Hardy modulates back yet again from the rich comedy of the search party's rustic chorus in the Sherton inn, to the murmured devotions of Marty South, whom they pass unreflectingly by upon their homeward journey. Marty's last lament for Giles and the world he represented has all the beauty and simplicity of a traditional folk-song, and her lone figure is finally recognisable as the 'incubus of the forlorn' which Hardy invoked upon the first page: the novel's form becomes circular and absolutely complete, one of Hardy's finest achievements.

As already remarked, this emphasis upon the quiet heroism of ordinary people, like Marty or Dilsey, is a fundamental common feature of the novelists' shared 'folk-historical' perspective. Before turning to examine this perspective in Faulkner's novels, it seems important to repeat that the positive aspects of Faulkner's exploration of the 'ache of modernism' depend, perhaps, rather more heavily than Hardy's, upon an awareness of a certain latent comedy running through the pattern of human suffering. Sometimes this wry humour is inherent in the events themselves, as in *Pylon* or *As I Lay Dying*, or it may be embodied in contrasting plots and stories. Even in *Sanctuary* humour is present, though muted, a persistent sardonic undercurrent of black comedy which rises into prominence in scenes such as Horace's conversations with Senator Clarence Snopes, or in the ironically 'prim decorum' with which Miss Reba and her colleagues conduct themselves off-duty. As one reads Faulkner's novels the 'ridiculous' and the 'terrible' are found, gradually, to be closely interwoven, as in the story of Lena and Byron which frames and contrasts Joe Christmas's torments. Faulknerian humour often subsists in the bizarre tension felt between the appearances and the actuality of human conduct, the case of the invaluable black mechanic who has to be brought from jail to repair a car providing a minor but typically Yoknapatawphan example: 'Mr. Connors [the deputy] came with a shotgun and Jabbo in handcuffs and they all went out to the car while Mr. Connors handed the shotgun to Jabbo to hold while he got out the key and unlocked the handcuffs and took the shotgun back' (*TTO*, p. 63).

Faulkner takes an especial delight in exposing a sense of honour lurking in obscure crannies of the human spirit. Another intemperate mechanic, the wretched Jiggs of *Pylon*, is furtively swigging the unconscious Reporter's absinthe at nine in the morning. He is perfectly willing to rifle his host's pockets, but when the idea of filling a bottle to take with him runs through his mind, he fiercely rejects temptation with the immortal line, 'It's because even if I am a bum there is some crap I will not eat' (*Pylon*, p. 119). Faulkner's intention is clear. As in the case of Ruby Lamar, or the idiot Snopes and his beloved cow, human virtue is sufficiently precious to be revered in whatever context it appears, as Hardy defiantly asserted by subtitling *Tess* 'A Pure Woman'. This quiet respect often underlies the occurrence of Faulkner's humour – Connors's familiarity with Jabbo, or Jiggs's thief's honour, are none the less valuable for appearing clumsy or silly. The grim quality of this humour, of course, also reflects the folk-traditions of a primitive and isolated region where, as in Hardy's Dorset, misfortune was shrugged aside with little comfort other than stoical courage or a wry quip.[75] Both are demonstrated by the episode of Cash's broken leg, hideously set in a home-made concrete cast, which shocks the veteran Dr Peabody even as he masks his concern with pungent sarcasm.[76]

The relationship between Faulknerian and Hardeian humour is deepened by the fatalism which colours the outlook of both groups of country folk, and by the two writers' common agnosticism and religious scepticism.[77] Faulkner and Hardy were each among the first generation of their respective cultures to experience the wholesale modernistic crumbling of Christian faith, as effected by the 'cultural lag' aligning Faulkner's Deep South with nineteenth-century England,[78] and Cleanth Brooks's explanation of the subsequent ideological process helps us to perceive the two writers' common preoccupation with the problem of suffering: 'we need not be much puzzled as to how Faulkner came by the "Stoical" elements that we find in his work. As Professor John Hunt ... has aptly put it: the first step backward from Christian orthodoxy is usually into some version of Stoicism.'[79] One might usefully add that for Faulkner and Hardy the second step was into the creation of art which would exact a full look at the worst, such as the conflict with nature and circumstance symbolically enacted by Hardy's malign coincidences, or the hapless struggles of Faulkner's protagonists against enormous physical difficulties. Viewed in this sombre context, the comic element of both men's work represents an affirmation of their faith in man's ability to endure. I should like, therefore, to look now in some detail at a fully developed example of Faulkner's blending of the 'ridiculous' and the 'terrible'. How is the Faulknerian protagonist shown to cope successfully with life, to grow and adapt like Gabriel Oak, rather than to fragment? And which Faulkner novel corresponds most closely to the 'pastoral' and epic narrative qualities of Hardy novels like *The Woodlanders* or *Tess*, and, like them, comprehensively explores the character of the rural community, examining the harshness and failings of its traditional values alongside the excesses of a disorientated modernism?

Light in August seems to offer the most suitable material for such an inquiry. Unlike *The Sound and the Fury, As I Lay Dying* or *Absalom, Absalom!*, its narrative is largely authorial, though with constant flashbacks and subjective commentaries. The unfolding of its several plots proceeds with the calmness and clarity of a Victorian novel,[80] richly portraying the varied town and country life of Yoknapatawpha as an ambiguous world of great physical immediacy and memorable, unpredictable characters:

> The wagon mounts the hill toward her.... The sharp and brittle crack and clatter of its weathered and ungreased wood and metal is slow and terrific: a series of dry sluggish reports carrying for a half mile across the hot still pinewiney silence of the August afternoon ... they draw slowly together as the wagon crawls terrifically toward her in its slow palpable aura of somnolence and red dust....

From beneath a sunbonnet of faded blue ... she looks up at him quietly and pleasantly: young, pleasantfaced, candid, friendly, and alert. She does not move yet.... In the halted wagon Armstid sits, humped, blackeyed....

'How far you going?' he says....

Apparently Armstid has never once looked full at her. Yet he has already seen that she wears no wedding ring.   (*LIA*, pp. 8, 10–11)

This opening scene anticipates many of the novel's areas of concern. Its extraordinary cinematic rendition of sensation and scene, aided by the use of the present tense, concentrates our fullest attention upon the reactions of the strangers to one another. The pregnant figure of Lena Grove has already been observed and discussed by Armstid and his neighbour back down the road, and gossip will remain a potent force throughout the novel. The scene's laconicism also introduces that Faulknerian interest in the gulf between the sexes, reflected in Armstid's thoughts (p. 13), and indeed his forebodings about his wife's reactions to the unmarried mother are eventually disproved. Finally, the emphasis upon Lena's patient journey, 'like something moving forever and without progress across an urn' (p. 8), suggests a poetic criterion for our assessment of the other characters' spiritual health: images of roads and motion continually recur.

The mood generated by Lena Grove and her journey reflects the novel's pastoral dimension, as does her name. Yet this tranquility is continually menaced by the unbalanced obsessions and abstractions of its society, so many of whose members are described as 'fanatical' (pp. 98, 186, 202, 258). All the major protagonists, save Lena, are obsessive idealists: all are essentially loners. Faulkner emphasises the crucial influence of social and familial conditioning through a series of remorselessly unhappy case-histories, in which recurrent motifs of emotional deprivation, intolerance and running away from home indicate the importance of Minter's 'betrayed children' thesis. The novel's exploration of father–son antagonism, fascinated fear of female sexuality and the fixation with a romanticised ancestor may well reflect some of the tensions of Faulkner's early life.[81] What is more certain is that his protagonists' various tragedies spring from malaises intimately associated with Faulkner's own regional environment – obsessive attitudes to the past, to women, sex, race and religion – while Lena's steady progress and influence upon others celebrates the equally stubborn virtues of traditional Southern society.

Light in August presents a dense variety of different stories, some apparently quite unrelated: it is possible, for example, that Joe never knows of Lena's existence.[82] They are, however, linked by common themes and images, the most prominent being the cancerous network of abstractions and prejudices which blight the lives of so many characters. Gail Hightower has elevated the legendary exploits of his Confederate grandfather into a form of private religion which Faulkner clearly intends to symbolise the South's nostalgic and escapist tendencies. Simon McEachern's religion is a cold, ruthless Calvinism which disdains all human compromise or pleasure and replaces love with a dehumanised work-ethic. Significantly, he scorns the qualities of softness, compassion and unpredictability which he associates with the other sex. His foster-son, Joe Christmas, inherits this distrust of women, his twin obsessions revolving ambiguously around the Southern taboos surrounding sex and race. He has inherited these also from his grandfather, the insane Eupheus Hines, who channels his religiosity into a fanatical hostility towards women and blacks, letting his unmarried grand-daughter die in childbirth, and urging a mob to lynch his supposedly 'nigger' grandson (pp. 185, 279). The Burdens' preoccupation with race and religion represents the opposite extreme, preaching the guilty and philanthropic necessity to 'raise' the Negro to remove God's curse on the whites. Where most of these dogmas are related to traditional Southern obsessions, Percy Grimm's monomania represents the worst of the New South, his neo-fascist glorification of regimented violence springing from an inner emptiness and the decay of any coherent traditional code.[83]

Another common theme throughout the different stories is that of an unhealthy escapism. Characters who are unable to muster those qualities of adaptability and compromise demanded by normal human relationships tend to retreat into isolation, abstraction or mindless repetition. Racism and dogmatic religion are the most common forms of escape from the complexities of reality. When Brown claims that Joanna Burden's murderer is a 'nigger', the marshal warns that 'You better be careful what you are saying, if it is a white man you are talking about.... I don't care if he is a murderer or not'. (p. 75), thus unconsciously revealing a lot about the moral priorities of his society. The man-hunt now takes on a new and terrible intensity, provoking some of Faulkner's most savage descriptions as we see the townsfolk revelling in sadism and sensationalism, 'a promise of something beyond the sluttishness of stuffed entrails and monotonous days' (p. 220).[84] Just as these men use 'law' and 'order' to justify their appetite for cruelty (p. 339), so Hightower exploits religion for his own perverse and escapist purposes: 'When he believed that he had heard the call it seemed to him that he could see his future, his life, intact and on all sides complete and inviolable, like a classic and serene vase, where the spirit could be born anew sheltered from the harsh gale of living' (p. 359). It is no accident that these images echo Faulkner's heavily ironic description of Percy Grimm's Pauline conversion: 'It was the new civilian–military act which saved him.... He could now see his life opening before him, uncomplex and inescapable as a barren corridor, completely freed now of ever again having to think or decide' (p. 339).

Joanna Burden resorts to another kind of idealism, a philanthropic urge to aid black schools and colleges, noble in itself were it not that she looks upon black people as 'a thing, a shadow in which I lived, we lived, all white people' (p. 190) – a violation of others' individuality which eventually costs her her life when she treats Joe as a convenient 'Negro' instrument in her design. Her other forms of escapism, an alternation between frantic nymphomania and a 'monotonous, sexless' religious fervour (p. 211), may remind us of the schizophrenia of that other social rebel, the equally self-destructive Sue Bridehead, and Joanna's final escape is indeed a death-wish, as the two bullets in her ancient pistol indicate.

When we first see him, Byron Bunch's existence is dominated by equally life-denying patterns, an escape from life through the rigid routines of church and work. This routine is disrupted when he falls in love; and when Lena gives birth he experiences a psychological crisis (clearly one of Faulkner's moments of epiphany), having to face two dreaded facts – the knowledge that Lena is not a virgin, and the duty to inform Lucas Burch of the baby. Byron survives his crises through his stoicism and by his new-found commitment to 'motion' and responsibility. After fighting the fleeing Burch, he lies stunned, his mind in a peaceful reverie until disturbed by a train whistle:

> This rouses him: this is the world and time too. He sits up.... It is getting late: it is time now, with distance, moving, in it. 'Yes, I'll have to be moving. I'll have to get on so I can find me something else to meddle with.' The train is coming nearer. Already the

stroke of the engine has shortened and become heavier as it begins to feel the grade ... the engine is in sight now, almost head on to him beneath the spaced, heavy blasts of black smoke. It has an effect of terrific nomotion. Yet it does move, creeping terrifically up and over the crest of the grade.   (p. 331)

Just as the country wagons in which Lena travels offer a powerful objective correlative for her patient, enduring quest, so the image of the labouring locomotive reflects something of Byron's stubborn energy and determination. The train's noisy appearance marks his re-entry into the confusion of existence and, moreover, Byron's curiosity rewards him with a vitally important glimpse of Burch leaping onto a passing car, thus vanishing from Lena's life.

The rueful comedy of Byron and Lena gives balance and contrast to the tragic centre of *Light in August*, the story of Joe Christmas. Living in a society obsessed by caste, Joe cannot identify himself as either white or black:[85] he is 'rootless', a lost and lonely spirit whose identity crisis makes him hate both whites and blacks (pp. 25, 82, 87, 88). Similarly, he fears and despises the reactions of the women to whom he is nevertheless repeatedly drawn (p. 83). Like those of the novel's other tragic protagonists, Joe's deepest impulses are escapist. Disillusioned in love, he seeks escape in travel, fleeing down 'a thousand savage and lonely streets' (p. 106); in swapping racial roles; in gratuitous violence; in a fatalistic philosophy ('Something is going to happen to me I am going to do something', p. 80); and eventually in a death-wish (p. 249). Joe's hatred lashes out sadistically at others, but his real victim is himself, as he seems partially aware, his compulsively repetitive violence always forbidding him the peace for which he yearns. His story possesses a powerful epic quality, like that of Lena. But where her journey is evoked as a Keatsian pastoral,[86] Joe's travels are set in a dimension not unlike the harsh *firm noir* world of *Sanctuary*, and are evoked as a suitably dark Byronic quest:

> He stepped from the dark porch, into the moonlight, and with his bloody head and his empty stomach hot, savage, and courageous with whiskey, he entered the street which was to run for fifteen years.
>
> The whiskey died away in time and was renewed and died again, but the street ran on. From that night the thousand streets ran as one street, with imperceptible corners and changes of

scene, broken by intervals of begged and stolen rides, on trains and
trucks, and on country wagons with he at twenty and twentyfive
and thirty sitting on the seat with his still, hard face and the clothes
(even when soiled and worn) of a city man. (p. 168)

Joe travels throughout the South, and into the cities of the North,
trying to 'escape from himself', 'doomed with motion' (p. 170). Joe
and Lena are linked by their associated habit of constant travel, as in
the passage above; their motion expresses a common attempt to find
a secure identity, to renounce their betrayed childhoods. Lena
succeeds effortlessly, since her 'doggedness has a soft quality, an
inwardlighted quality of tranquil and calm unreason and detachment' (p. 16), and she finds folks 'right kind'. Joe, who has no such
inner confidence, can only arouse hostility in others, as evidenced by
his very first appearance at the mill (p. 26). Faulkner pointedly
contrasts the sense of harmony integrating Lena's travels with the
physical world to Joe's alienation, in images which one would not be
surprised to find in a Hardy novel:

> The wagon now has a kind of rhythm, its ungreased and
> outraged wood one with the slow afternoon, the road, the
> heat. (p. 12)

> Overhead the slow constellations wheeled, the stars of which he
> had been aware for thirty years and not one of which had any name
> to him or meant anything at all by shape or brightness or
> position. (p. 81)

Faulkner's balanced conception of Joe's and Lena's quests, and the
epic tone which distinguishes them, deliberately reflects the
specifically Southern characteristics of Joe's tragedy. Like Quentin,
Joe is full of 'voices':

> it seemed to him ... that he was hearing a myriad sounds ... voices,
> murmurs, whispers: of trees, darkness, earth; people: his own
> voice; other voices evocative of names and times and places –
> which he had been conscious of all his life without knowing, which
> were his life. (p. 80)

Clearly, these voices, which recur just before he kills Joanna (p. 211),
whisper to Joe of all those Southern tensions and obsessions which

are so richly dramatised throughout the book; as with Hightower's personal visions, Faulkner is drawing upon the particular idiosyncracies of Southern experience (in this case, the scars left by a violent history, by slavery, by Calvinism) and using them to explore problems which are ultimately universal, as the Christ imagery which also clings around Joe suggests. In his account of Joe's restless wanderings, Faulkner evokes a comprehensive range of Southern experience, 'house or cabin, white or black' (p. 251),[87] a wide variety of jobs, life on the country farm or in the urban bar-room. This panorama reflects the passionate oppositions nor merely of Joe's life but of the 'ache of modernism' in the world of twentieth-century Yoknapatawpha, just as Tess's wanderings throughout Wessex reflect the tensions in her world. These confusing oppositions are re-enacted in miniature in the splendid taut narrative of chapter 5. Here we see Joe living in an austere country cabin, but dressing in city clothes; working in a country saw-mill, but also distilling homemade whiskey which links him to the Memphis underworld; sleeping in a ruined stable to savour the smell of horses, then avidly reading 'a magazine of that type whose covers bear either pictures of young women in underclothes or pictures of men in the act of shooting one another with pistols' (p. 85); roaming amongst the 'fecundmellow voices of negro women' in Freedman Town, and then the suburban gardens of prosperous white people, feeling alien in each; exposing himself by the roadside to 'white bastards' and their 'bitches' in passing cars, and then menacing a group of black passers-by. Through this vivid narrative form, Faulkner expresses his sense of regional and modernistic imbalance, a tragedy of frustrated harmony which is also symbolically realised by Hightower's vision of Joe's face blending with that of his murderer, in superb epiphany of the tragic Southern experience encapsulated in Joe's life and death.[88]

One of the most remarkable achievements of *Light in August* lies in persuading the reader to sympathise with such a harsh and loveless soul as Joe. As with Mink Snopes, Faulkner shows the protagonist at his worst before providing explanatory details, in this case the story of a terrible childhood, which force the reader to revise his first impressions. It is debatable whether Joe could be properly regarded as a tragic hero, for he shows only faint signs of a possible self-knowledge or moral growth. However, they should not be ignored, and it seems to me highly significant that these suggestions of redeeming human potential are all associated with Joe's isolation from society in the final stages of his flight across the country. Faulkner builds up to this episode slowly and deliberately. First come numerous protracted descriptions of Joe's pursuers, and all 'the sound and the fury of the hunt' (p. 248). When we finally see Joe, he exhibits the calm detachment of those other Faulknerian protagonists who strain themselves beyond the limits of physical endurance in a wild natural setting – the tall convict, Mink Snopes, the slave in 'Red Leaves'. As in the latter, Joe's flight takes on a nervous and sinister beauty, as when he falls asleep in a field in the act of running (p. 250). Like these protagonists too, Joe seems to have escaped from the realm of ordinary time. Each of his encounters with strangers is marked by an eerie quality, as if he were a creature from another planet; and Joe shows a glimmering awareness of the need for human communion as he remembers the terrified reactions of a black family from whom he demands a meal, his reflections all the more poignant and ironic in view of the reluctance with which Joe has always accepted food from others (p. 252).

Joe simultaneously realises the need for man's communion with nature, to which he now feels closer than ever before, the sense of intimacy and serenity emphasised by bursts of present tense:

> It is just dawn, daylight: that grey and lonely suspension filled with the peaceful and tentative waking of birds. The air, inbreathed, is like spring water. He breathes deep and slow, feeling with each breath himself diffuse into the neutral greyness. (p. 249)

The frozen, epic tranquillity of Joe's journey is oddly reminiscent of the fragile Indian-summer quality which distinguishes the flight across country of that other doomed murderer, Tess, with Angel. 'It is as though he desires to see his native earth in all its phases for the first or last time' (p. 254); and the quietness which Joe experiences seems closer to that peace for which he has always longed than anything he had known 'inside' society. And yet Faulkner's ambivalence, especially towards the relationship between man and nature, cannot quite allow an unequivocal idyll, and Joe realises that it is not solely his new-found intimacy with nature which has given him 'peace and unhaste and quiet', but also lightheadedness from lack of food and sleep. Nature has its splendours, but recourse to these alone is no solution to the problems of human society; by becoming absorbed in nature and ignoring his body's necessities, Joe has, like Giles Winterborne beneath his hurdles in the rain, already begun a slide towards death.[89] As he draws near to Mottstown, and his capture, Joe achieves his last epiphany:

> he is entering it again, the street which ran for thirty years ... during the last seven days he has ... travelled further than in all the thirty years before.... 'But I have never got outside that circle. I have never broken out of the ring of what I have already done and cannot ever undo,' he thinks quietly.   (p. 255)

Joe realises, finally, the erroneous nature of his attitudes to time. For most of his life he has been isolated in a manic, chaotic time-present, where he has submitted to sudden violent and fatalistic compulsions ('Something is going to happen to me.... I had to do it'). More recently he has endeavoured to escape time completely. But he now sees that the past, present and future of a man's life are one organic unity, that man must accept responsibility for his past actions; and so he drives on into Mottstown, where – unknown to both of them – his mad grandfather awaits him. Gail Hightower, who has spent most of his life isolated by an imaginary past, will experience similar insight into the patterns of his own misshapen life, and this realisation of the interrelation of one's past and present (which is more than the proud Thomas Sutpen ever achieves) provides a not ignoble climax to both men's tragic existences.

Considerable space could be devoted to a discussion of the treatment and the role of time in *Light in August*. Byron, for example, tries to establish his own artificial scheme of time, and hence control the random circumstances of his life, by a rigid weekly routine. Lena's patient, ongoing progress, and the determination 'to be moving' which Byron learns from her, indicate the importance which Faulkner attaches to purposeful motion, symbolised in the 'wheel' of thought which brings Hightower's regeneration, or in the continuing mobility and endurance of Lena and Byron at the novel's close. Such motion does not imply a neglect of the past – indeed, Len's pursuit of Lucas Burch proves that she is only too vividly aware of its repercussions. Rather, it acknowledges the past's influence while striving to make sense of the present. Both the structure and the dramatic content of *Light in August* affirm, like *The*

Mayor of Casterbridge, what Gavin Stevens preaches rather too baldly and clumsily in *Requiem for a Nun*: 'you – everyone – must, or anyway may have to, pay for your past' (*RFAN*, p. 138).

Faulkner's narrative technique in *Light in August* makes use of a fairly complex succession of flashbacks, creating an awareness of events by way of people's memories and thus anticipating the more radical and ambitious structure of *Absalom, Absalom!* This fictional strategy of overlapping stories in a rich variety of tones, featured throughout Faulkner's work, may be compared to the practice of the Southern folk-tradition of oral story-telling, the recounting of memories, anecdotes, tall tales and gossip to which the novelist had been accustomed since boyhood. *Light in August* amply demonstrates the influence of this tradition. Much of its story-telling, especially its eager modulations in and out of the present tense, exactly resemble a relaxed, contemplative voice, spinning familiar tales and remembered conversations out of an apparently bottomless memory.[90] Faulkner continually introduces new stories and characters, even as the novel nears its end, and they make their entrance with the quiet ease and gravity of figures in a traditional folk-tale: 'On that Friday when Christmas was captured in Mottstown, there lived in the town an old couple named Hines' (p. 256); 'In the town on that day lived a young man named Percy Grimm' (p. 338).

Other cameos provoke the reader's imagination by their customary Faulknerian ambivalence, reflecting the mysteries of paradoxical human nature and of the conflicting Southern character in particular. What are we to make, for example, of Sheriff Watt Kennedy, 'a fat, comfortable man with a hard, canny head and a benevolent aspect ... with little wise eyes like bits of mica embedded in his fat, still face' (pp. 216, 316)? Kennedy acts briskly to ascertain who lived in the Burden cabin:

> 'Get me a nigger,' the sheriff said. The deputy and two or three others got him a nigger. 'Who's been living in that cabin?' the sheriff said.
> 'I dont know, Mr. Watt,' the negro said. 'I aint never paid it no mind.'

He does have some vague notion, of course, and Kennedy and his deputy extract the information with a belt wielded 'buckle end outward' (p. 220). One gathers that the method is very simple:

apparently any nigger will do. For the world of _Light in August_, such brutality is relatively minor, and Faulkner reports the incident with studied detachment, but it quietly supplies another piece in the jigsaw of social and psychological malaise, all the more disturbing since Kennedy appears in other respects to be a decent enough man, who speaks kindly to Byron in his misery and expresses sympathy for Molly Hines (p. 318).

By comparing and contrasting the novel's case-histories, the reader can frequently perceive ironic paradoxes of which the characters seem unaware. Hines, who despises black people, is dependent upon 'the bounty and charity of negroes for sustenance' (p. 258). One soon notices that even those holding diametrically opposing views are often more alike than they could possibly imagine, an insight indicative of the novel's tragi-comic vision of humanity.[91] Conversely, the grandfather whom Hightower idolises was in reality quite different from the fond romantic imaginings of his descendant.[92]

Hightower's delivery of Lena's baby, his attempt to shield Christmas, and the 'wheel' of self-scrutiny acknowledging his social and personal sins, are a tacit admission that choice, involvement and responsibility are necessary to make man's existence meaningful. And the tendency of humanistic values to spread outwards from the influence of the unassuming girl from Alabama demonstrates that surer faith in human nature which distinguishes _Light in August_ from the moral darkness of _Sanctuary_. The 'logical pattern to evil' which devastated Horace Benbow is still visible in the self-perpetuating perversions of Joe's or Joanna's upbringing, but in this novel they are at least balanced and opposed.

The novel's positive values are perhaps most clearly expressed by that customary Faulknerian distinction between 'words' and 'doing'. Byron and Lena personify a stoical commitment to 'doing' and motion which silently rebukes the abstract or mindless exercise of 'words' inherent in the community's religious and racist hysteria, Hightower's romanticism or Lucas Burch's shallowness. Byron's traumatic recognition of the awful gulf between words and doing, comparable to Addie Bundren's great soliloquy, occurs fittingly enough as Lena gives birth, when Byron must cope with the harsh and inescapable facts of man's (and, more especially, woman's) existence –

> It was like me, and her, and all the other folks that I had to get mixed up in it, were just a lot of words that never even stood for anything, were not

even us, while all the time what was us was going on and going on
without even missing the lack of words.   (p. 302)

It is important, therefore, to note that the novel's 'restorations' are
enacted not so much by discussion as by example. This, it seems to
me, is where a protagonist such as Byron is far more satisfying as a
literary creation, and as a human being, than Faulkner's later
verbose philosophers, principally Gavin Stevens. Byron's ability to
cope is reflected by a rueful laconicism drawn from his traditional
'austere ... country raising' (p. 38):

> The mild red road goes on beneath the slanting and peaceful
> afternoon, mounting a hill. 'Well, I can bear a hill,' he thinks. ...
> 'It seems like a man can just about bear anything.... He can even
> bear the thinking how some things is just more than he can
> bear.... He can even bear it to not look back, even when he knows
> that looking back or not looking back wont do him any good.'
>   The hill rises, cresting. He has never seen the sea, and so he
> thinks, 'It is like the edge of nothing....'
>   ... But then from beyond the hill crest there begins to rise that
> which he knows is there ... the terrific and tedious distance
> which, being moved by blood, he must compass forever and ever
> between the two inescapable horizons of the implacable earth.
> Steadily they rise, not portentous, not threatful. That's it. They
> are oblivious of him.   (pp. 318–19)

Byron grimly decides that 'if that's all it is, I might as well have the
pleasure of not being able to bear looking back too' (p. 319); and only
because he has the courage to do this does he glimpse the fleeing
Lucas Burch, and thereby finds himself eligible to return to Lena.
The moral profile of Byron's character which emerges is thus rooted,
like that of Lena, in the interrelation of character and environment.
His stoicism reflects his familiarity with the 'implacable earth';
Faulkner does not so much tell us about Byron's resilience as show it
by a Hardeian 'conjunction of things', the tribulations of a man's life
outlined by his own native hills and horizons, exactly as Hardy
frequently symbolises the human plight by contrasting a small,
suffering human figure with the massive and indifferent force of
nature.

Asked whether he ever identified with any of his characters, 'for
instance someone like Gavin Stevens', Faulkner replied that
occasionally the writer's and character's ideas coincide but 'when

you do that they'll become his … you're not trying to preach through the character … you're too busy writing about people'.[93] One may notice echoes of his description of Don Quixote entering reality by being 'so busy trying to cope with people':[94] both pronouncements are amply applicable to his portrayal of Byron and Lena. Gavin Stevens is, of course, often viewed critically, and cannot be simply identified as an authorial spokesman.[95] Yet he plainly *is* an explicit spokesman for one perspective upon both Southern society and the human plight, if not always Faulkner's own, and his increasing prominence in Faulkner's later work points to an important distinction between the final perspectives upon the human condition developed by Faulkner's and Hardy's novels. While Hardy's last two novels become increasingly critical of social injustices, and darker and more unrelievedly tragic in tone, Faulkner's work shows a comparable concern with social justice but grows mellower, more steadily hopeful in its emphasis upon the efficacy of human values. Regrettably, as this happens his work grows simultaneously less psychologically gripping and less artistically satisfying; it is noticeable, for instance, that the *formal* elements of disorder and disintegration grow less challenging in his later work as the content mellows. This creative decline is, I think, directly related to Faulkner's increasing preoccupation with the fictional discussion of 'ideas'. In his finest work, that of the period between 1929 and 1940, which includes *Light in August*, Faulkner seems to be writing from instinctive sources, guided only by fidelity to his conception of character.[96] To his imagination these characters appeared suddenly, intuitively, in isolated, dream-like images, such as the one that inspired *The Sound and the Fury*,[97] and they spoke in actual living, autonomous voices.[98] His task, as he saw it, was to give them some artistic coherence and to record them with disinterested fascination.[99]

Perhaps this 'demon-driven' inspiration could not be expected to maintain its intensity or 'fire' for many years. Certainly, the moralising ruminations of Gavin and Chick in *Intruder in the Dust*, or of the corporal and the old general in *A Fable*, function on a lower creative plane than the innate moral drama of *Light in August* or *Absalom, Absalom!* Wittenberg suggests that by the time of *Go Down, Moses* Faulkner had made an 'ultimate transformation from a novelist of consciousness to one of conscience'.[100] Where the works of 1929–40 had dramatised human virtues and vices, Faulkner's later novels tend to sermonise about them in voices that, if not reproducing his own views verbatim, at least seem frequently to be doing so. Hardy's novels had always been prone to break off suddenly from a vivid narrative, landscape description or dialogue into a sudden, brief discussion of Novalis's views, or the conduct of the President of the Immortals. But this instability is part of their peculiar charm, the 'harmony of separates'[101] which may be seen as a counterpart of Faulkner's multiple perspectives, since it encourages the reader in a simultaneous intimacy with, and detached scrutiny of, the world of Wessex. Stevens's philosophisings, on the other hand, are sometimes (though not always) long and tedious, their tendencies towards generalisation and didacticism often resulting in a sluggishness of narrative despite the balancing viewpoints of Chick or Ratliff, or Lucas Beauchamp's inscrutable presence. At their slightest, Hardy's tragic denouements are weakened by an over-strenuous ironic tone (as in *Two on a Tower*, *The Hand of Ethelberta* or even the final paragraph of *Tess*), while some of the most heartfelt sentiments to be voiced in Faulkner's novels are marred by the self-conscious portentousness of their exponents.[102] The two writers' visions of humanity seem most homogenous as well as most valuable when they subsume their wisdom within the characters' 'doing', or seeing, rather than their 'words', and the reader's most memorable impressions of life in Yoknapatawpha flow from the contemplation of scenes such as Quentin handing his letter to Deacon, or Charles Bon's (very Hardeian) substitution of the photographs of Judith and his mistress, or Byron watching a train with 'the rapt and boylike absorption ... of his country raising' (*LIA*, p. 331).

Such images offer the reader paradigms of meaningful human experience which show, rather than tell, the reader that man should balance his fondness for abstract ideas and 'words' against the experiential necessity for flexibility, change, motion and 'doing'. As in Hardy's novels, the characters best able to establish such equilibrium are those whose daily experience represents a 'folk-historical' dimension, those whose lives involve intimate contact with the rhythms of nature, whose work demands a patient and enduring accommodation with their environment. They are not so much 'ideal' as *necessary* characters, who demonstrate Hardy's 'simple loving-kindness', and represent what Lyall Powers has termed (adopting Matthew Arnold) 'a Saving Remnant – those in whom our hope may safely reside'.[103] Women figure prominently in this group, in both writers' novels. So do small farmers, agricultural workers, independent craftsmen, tradesmen and yeomen (Ratliff supplying an interesting equivalent to the roles of Dick Dewy and Diggory Venn), black people in Faulkner's work and the poor and oppressed in Hardy's, aged story-tellers and various primitives who live on the fringes of society.

At this point we might remark a curious conundrum, one implicitly acknowledged by Faulkner's often rather distant treatment of the 'Saving Remnant'. This is simply that most of his readers will not be small farmers or itinerant labourers, any more than were Hardy's. Equally, neither were the novelists. The modern, probably urban and relatively cerebral reader is therefore confronted by an intriguing paradox: how can these moving paradigms of relatively obscure or exotic folk be most usefully and positively related to his or her own moral dilemmas? For however much Faulkner's novels stir the imagination and reflect universal emotions, it is probably much easier for the modern reader to identify imaginatively with Quentin, Dr Peabody, Gavin or Isaac than to penetrate the consciousness of a Dilsey, Cash, Lena or Sam. Possibly, too, the dilemmas which most of us experience are closer to those of Grace or Angel than to those of Marty or Tess, even though we might not like to admit it.

It is true that it would be uncharacteristic, not to say crass, if Faulkner offered us a prototype modern man who *could* wholly cope with the transitional flux of the New South in Yoknapatawpha; Ratliff probably comes closer than any other protagonist to this impossible requirement.[104] Hardy's corresponding realisation of these problems finds its most obvious expression in the elegiac mood of his greatest tragedies, the sense of a diminution in the quality of life afforded by the loss of Henchard, Giles, Tess and Jude; consequently his particular 'ache of modernism' is, as I have remarked, more unequivocally tragic than that of Faulkner. Meanwhile, his awareness of the gulf between modern, educated reader and obscure, humble protagonist is also reflected, as I have stressed, by the continual modulations of tone; and Faulkner finds his most forceful answer to this paradox in the same quarter. It is located in his style, which in his finest work boldly integrates the reader into the very processes of creative fiction itself, establishing alternative points of view, undermining certainties, stressing the ambiguities of events, and forcing the reader to acknowledge the ambivalent and ever-changing nature of experience.

In my final chapter I should like, therefore, to re-examine some of the major ideas which have grown out of my comparative analysis, and to attempt to gather them together in a brief account of the relationship between form and content in the novels; I hope, however, that it will already have become clear that what Faulkner and Hardy want to say emerges very much through the way that they say it, and that while Faulkner does not supply an 'ideal' character, the structure of the novels themselves – the shape and texture of the narratives, constantly emphasising the richness and complexity of experience – encourages us to avoid the blinkered over-simplification practised by the tragic protagonists, and to evaluate a balanced view of life which corresponds in spirit with that of his 'Saving Remnant'.

5

'A series of seemings': the Marriage of Form and Content

an endeavour to give shape and coherence to a series of seemings, or personal impressions

('Preface' to *Jude*)

the truth is what they saw though nobody saw the truth intact
(*Faulkner in the University*, pp. 273–4)

It seems useful at this point to attempt to draw together some of the correlations between Hardy's and Faulkner's lives and work which have emerged from previous chapters, thereby approaching some brief discussion of formal achievement through a reacquaintance with those factors which inspired their content.

Their novels grew out of a problematic engagement of character and environment, prompting an imaginative endeavour to explore the tension between the native's estrangement and his return. Both men started their literary careers as poets, and only gradually discovered inspiration in their regional worlds, and a vocation as novelists, following tentative urban exiles. A return to their roots became a necessary condition of artistic creativity, but each writer developed a curiously ambivalent relationship with his native environment, reflected throughout the content and form of his fiction. Both men pursued a lifestyle characterised by duality. Faulkner lived for the rest of his life in Oxford, but always remained something of an outsider; Hardy eventually settled in Dorchester but spent part of each year in London. Both were troubled by the contrast between the unworldliness of their literary vocation and the sturdy practicality of their ancestors and fellow-citizens. Hardy expressed a wistful desire to have been a country architect, Faulkner adopted the roles of hunter, farmer or pilot. Both writers show a strong interest in social misfits as protagonists, those who occupy the fringes of conventional rural society; this imaginative stance becomes a way of exploring that society in fiction, while resisting identification with its norms. Not surprisingly, both writers' work caused bitter controversy and disapproval, not least in their local communities: Hardy by his outspoken views on sexual morality, Faulkner by his critique of Southern racism. In coming to terms with the clash between tradition and modernity, the central strategy was not merely one of imaginative literature, a 'series of seemings', but specifically the creation of a fictional world, a 'cosmos of my own'.

Accordingly, their protagonists continually enact this experience of tension and ambivalence. The dissension and rivalry between Michael Henchard and Donald Farfrae dramatises the clash of traditional and modern consciousnesses, the one crude, anachronistic, excessively personal, over-emotional and yet redolent of a certain rough grandeur; the other innovatory, impersonal, dispassionate, sensible, but somewhat mean-spirited.[1] The reader is encouraged to consider whether the quality of life in Casterbridge is improved or diminished by the passing of Henchard. The question is sometimes reflected by the gossip of the community:

> His accounts were like a bramblewood when Mr. Farfrae came. He used to reckon his sacks by chalk strokes all in a row like garden-palings, measure his ricks by stretching with his arms, weigh his trusses by a lift, judge his hay by a chaw, and settle the price with a curse. But now this accomplished young man does it all by ciphering and mensuration.   (TMOC, p. 136)

and sometimes by Hardy's own ambivalent tone.[2] The counterpart to this social and commercial displacement is found in Faulkner's rather less equivocal description of the contrast between the business methods of Jody Varner and Flem Snopes;[3] while a Hardeian sense of imminent loss permeates the conversations between Sam Fathers and his young friends Quentin or Isaac. In all these relationships the writers gently intimate that we are not simply seeing a choice between alternative, readily available cultures; rather the contrasts express that poignant hiatus between incompatible forms for which I have adopted Hardy's phrase 'the ache of modernism'. For one thing, the contrasts involve *time*: the inevitability of change forbids our easy inheritance of our ancestors' patterns, and the reader recognises that however much we admire some of them, the ways of Henchard or Sam are doomed.

Society poses other difficulties. Due to the imperfections, separations and confusions of human intercourse (especially virulent in the disorientated social worlds explored by Hardy and Faulkner) it is hard for people to find meaningful communion with one another. Hardy's protagonists yearn vainly to cross the barriers of social class; Faulkner's black and white characters are hampered by prejudice and stereotype. Sexual misunderstandings are another stumbling-block: both writers' male protagonists tend to paint idealistic portraits of womanhood which distort the reality of women's lives, and bring misery to both sexes.

Pursuing different ways of life, traditional and modern protagonists also necessarily develop disparate sensibilities. As I suggested earlier, the 'Saving Remnant' often seem rather remote from the actual experience of both reader and author. Again, the problem is one widely felt in modern life. It finds eloquent expression in H. J. Massingham's essay describing the life and craftmanship of Samuel Rockall, a 'wood-bodger', or wood-turner. Rockall finds three old knife-blades thrown away and fits new wooden handles to them, and Massingham comments:

> there is a secret of life in this peasant-craftsman which the modern world must rediscover. I cannot rediscover it myself because I am too much of this moden world. But I constantly see symbols of it like that of the abandoned knife-blade raked out of the midden and made into a thing of beauty.[4]

It is exactly this tension which informs Faulkner's reiterated distrust of 'words' and advocacy of 'doing', reflected in Addie Bundren's soliloquy or Hightower's 'thinking ... as every other man has thought: how false the most profound book turns out to be when applied to life' (*LIA*, p. 361). Hardy's critique of intellectual idealists like Clym or Fitzpiers suggests similar misgivings, and points to an ironic paradox: how can a writer celebrate 'doing' and deprecate mere 'words', in his chosen medium of words? This problem is felt in the severe dislocation of the different protagonists, where often no middle ground seems attainable. We may well feel, for example, that Lena Grove's quality of 'tranquil and calm unreason' is simply not an available option in most of our daily circumstances, and that perhaps she is a little *too* mindless; while

Quentin and Darl alarm us because they can't ever *stop* thinking. As introspective artists, Faulkner and Hardy are naturally enough fascinated by cerebral, self-conscious characters of the sort they frequently deplore, and, like Massingham, feel cut off from the taciturn men of action whom they admire. We may suspect that we hear the authors' own rueful thoughts when Henry Knight explains that 'it is only those who half know a thing that write about it. Those who know it thoroughly don't take the trouble' (*APOBE*, p. 162), or when Bayard II 'realised ... the immitigable chasm between all life and all print – that those who can, do, those who cannot and suffer enough because they can't, write about it' (*TU*, p. 157).

Clym Yeobright and Edred Fitzpiers seem to reflect other fantasised incarnations of Hardy's own personality (certainly they all share a taste for philosophical literature and picturesque rusticity) just as Darl and Quentin and Isaac suggest imaginary versions of their creator had he not found his imaginative outlet in fiction. For despite the delicate and continual balancings of his story-telling, Faulkner inevitably seems closer to some of his fictional consciousnesses than others; some, such as Quentin, are intimately rendered, others, such as Lena, remain a little distant, however warm his approbation. Hardy's protagonists are treated with a similar variation of intimacy.

One instinctive solution to the problematic balance of 'words' and 'doing' in each man's writing is the imaginative resource of nature. It seems significant, for example, that Faulkner's first, and highly explicit, discussion of the writer's dilemma, in *Mosquitoes*, couches its defence of 'words' in images of natural fertility (and oddly fitting, too, that Fairchild's theory may remind us of Hardy's 'familiar conjunctions of things'):

> 'Well, it is a kind of sterility – words,' Fairchild admitted. 'You begin to substitute words for things and deeds, like the withered cuckold husband that took the Decameron to bed with him every night, and pretty soon the thing or the deed becomes just a kind of shadow of a certain sound.... But you have confusion, too. I don't claim that words have a life in themselves. But words brought into a happy conjunction produce something that lives, just as soil and climate and an acorn in proper conjunction will produce a tree.' (*Mosquitoes*, p. 175)

A concentrated evocation of nature in 'words' enables Faulkner to

explore the state of mind of a wholly inarticulate character, such as
the mentally subnormal Ike Snopes in *The Hamlet*, in language far
beyond Ike's reach, thus simultaneously reminding us of the gulf
between his 'primitive' consciousness and our own, and yet
momentarily bridging it:

> he discovered ... that dawn, light, is not decanted onto earth from
> the sky, but instead is from the earth itself suspired. Roofed by the
> woven canopy of blind annealing grass-roots and the roots of
> trees ... it wakes, upseeping, attritive in uncountable creeping
> channels: first, root; then frond by frond, from whose escaping
> tips like gas it rises and disseminates and stains the sleep-fast
> earth with drowsy insect-murmur; then, still upward-seeking,
> creeps the knitted bark of trunk and limb where, suddenly louder
> leaf by leaf and dispersive in diffusive sudden speed, melodious
> with the winged and jewelled throats, it upward bursts and fills
> night's globed negation with jonquil thunder. Far below, the
> gauzy hemisphere treads with herald-cock, and sty and pen and
> byre salute the day. (*TH*, pp. 168–9)

Unlike Faulkner's earlier depiction of the subnormal Benjy Compson, this does not even attempt to reproduce Ike's thought-pat-
terns literally. Rather it reflects, precisely in the manner of Hardy's
urge to 'intensify the expression of things' in the 'mad, late-Turner
rendering',[5] the ecstasy which Ike experiences in this May dawn,
fleeing with a stolen cow with which he has fallen in love. The
practical circumstances may verge upon the ludicrous, yet the sheer
opulence of the language, its urgency and repetitions, defies the
reader to withhold sympathy; indeed, the novel's structure
encourages us to compare Ike's blind devotion favourably with the
preoccupations of other less ingenuous protagonists, principally
the other Snopeses. An unchanging world beyond man's control,
nature throws human activities into revealing focus. But neither
novelist suggests that an intimacy with nature alone can solve man's
moral crises, as Clym and Isaac McCaslin discover; and Ike is, after
all, an idiot, lacking a 'conscience to keep him awake at night' (*TH*,
p. 170).

It is, therefore, in the structure and the style of their novels, and in
their marriage of form and content, that Faulkner and Hardy
achieve many of their most subtle and enlightening renditions of
experience through words. In Hardy's case this is expressed

primarily by that continual, hesitant fluctuation of the authorial voice between engagement and detachment. Ian Gregor's introductory essay on *The Mayor of Casterbridge* offers a perceptive analysis of this movement which helps us to see its nascent relationship to Faulkner's more radical narrative strategy. Gregor draws our attention to

> the compassionate presence of the narrator, whose mediating consciousness is an integral part of the drama.... In the very elements that go to make up his fiction – the narrative trajectory, the sudden moment of symbolic concentration, the oscillations between story and commentary ... Hardy is acting out his own impression of life as a series of seemings ... communicated most frequently in that air of ambivalence which hangs over so many incidents in the novel ... [and] which creates in the reader not so much an awareness of complexity as a desire to suspend judgement and to sense a more inclusive view.[6]

This, it seems to me, shows very usefully the strong emotional unity of the two writers' conceptions of experience, and the demand for continual flexibility in the novelist. Where they differ appreciably is in the precise psychological projection and technical expression of that characteristic ambivalence. Hardy's attitude to experience remains primarily introspective and detached, studying his own imaginative responses to 'flux and reflux – the rhythm of change' (*Tess*, p. 399), 'the persistence of the unforeseen' (*TMOC*, p. 354), and therefore maintaining the authorial voice throughout continual fluctuations. Hence, as Gregor emphasises, and the 'Preface' to *Jude* declares, Hardy's fiction is 'an endeavour to give shape and coherence to a series of seemings, or personal impressions, the question of their consistency or their discordance, of their permanence or their transitoriness, being regarded as not of the first moment'.[7]

Faulkner's imaginative responses to experience are rather directed *outwards*, moving from introspective sources towards the relativity of 'seemings' as they occur to different individuals, and frequently expressed through a series of multiple perspectives, for he considered that

> no one individual can look at truth. It blinds you. You look at it and you see one phase of it. Someone else looks at it and sees a

slightly awry phase of it. But taken all together, the truth is what they saw though nobody saw the truth intact ... when the reader has read these thirteen ways of looking at the blackbird, the reader has his own fourteenth image of the blackbird which I would like to think is the truth.[8]

In order to compare briefly the relationship of form and content in the two novelists' work, I should like to examine some interesting parallels between *Absalom, Absalom!* and *The Mayor of Casterbridge*. These novels show some extraordinary similarities, both of plot and of philosophical implication. It is, of course, possible that such striking echoes are semi-conscious ones on Faulkner's part,[9] but equally they may be simply indicative of the essentially emotional, psychological and philosophical bonds uniting the two writers' work.

Each novel shows the historical rise and fall of a powerful, lonely man, ambivalently portrayed, whose career is embellished by mythical overtones[10] and who may be inspired by the novelist's fascination with a colourful, violent ancestor.[11] Certainly the protagonist personifies the virtues and vices of a vanished traditional world. But his rise to power is achieved through a ruthless 'design', and the cost of his success is a guilty secret, a 'skeleton ... in the closet' (*AA*, p. 13) unknown to society, which eventually contributes to the protagonist's downfall. In each case, the secret concerns the betrayal of love for the sake of ambition, each protagonist heartlessly abandoning his wife and child to further his career; and each wife and/or child reappears years later, with dramatic results. Each protagonist fails disastrously to learn from his previous mistakes; for example, Henchard's impulsive reading of his dead wife's letter about Elizabeth-Jane exemplifies his susceptibility to rash and wilful actions, while Sutpen continues to treat other vulnerable women (Rosa, Milly) with careless contempt. The cyclical nature of each man's career and the significant repetition of important features in their lives emphasise that these two novels, like *Light in August*, are concerned to investigate the relationship of the past and present: indeed, the pervasive influence of the past shapes the structure of these novels and suggests their common philosophical theme. This is the realisation that events do not merely occur and cease in an experiential vacuum, but interlock with all other events in a 'great web of human doings' (*TW*, p. 52) which reverberates in other people's lives and memories. Hardy's 'great web' is identical with Judith Sutpen's idea of human lives entangled on a loom:

> you are born at the same time with a lot of other people, all mixed up with them, like trying to … move your arms and legs with string only the same strings are hitched to all the other arms and legs … like five or six people all trying to make a rug on the same loom only each one wants to weave his own pattern into the rug. (*AA*, p. 127)

It is echoed too by Quentin's reflection that

> *Maybe nothing ever happens once and is finished … but like ripples maybe on water after the pebble sinks, the ripples moving on, spreading, the pool attached by a narrow umbilical water-cord to the next pool … that pebble's watery echo whose fall it did not even see moves across its surface too. (AA, p. 261)*

This holistic view of life clearly carries a moral as well as philosophical imperative, that belief in karma remarked upon earlier in this study, which suggested that one's present actions cryptically determine one's future destiny with an ironic appropriateness. Again, Gregor's comments upon *The Mayor of Casterbridge* prove highly pertinent to *Absalom, Absalom!*:

> the opening of *The Mayor of Casterbridge* reveals in a remarkably pure way the characteristic Hardy stance towards experience. Within each chapter a set of reverberations is released from a single violent act – the sale of the wife, Henchard's vow. A perspective on the human deed is established. The act of an individual person cannot be contained by that individual's life; it leads persistently outwards to the whole social context, a context both personal and social.[12]

Sutpen's tragedy is partly that he can never achieve this holistic vision of life, primarily because of his 'innocence', which 'believed that the ingredients of morality were like the ingredients of pie or cake and once you had measured them … and put them into the oven it was all finished and nothing but pie or cake could come out' (*AA*, p. 263). The tragic epiphany is left to the heir of Sutpen's spiritual legacy, Quentin, whose final despair stems from a double recognition of life's 'ripples': that given Sutpen's 'innocence', his failure was inevitable, and furthermore that the ripples continue to spread, touching Quentin's own personal traumas, and the general defects of Southern society. The great web and the ripples are equally visible to the reader in the novelists' sense of place linking character and environment (for example, the emotional unity of Sutpen and Henchard with their respective houses),[13] and in other uncannily repetitive tricks of history: the psychological 'doubling' of the divided Quentin with the conflicting Charles and Henry; the karmic appearance of Bon at Sutpen's door, and a repetition of humiliating rejection;[14] Mrs Newson's eerie second sighting of the furmity woman at the fair, and the latter's arrival in Casterbridge; Henchard's discovery of his 'drowned' likeness, or his shocked glimpse of Lucetta appearing like Susan in the Ring. Social consequences percolate outwards from these private dramas, both novels involving the reader in a busy awareness of the conscious-nesses of witnesses and reporters. A curious, gossiping local community scrutinises each protagonist's career,[15] and marvels at his fall. In *Absalom, Absalom!*, of course, the most important audience is the 'modern' consciousness of Quentin,[16] and this demands consideration of the one fundamental distinction between the two novels, that of authorial perspective and narration. The ambivalence of experience and the power of the past are expressed by a much more radical narrative method than Hardy's authorial fluctuations afford, since Faulkner frames the historical story inside the 'modern' reinterpretations of 1909–10: unlike *The Mayor of Casterbridge*, we are confronted by a story inside a story. Hardy's linear plot must obviously rely more heavily than Faulkner's jigsaw puzzle upon symbolic incident and authorial commentary. But *The Mayor of Casterbridge*, too, is rich in voices. Hardy's gift for authentic vernacular gives us, through the Casterbridge community's role as chorus, both a dense awareness of traditional folk-life and a continual reminder of the influence of 'Time, the magician':

> 'tis said 'a was a poor parish 'prentice ... that began life wi' no more belonging to 'en than a carrion crow!   (p. 113)

> Cuxsom's gone, and so shall leather breeches!   (p. 114)

> And all her shining keys will be took from her ... and her wishes and ways will all be as nothing!   (p. 149)

As the novel progresses, the reader also notices an increasing tendency for the authorial 'series of seemings' to merge with the consciousness of Elizabeth-Jane, whose resilient and unassuming personality experiences poverty and prosperity, the fierceness of Henchard's temper and the bland frigidity of Farfrae's pragmatism:

> She looked from the window and saw Henchard and Farfrae in the hay yard talking.... Friendship between man and man; what a rugged strength there was in it, as evinced by these two. And yet the seed that was to lift the foundation of this friendship was at that moment taking root in a chink of its structure.
>
> It was about six o'clock; the men were dropping off homeward one by one. (p. 126)

The voice here shows a characteristic Hardeian modulation between ironic philosophical reflections and a vigorous deployment of dramatic incident. At this early point in the novel, the voice is wholly authorial, the girl a mere convenient observer. Yet the quiet tone of philosophical detachment is very much that which one learns to associate with Elizabeth-Jane, who gradually comes to resemble one of the stoic, enduring survivors of Faulkner's 'Saving Remnant'. Not only does her perspective encourage a balanced assessment of events, but she is seen, like Byron Bunch, to grow in self-knowledge and in her ability to cope with misfortune, 'discovering ... the secret ... of making limited opportunities endurable' (pp. 353–4). It therefore seems wholly fitting that Hardy's description of her subsequent life closes the novel in a tone of heavy, earnest solemnity which exactly matches her worthy but rather prim sensibility.

Just as this mood of awkward anticlimax and mediocrity deliberately echoes the reader's emotional pitch following Henchard's death, so a rather cruel question and a desperately evasive reply convey precisely the psychological impasse reached by the end of *Absalom, Absalom!* Faulkner's integration of form and content throughout the novel represents his most ambitious and successful experiment in style; he manages simultaneously to match the tone and personalities of individual sections, as in *The Sound and the Fury*, and to create out of the whole a kaleidoscope of stories whose configurations of meaning are seemingly endless. The effect is radically new, though the inspiration for Faulkner's narrative structure is a very traditional one indeed, being his regional inheritance of orally-told stories, their patterns and rhythms forming a powerful concrete universal for that accumulated weight of Southern history, voices and observations which oppresses Quentin:

> But you were not listening, because you knew it all already, had learned, absorbed it already without the medium of speech somehow from having been born and living beside it... so that what your father was saying did not tell you anything so much as it struck, word by word, the resonant strings of remembering. (pp. 212–13)

The tension between tradition and modernism is sustained in both the story and the formal texture of the historical enigma which the protagonists of 1909–10 struggle to solve. Traditionally Southern 'tellings' of Sutpen's story, comprising the Gothic emotionalism of Miss Rosa and the elegant, languid fatalism of Mr Compson, are held up against the new insights of the younger generation, comprising Shreve's detachment and irreverence, and Quentin's anguished transitional consciousness. Suspended somewhere between the two worlds, Quentin is the repository for all the South's sentimental longings for a 'tradition' that never really was (Sutpen, after all, was not even a real gentleman),[17] yet he is also sensitive and observant enough to find convincing historical explanations for the actual causes of Sutpen's failure, and that of Southern society. His problem is that the knowledge is a terrible one, with no readily apparent solution.

But, *Absalom, Absalom!* is not only Quentin's story, for the reader is likewise involved in the detective work, and inherits something of Quentin's confusion and ambivalence, if not his terror, at the end. As each of the narrators brings different information and subjective bias to bear upon the story of Thomas Sutpen, we find ourselves peering through a series of powerful but unfocussed lenses, capable of infinite variations of perspective, which each reader must carefully test and adjust according to individual sensibility. Our insights into the novel's subject grow directly out of an immersion in the texture of its form, so that to put a small section of this organic narrative under a critical microscope is to reveal, in microcosm, the novel's larger themes, much as Faulkner's Yoknapatawpha mirrors the South, and humanity. Each different layer of narrative contributes to our continual sense of discovery, about Sutpen and his family, the narrators, the South, the creative and historical imagination:

> They stared – glared at one another. It was Shreve speaking, though save for the slight difference which the intervening degrees of latitude had inculcated in them ... it might have been either of them and was in a sense both: both thinking as one, the voice which happened to be speaking the thought only the thinking became audible, vocal; the two of them creating between them, out of the rag-tag and bob-ends of old tales and talking, people who perhaps had never existed at all anywhere ... shadows not of flesh and blood which had lived and died but shadows in turn of what were (to one of them at least, to Shreve) shades too.... The chimes now began to ring for midnight, melodious, slow and faint beyond the closed, the snow-sealed window.   (p. 303)

This passage's first object of attention appears to be the different intuitive responses of two young men to a historical puzzle; and the carefully ambivalent tone establishes that the differences between their contributions are negligible, that *both* contributions are essential to the reconstruction, and yet that differences in regional consciousness *will* eventually lead to different results. For the second layer of subject examines the 'shadows' of historical personages whom Shreve and Quentin create, the most notable being those of Charles Bon and Henry Sutpen, and while these may merely seem 'to one of them at least, to Shreve', to be 'shadows ... of what were ... shades', Faulkner obliquely hints that to Quentin they represent more palpable and ominous presences, of urgent relevance to his Southern consciousness. Thirdly, the passage can be seen as a paradigm of the Faulknerian approach to historical interpretation, in that the two young men's imaginative reconstruction of characters from 'old tales and talking' is essentially Faulkner's own novelistic method. The form of the text thereby represents an argument for the validity of the techniques of the novelist as a means of discovering the truth of historial experience, and the ultimate effect of the novel's wider kaleidoscopic patterns is to encourage the reader to adopt those techniques himself, in order to discover his own interpretation of the mysteries of the human heart. Finally, it should be remarked that Shreve's and Quentin's perspectives on the story are shown to be themselves subject to the limitations of time and distance (the midnight chimes, the alien New England snow) and are therefore themselves part of the historical process. Nothing remains stable.

The effects of these discoveries swiftly become more evident. Shreve creates out of these 'shadows' a scene in which Bon travels up the Mississippi en route for Oxford, wondering why his mother's lawyer has arranged for him to attend this obscure provincial university:

> maybe leaning there in that solitude between panting smoke and engines and almost touching the answer, aware of the jigsaw puzzle picture integers of it waiting, almost lurking, just beyond his reach, inextricable, jumbled and unrecognizable yet on the point of falling into pattern which would reveal to him at once, like a flash of light, the meaning of his whole life, past – the Haiti, the childhood, the lawyer, the woman who was his mother. And maybe the letter [a secret letter of introduction from the lawyer to Henry, recommending Charles] itself right there under his feet, somewhere in the darkness beneath the deck on which he stood.... One day Henry showed it to him and there was no gentle spreading glow but a flash, a glare ... in which he stood looking at the innocent face of the youth almost ten years his junior, while one part of him said.... *Wait. Wait. You cant know yet. You cannot know yet whether what you see is what you are looking at or what you are believing.* (pp. 313–14)

Here the reader experiences a sense of identification with the immediate subject, Charles Bon, which steadily strengthens from the tentativeness of 'maybe' through the growing narrative certainty ('One day Henry showed it to him') to a dramatic epiphany, its internalised thoughts denoted in italics. This process of discovery is reinforced by the passage's theme of a symbolic journey which is both actual (a voyage by steamboat), psychological (in Charles's gathering suspicions about his parentage) and perhaps even capable of literary allusion.[18]

The passage's second layer of subject envisages the enigmatic and subtly interrelated patterns of a human life as a 'jigsaw puzzle', with its teasing sense of elusive meaning so near and yet so far from attainment. Again we are reminded of the significance of the entire novel's form and content, while the passage itself suggests that these enigmatic patterns can be deciphered by imaginative intuition, by epiphany ('a flash, a glare'), especially if, like Quentin and Shreve, we are capable of imaginative identification with others.

Lastly, Charles's internalised thoughts suggest the problem of distinguishing meaningfully between objective and subjective reality – does one see what one is actually looking at, or what one *believes* to be reality? Within the context of the passage, the implication is simply that Charles longs for a solution to the mystery of his origins, and *wants* to believe that he has identified his father. But his thoughts also forcibly confront the reader with several of the novel's major themes. Firstly, they remind us of Quentin's personal problems, his fastidious and unworldly idealism, his sexual insecurity, and his ambivalent feelings about the South. For Quentin has noticed the uncomfortable parallels between the historical reconstruction and his own circumstances, parallels which explode in his hysterical denial at the end of *Absalom, Absalom!* and which are explored more explicitly in *The Sound and the Fury*. Meanwhile his tormented discovery of Charles's and Henry's crises, and those of other historical characters, remind the reader of the ongoing influence of the past, particularly in a Southern consciousness like that of Quentin.[19] Secondly, therefore, Faulkner's novel points obliquely towards the tendency of his contemporary Southern society of 1936 to believe what it wanted to believe, rather than to consider the complex and problematic nature of reality. Obviously, this is of special relevance to race relations, and eventually the Sutpen tragedy, like Quentin's repressed horror, is traced to a series of dogmatic responses to human dilemmas dictated by racism.

Finally, Charles's uncertainty emphasises once again the multifaceted nature of 'truth': 'Wait. Wait. You cant know yet' expresses both the philosophical subject and the narrative method of *Absalom, Absalom!*, as it continually confounds our attempts to confine or stereotype experience by suggesting new possibilities. As with Hardy's novels, every rereading brings fresh insights and glimpses of unsuspected interrelations; while Faulkner's more unique gift is to offer the reader, via his role in considering, comparing and balancing the conflicting viewpoints of the multiple narration, a valuable paradigm of the means by which man may best cope with the slippery and paradoxical nature of experience.

Although Hardy's stylistic techniques are less radical than those of Faulkner, his sensitivity to the unexpected and imponderable qualities of life finds expression in an idiosyncratic narrative style whose subtle changes of tone and texture achieve a restrained Victorian equivalent of a modernist's multiple perspectives. For example, his style mirrors the consciousness of his protagonists to an uncanny degree; hence, as previously remarked, the rather self-conscious sobriety at the close of *The Mayor of Casterbridge* seems to show us into the mind of Elizabeth-Jane, while Hardy's lavish opening description of Eustacia, in *The Return of the Native*, is even more perilously successful. She is variously compared to an Olympian goddess, the Sphinx, a classical marble, 'Bourbon roses, rubies and tropical midnights'; the list could be continued. But rather than seeming merely ludicrous, this literary junk-shop of extravagant curiosities strikes us as exactly the sort of imaginative storehouse where a romantic daydreamer like Eustacia would enjoy browsing, trying on 'a diadem of accidental dewdrops', or making a mental note to listen to some Mendelssohn (*TROTN*, pp. 93–4). At the same time, Hardy gives a little metaphysical cough to let one know that he is still minding the shop, closing a sensuous description of Eustacia's lips with the observation that, 'that mouth did not come over from Sleswig with a band of Saxon pirates whose lips met like the two halves of a muffin' (p. 94). It is just the sort of quiet witticism which Faulkner would have relished, and while it nicely balances the portentousness of the rest of the passage, it reminds us too of Eustacia's very real exoticism, and its contrast with her gauche provincial neighbours.[20]

Hardy's fluctuations of tone are capable of an astonishingly flexible range of effects, despite the nominally ever-present authorial voice. His anthropomorphism and 'familiar conjunctions of things' form another imaginative resource which often corresponds precisely with Faulkner's art; their sensitive responses to the qualities of *things* are able to convey poetic impressions of a kind which continually transcend the workaday requirements of narrative fiction. In the story 'The Romantic Adventures of a Milkmaid', the Baron takes Margery's jacket and 'rolled and compressed it with all his force till it was about as large as an apple-dumpling, and put it in his pocket' (*ACM*, p. 326).[21] In *The Hamlet*, Jody Varner 'drew from his hip a leather purse about the size and shape and colour of an eggplant' (p. 51). Here is that artistic dedication to 'form solidity color' pledged at the end of *Mosquitoes* (p. 281), even in the minutest particular, which adds so much to the reader's enjoyment of the novels' texture; while on a larger scale each writer demonstrates a quality defined by one Faulkner critic as 'a velocity of memory ... [an] insistence on embracing all actuality in the moment ... an attempt to realize continuity with all our genesis, our "progenitors" ... with all we have touched, known, loved'.[22] This attempt relies upon techniques whereby the reader's absorption in specific naturalistic details is suddenly expanded to accommodate a larger, if nebulous, significance. These moments of heightened consciousness seem to take two distinct forms. One resembles those Joycean epiphanies in which a character betrays himself to the reader by an apparently trivial remark or action. Such moments are often straightforwardly symbolic, as Giles holds his apple-tree erect in Sherton market, or Quentin smashes his watch. Sometimes the protagonist is unaware of the significance of his remarks, as in Farfrae's wonderfully bathetic response to the story of Henchard's last hours ('Dear me ... is that so!' – *TMOC*, p. 352), or in Jason Compson's tortured syntax: 'I've got every respect for a good honest whore because with Mother's health and the position I try to uphold to have her with no more respect for what I try to do than to make her name and my name and my Mother's name a byword in the town' (*TSATF*, pp. 208–9).

More unique to Hardy and Faulkner are those epiphanies where a character broods over the implications of his own reverie, and the reader is invited to share in the imaginative process, which may have no immediate resolution. Angel Clare says to himself, 'What a fresh and virginal daughter of Nature that milkmaid is!'

> then he seemed to discern in her something that was familiar, something which carried him back into a joyous and unforeseeing past, before the necessity of taking thought had made the heavens gray. He concluded that he had beheld her before; where he could not tell.   (*Tess*, pp. 158–9)

Angel's stereotype of Tess is ironically both wrong and right; and while we know where he has seen her before, the 'joyous ... past' may connote not merely his student days, but also a yearned-for golden age when men were 'natural', unclouded by the Victorians' 'necessity of taking thought'; a world, moreover, in which Angel would perhaps not have rejected his loving, unvirginal wife. Faulkner presents a comparable moment in the inner life of another misguided idealist when Quentin, having remarked that 'a nigger is not a person so much as a form of behaviour; a sort of obverse reflection of the white people he lives among', travels home to

Mississippi for Christmas. He awakes to find the train halted somewhere in Virginia, and gazing from the window notices 'a nigger on a mule ... like a sign put there saying You are home again. He didn't have a saddle and his feet dangled almost to the ground. The mule looked like a rabbit.' Quentin chaffs the old man and throws him a quarter, 'Christmas gift'; the train moves on,

> and they passed smoothly from sight ... with the quality about them of shabby and timeless patience, of static serenity.... And all that day ... I thought of home ... and my insides would move like they used to in school when the bell rang.   (*TSATF*, p. 81–3)

Quentin's reflections, like those of Angel, are both patronisingly wrongheaded and of unforeseen relevance to his story, redolent of an agreeably nostalgic self-indulgence which, the reader may faintly intuit, promises ill for his future.

The other key moments I have in mind tend to shade imperceptibly into the more extended epiphanies, but are distinguished from them by a more prominent authorial voice and a rapt, even rhetorical, style. Millgate identifies these as 'experiential moments'[23] in Faulkner's novels, but the term seems just as applicable to Hardy's work, forming as these moments do a noticeable transcendence of narrative which strains to express the 'heart and inner meaning' of the novelist's vision, to find 'words' the equal of 'doing'. Examples will, I hope, spring to mind from earlier chapters: Hardy's lavish evocation of Mrs Yeobright's last moments or Tess's experience in the overgrown garden, already amply discussed, depend upon the same use of nature for a touchstone to emotion, and experimentation with lushly mimetic prose, as Faulkner's exploration of Dewey Dell's confused unconscious mind:

> I feel my body, my bones and flesh beginning to part and open upon the alone, and the process of coming unalone is terrible. Lafe, Lafe ... I feel the darkness rushing past my breast, past the cow; I begin to rush upon the darkness but the cow stops me and the darkness rushes on upon the sweet blast of her moaning breath, filled with wood and with silence....
> ... The cow breathes upon my hips and back, her breath warm, stertorous, moaning. The sky lies flat down the slope, upon the secret clumps. Beyond the hill sheet-lightning stains upwards

and fades.... I said You don't know what worry is. I don't know what it is. I don't know whether I am worrying or not. Whether I can or not. I don't know whether I can cry or not. I don't know whether I have tried to or not. I feel like a wet seed wild in the hot blind earth.   (*AILD*, pp. 51–3)

Faulkner's use of interior monologue obviously claims a greater intimacy with his protagonist than Hardy's authorial voice, but it is probable that imagery such as 'the rank-smelling weed-flowers glowed as if they would not close for intentness, and the waves of colour mixed with the waves of sound' (*Tess*, p. 162) offers the reader an approximation of Tess's semi-conscious reverie just as vivid and persuasive as 'I feel like a wet seed wild in the hot blind earth.' Faulkner's mimetic passages are in any case often third-person: the fine evocation of Jack Houston's last sensations, dying of a shot-gun wound, provides an apt example.[24] Both novelists also endow their protagonists' consciousnesses with an extravagant vocabulary realistically unavailable to them: it is unlikely that Dewey Dell would call the cow's breathing 'stertorous' or that Tess would think of herself as 'undulating' upon the notes of Angel's harp, but the reader willingly acquiesces to the texts' determination to express the inexpressible.

Finally, Faulkner and Hardy are most memorable, and perhaps most alike, in their creations of entire imaginative worlds which cannot ever be fully described or contained. The power of their novels moves us not despite but because of their peculiar untidiness, their fluctuations and unexpected balancings, their ironic interrelations and odd tangential developments. Often a compelling story is glimpsed only in tantalising fragments, such as the drunken farmer turned night-poacher in *Desperate Remedies*, the forgotten history of the corn-field in *Jude*, or the nameless hill-farmer who pursues Ike Snopes in *The Hamlet*. Yoknapatawpha and Wessex gain immeasurably in imaginative potency through the awareness of other unexplored stories like these hidden in the shadows of the narrative; the effect is much like that of the traditional ballad's ability to suggest, in its laconic and understated way, a vast dim tapestry of folk-history from which it has emerged and into which it will be seamlessly reabsorbed. Thus both men's created worlds continually expand and reassemble in our imaginations on subsequent re-readings, new horizons glimpsed, their inhabitants recognisable but often a little changed. Hardy's heart-felt personal solicitude for Tess ('I have not been able to put on paper all that she is, or was, to me')[25] reflects not only the modesty of an artist who defined his novels as merely 'a series of seemings', but also a tormented awareness of the ineffability of every individual. Faulkner, too, continued to brood over his protagonists' lives, readily admitting the vivid presence of his inner world: '[my characters] exist. They are still in motion in my mind. I can laugh at things they're doing that I haven't got around to writing yet.'[26]

Faulkner's delight in human idiosyncracy is of a piece with the quiet watchfulness of the country folk whom his novels celebrate, such as Vernon Tull of *As I Lay Dying* who reminds us that, 'Well, folks are different' (p. 21); and with characteristic generosity, Faulkner genially acknowledges the writer's own fallibility, and the exhilarating unpredictability of human nature: 'The writer is learning all the time ... from his own people ... they surprise him, they teach him things that he didn't know, they do things and suddenly he says to himself, why yes, that is true, that is so.'[27] Just so, the stories of Hardy and Faulkner continue in our imaginations after we have finished the novels; it is singularly appropriate, and also strangely moving, to know that their creators evidently shared in our experience.

Notes

NOTES TO CHAPTER 1. DORSET: 'THE LOST SENSE OF HOME'

1. Charles J. Longman, editor of *Longman's Magazine*, to Richard Jefferies, quoted in Samuel J. Looker and Chrichton Porteus, *Richard Jefferies, Man of the Fields: A Biography and Letters* (London, 1965) pp. 125–6. See also Michael Millgate, *Thomas Hardy: His Career as a Novelist* (London, 1971) p. 206.
2. 'Livier' was the traditional term which Hardy generally used for this intermediate class of tradesmen and independent cottagers, and I shall use it in future to cover both villagers who are cottage 'life-holders' and (not strictly accurately) 'copy-holders'. The former indicates a person holding a property on a lease lasting for one or more (usually three) lives, hence 'livier'; the latter indicates the more secure tenancy regulated by a 'copy of court roll' administered by the lord of the manor, and is hence not literally a livier, but a small freeholder. 'Livier' is, however, the most convenient term to indicate this ancient and varied group.
3. Richard Gray, *The Literature of Memory: Modern Writers of the American South* (London, 1977) pp. 3, 7–8.
4. *Tess*, p. 156; cf. also *The Dorsetshire Labourer*, p. 3.
5. Merryn Williams, *Thomas Hardy and Rural England* (London, 1972) p. 90. Williams's study usually, however, serves as a rare and valuable corrective to such misunderstandings. And see the later essay, Merryn and Raymond Williams, 'Hardy and Social Class', in *Thomas Hardy: The Writer and his Background*, ed. N. Page (London, 1980) p. 36, where Tess's education is placed in its true perspective.
6. Douglas Brown, *Thomas Hardy* (London, 1954) pp. 30, 36.
7. *The Dorsetshire Labourer*, and the important letter from Hardy to Rider Haggard, printed in *Life*, pp. 312–14.
8. See, for example, the interview in *Cassell's Saturday Journal*, 25 June 1892; *The Dorsetshire Labourer*, p. 7; or *Tess*, p. 275, where the word is, significantly, put into the mouth of Angel Clare.
9. Brown, *Thomas Hardy*, pp. 32, 31.
10. *Under the Greenwood Tree* is set in the 1840s; see p. 54 of the novel itself, and p. 27 of the Preface, where Hardy mentions a setting of 'fifty or sixty years ago' – he was writing in 1896. See also F. B. Pinion, *A Hardy Companion: A Guide to the Works of Thomas Hardy and their Background* (London, 1968) p. 21. Pinion sets *The Return of the Native* in either 1842–3 or 1847–8 (see *A Hardy Companion*, p. 31), and suggests that the main story of *The Mayor of Casterbridge* begins about 1850; and the whole action lasts 25 years.
11. See Millgate, *Hardy: His Career*, p. 102, for a discussion of this point; and for the suggestion that the novel may in any case be set about 1860, though F. B. Pinion and Carl Weber agree upon 1869–73.

12. See pp. 407–9 of the New Wessex Paperback Edition of *The Woodlanders* for an important and definitive discussion of the novel's time-scheme; also Millgate, *Hardy: His Career*, pp. 245–6.
13. According to Hardy himself (see *Life*, p. 433).
14. In *The Dorsetshire Labourer*, p. 17, Hardy says, 'I am not sure whether, at the present time [1883], women are employed to feed the [threshing] machine, but some years ago a woman had frequently to stand just above the whizzing wire drum, and feed from morning to night.' Gittings also argues for an early setting: see his *Young Thomas Hardy* (London, 1975) p. 216.
15. About half of the total area of England and Wales in 1873 belonged to a group of just over 4000 people (see Pamela Horn, *The Rural World 1780–1850* (London, 1980) p. 223).
16. Typical of many such portraits is the Squire in 'Netty Sargent's Copyhold', part of the story 'A Few Crusted Characters' in *Life's Little Ironies*: 'How that wretched old Squire would rejoice at getting the little tenancy into his hands! He did not really require it, but constitutionally hated these tiny copyholds and leaseholds and freeholds, which made islands of independence in the fair, smooth ocean of his estates' (p. 263).
17. Interview in *Cassell's Saturday Journal*, called 'Representative Men at Home: Mr Thomas Hardy at Max Gate, Dorchester' (25 June 1892).
18. Preface to *The Hand of Ethelberta*, p. 31.
19. 'In the nineteenth century only a little over a tenth of the land was in the hands of owner-occupiers. Many of the small owners were in fact tradesmen and middle-class country residents who bought land as a convenience for their occupation, or for pleasure-grounds' (see G. E. Mingay, *Rural Life in Victorian England* (London, 1976) p. 56 *et seq.*).
20. Letter from Hardy to the English Folk Dance Society, quoted in *Journal of the English Folk Dance Society* (1927) pp. 53–4, and in Millgate, *Hardy: His Career*, pp. 55–6.
21. *The Dorsetshire Labourer* (1883) p. 18; *Tess* (1891) p. 401; and the letter to Rider Haggard (1902), in *Life*, p. 314.
22. Sir James Caird, *English Agriculture in 1850–51* (London, 1852). My reference is taken from the new edition (London, 1968) p. 72; all subsequent references are also from this edition. The 'proverb' to which Caird alludes is also featured in Charles Kingsley's assertion that the Victorians were perfectly well off, unless they happened to be 'Dorsetshire labourers or Spitalfields weavers – or colliery children – or marching soldiers – or, I am afraid, one half of English souls this day' (see Kingsley, *Yeast: A Problem* (1851), in vol. II, *Works*, 28 vols (London, 1880–5) ch. 2, p. 29; quoted in Walter E. Houghton, *The Victorian Frame of Mind 1830–1870* (New Haven, Conn., 1957) p. 414.
23. Barbara Kerr, *Bound to the Soil: A Social History of Dorset 1750–1918* (London, 1968) p. 107.
24. Caird, *English Agriculture*, p. 72.
25. Ibid., p. 518, 84.
26. Alexander Somerville, *The Whistler at the Plough* (Manchester, 1852) pp. 37–40.

27. *Life*, p. 312.
28. The only other exponent of such unflinching realism in Hardy's day was that other great Wessex writer, Richard Jefferies: e.g. the essays *John Smith's Shanty* (*Fraser's Magazine*, February 1874) or *A True Tale of the Wiltshire Labourer* (written about the same time as the former, and published for the first time with it in *The Toilers of the Field* (London, 1892) after Jefferies's death).
29. Interview in *Cassell's Saturday Journal* (25 June 1892).
30. John Saville, *Rural Depopulation in England and Wales, 1851–1951* (London, 1957) p. 2.
31. Kerr, *Bound to the Soil*, p. 134.
32. For a useful discussion of this point, see Millgate, *Hardy: His Career*, pp. 211–12; and note also William Barnes's poem *'Eclogue: Two Farms in Woone'*, which Hardy would have known:

> If a young chap, woonce, had any wit
> To try an' scrape together zome vew pound,
> To buy some cows an' teake a bit o' ground,
> He mid become a farmer, bit by bit.
> But hang it! now the farms be all so big,
> An' bits o' groun' so skea'ce, woone got no scope.

(from *Poems of Rural Life in the Dorset Dialect* (London, 1879) pp. 102–4)

33. Interview in *Cassell's Saturday Journal* (25 June 1892).
34. Richard Jefferies, in *Hodge and his Masters* (London, 1880).
35. See Gittings, *Young Thomas Hardy*, pp. 112–13; and the essay 'Hardy and Sparks Family Portraits by Nathaniel Sparks and James Sparks', by Celia Barclay, in *Thomas Hardy Year Book*, No. 6 (1976) (St Peter Port, Guernsey, 1977).
36. *Life*, pp. 214–15.
37. See Saville, *Rural Depopulation*, pp. 66–8; and his quotations of statistics from A. L. Bowley, 'Rural Depopulation in England and Wales: a Study of the Changes of Density, Occupations and Ages', in *Journal of the Royal Statistical Society*, vol. LXXVII (May 1914) pp. 597–645.
38. *The Dorsetshire Labourer*, p. 19; and see also *Tess*, p. 401: 'The Durbeyfield … household had not been shining examples either of temperance, soberness, or chastity.'
39. For examples, see *The Trumpet-Major*, p. 345; or the story 'The Doctor's Legend', in *Old Mrs Chundle and Other Stories*, p. 46.
40. H. J. Massingham, *The Wisdom of the Fields* (London, 1945) p. 84.
41. Mingay, *Rural Life*, p. 183.
42. Even Creedle's lament for the vanished Winterbornes includes the gratuitous information that Giles's father was a cripple in his last days. Like the undefined 'wrong' by which Melbury had cheated the latter of Giles's mother, this functions as a firm, convincing personal detail (we seem to *see* Winterborne senior on his crutches) which quite deliberately undercuts any possible image of Giles's father, and Melbury, as participators in a wholly idealised, pre-Fitzpiers Hintock idyll.

43. F. R. Southerington, *Hardy's Vision of Man* (London, 1971) p. 123.
44. Ibid.
45. Millgate, *Hardy: His Career*, p. 210.
46. John Bayley, *An Essay on Hardy* (Cambridge, 1978) pp. 2, 198.
47. Raymond Williams, *The Country and the City* (London, 1973) p. 240.
48. *Life*, pp. 31–2.
49. Ibid., p. 56.
50. That is, the date of the journal entry quoted above.
51. Williams, *The Country and the City*, pp. 249–50.
52. Gittings, *Young Thomas Hardy*, pp. 4, 210.
53. Michael Millgate, *Thomas Hardy: A Biography* (Oxford, 1982) pp. 530–1.

NOTES TO CHAPTER 2. MISSISSIPPI: 'IMPLACABLE AND BROODING'

1. Many critics have discussed this aspect of Faulkner's South, though without comparing it to Hardy's Dorset. Irving Howe, for example, says of the South: 'It had been left behind. It was living on the margin of history – a position that often provides the sharpest perspective on history. Some decades after the defeat of the South, its writers could maintain a relation to American life comparable, in miniature, to the relation in the nineteenth century between Russian writers and European life. For while nineteenth-century Russia was the most backward country on the continent, its writers managed to use that backwardness as a vantage-point from which to observe West-European life and, thereby, to arrive at a profound criticism of bourgeois morality' (see Irving Howe, *William Faulkner: A Critical Study*, 2nd edn, revised (New York, 1951) p. 23).

   Howe himself quotes Allen Tate, who also claims that the Southern Renaissance is the result of the historical disunity between the South and the rest of America: 'It has made possible the curious burst of intelligence that we get at a crossing of the ways, not unlike, on an infinitesimal scale, the outburst of poetic genius at the end of the sixteenth century when commercial England had already begun to crush feudal England' (Allen Tate, *Virginia Quarterly Review* (April 1935) quoted in his later essay 'The New Provincialism', in *The Man of Letters in the Modern World* (New York, 1955) pp. 292–3). It is the major premise of this study that the special affinities of Hardy and Faulkner exist largely because Hardy also wrote at 'a crossing of the ways'.

2. 'Mississippi', in *Essays, Speeches & Public Letters by William Faulkner*, ed. James B. Meriwether, pp. 11–43 (hereafter referred to as *Mississippi*). 'It is not exactly a historical essay … he mingles an increasingly important autobiographical element with the historical and geographical materials of the piece … bringing fiction, Faulkner's own

previously written fiction, into the work' (Meriwether, 'Faulkner's "Mississippi"', *Mississippi Quarterly*, vol. 25 (Spring 1972) pp. 16–17).
3. For example, Faulkner said of *Sartoris*, his germinal Yoknapatawpha novel, that it represented an attempt 'to recreate between the covers of a book the world as I was already [*sic*] preparing to lose and regret' (see Joseph L. Blotner. *Faulkner: a Biography* (New York, 1974) pp. 531–2). In a letter to Malcolm Cowley, Faulkner said that after the First World War he had returned home to find that he was 'at home again in Oxford, Mississippi, yet at the same time ... not at home' (see Malcolm Cowley (ed.), *The Faulkner–Cowley File: Letters and Memories 1944–1962* (New York, 1966) p. 74).
4. This was a conscious recognition on Faulkner's part: he describes his confrontation of tensions, and extreme fictional reactions, in his 'Introduction' to *The Sound and the Fury*: 'We [Southerners] need to talk, to tell, since oratory is our heritage. We seem to try in the simple furious breathing (or writing) span of the individual to draw a savage indictment of the contemporary scene or to escape from it into a makebelieve region of swords and magnolias and mockingbirds which perhaps never existed anywhere. Both of the courses are rooted in sentiment; perhaps the ones who write savagely and bitterly of the incest in clay floored cabins are the most sentimental. Anyway, each course is a matter of violent partizanship ... I seem to have tried both courses. I have tried to escape and I have tried to indict' ('Introduction to *The Sound and the Fury*', ed. James B. Meriwether, *Mississippi Quarterly*, vol. 26 (Summer 1973) p. 412).
5. As in note 4, above.
6. Richard Gray, *The Literature of Memory: Modern Writers of the American South* (London, 1977) p. 254.
7. David Minter, *William Faulkner: His Life and Work* (Baltimore, Md., 1980) p. 80.
8. As in note 4, above.
9. Due mainly to the decline of the tobacco plantations, and to a growing lack of enthusiasm for slavery among Southern planters, who increasingly freed slaves between 1780 and 1820. See Francis Butler Simkins and Charles Pierce Roland, *A History of the South*, 4th edn, revised (New York, 1972) pp. 114–15; hereafter referred to as 'Simkins'. An uneasy attitude to slavery was demonstrated by the Mississippi Supreme Court in 1818 – 'Slavery is condemned by reason and the laws of nature. It exists and can only exist, through municipal regulations.' (Quoted in John Ray Skates, *Mississippi* (New York, 1979) p. 73; hereafter referred to as 'Skates'.) In a few years' time, such an attitude would be unthinkable in the state.
10. This was especially true in Mississippi, where probably 60–70 per cent of ante-bellum whites were yeoman farmers, depending on subsistence crops and livestock rather than cotton and owning few if any slaves (see Skates, pp. 92–3).
11. See Simkins, pp. 334–5; W. J. Cash, *The Mind of the South* (New York, 1941) pp. 151–2, 161, 287–8; Skates, p. 126. Again, Mink Snopes

provides a poignant example.

12. 'Farm tenancy and King Cotton dominated Mississippi more in 1920 than in 1870.... Six out of every ten Mississippians lived on farms. Of these, 65 per cent did not own their land, 68 per cent of all Mississippi farms in 1925 were tenant-operated, and 60 per cent of these tenants were sharecroppers' (Skates, pp. 133–5).

13. In 1880, the *per capita* income of the South generally was $376, compared with $1086 in the rest of the USA. The average nationally was $870; in Mississippi, it was $286. In the 1920s, the state's *per capita* income had only risen to $396, one-third of the national average (see C. Vann Woodward, *The Origins of the New South, 1877–1913* (Baton Rouge, La., 1951) p. 111, and Skates, 134.

14. Cash, *The Mind of the South*, pp. 295, 338.

15. Skates, pp. 149, 137.

16. For this concept of the smug moral 'complacency' felt by America at large, in contrast to Southern insecurity and introversion, I am indebted to C. Vann Woodward's remarks in *The Burden of Southern History*, revised edn (Baton Rouge, La., 1968) especially pp. 17–21.

17. W. R. Taylor, *Cavalier and Yankee: The Old South and the American National Character* (Cambridge, Mass., 1961) p. 160; see especially pp. 145–76.

18. Ibid., pp. 300–13.

19. For example, James Kirke Paulding, *Westward Ho! A Tale* (New York, 1832) discussed by Taylor, in *Cavalier and Yankee*, pp. 303–4.

20. C. Vann Woodward, *The Strange Career of Jim Crow* (New York, 1955) provides the most succinct study of this process. See especially ch. II, 'Capitulation to Racism', pp. 49–97.

21. See *Mississippi*, pp. 16–17, 39–42; Blotner, *Faulkner: A Biography*, pp. 76–8, 112–13, 1034–6.

22. For example, the almost hysterical Southern counterblast to the publication of *Uncle Tom's Cabin* in 1852. No fewer than 14 Southern novels between 1852 and 1855 offered apologies for slavery by vehemently denouncing the iniquities of Northern industry as more inhumane than the 'peculiar institution', and suggesting that the white Northern working-classes were 'wage-slaves' more oppressed than blacks. William John Grayson's poem of 1856, 'The Hireling and the Slave', presents the same argument by ingenuously contrasting the squalid lives of the European proleteriat with idyllic rural images of contented slaves enjoying the sort of existence conjured up by today's advertisements for dry martini: fishing from canoes, gathering turtle eggs on the beach, or hunting wild turkey and possum 'among the breezeless pines'. Grayson carefully points out that the black slave, unlike the wretched English poacher, need have no fear of gamekeepers. See Edmund Wilson, *Patriotic Gore* (New York, 1962) pp. 336–41, for an interesting account of these works. And see William Grayson, *The Hireling and the Slave, Chicora, and Other Poems* (Charleston, 1856). Edgar Allan Poe's *The Narrative of Arthur Gordon Pym* (1838) arguably offers a more powerful, symbolic exploration of white racial guilt and fear,

in its story of a dreamlike journey towards the unknown Southern pole, where the coastline bears 'a stong resemblance to corded bales of cotton', the climate grows surprisingly warmer, and the natives are black, boisterous, promiscuous, outwardly friendly and inwardly bloodthirsty. Poe is, unconsciously or semi-consciously, reproducing the paternalistic Southerner's traditional dual image of the slave as both childlike 'darky' and ferocious savage. W. R. Taylor's emphasis upon an inbred cultural fear of treacherous slave uprisings seems pertinent once again. Poe's racial symbolism in the *Narrative* is discussed in Leslie Fiedler, *Love and Death in the American Novel* (London, 1967) pp. 398–400.

23. For example, the faithful black retainers of Thomas Nelson Page's romantic stories, or the comic Uncle Remus of Joel Chandler Harris. Uncle Remus, however, is an interestingly ambivalent figure, a seemingly genial old black 'uncle' telling amusing animal stories to 'the Boy', a representative young white Southerner. When carefully examined, however, the stories in which the weak but cunning Brer Rabbit wreaks a humiliating and often bloody revenge upon the strong but stupid Brer Fox, are clearly a fantasised allegory of persecuted blacks triumphing over their white oppressors – as Harris was probably aware (see Louise Dauner, 'Myth and Humor in the Uncle Remus Fables', *American Literature*, vol. 20 (1948–9) pp. 129–43; and John Stafford, 'Patterns of Meaning in *Nights with Uncle Remus*', *American Literature*, vol. 18, (1946–7) pp. 89–108).

24. Or if, like Charles Bon, they pass for white (or like Joe Christmas, alternate their racial identity) they cannot escape the psychological strain of an identity crisis, all too evident in Bon's and Christmas's lives.

25. Darwin T. Turner, 'Faulkner and Slavery', in *The South and Faulkner's Yoknapatawpha*, (ed.) Evans Harrington and Ann J. Abadie (Jackson, Miss., 1977) p. 64.

26. I refer, of course, to the post-war movement for black civil rights and the wave of violence that it provoked in the South during the 1950s and 1960s. Cf. Faulkner's essays *On Fear: Deep South in Labor: Mississippi, 1956* and *A Letter to the Leaders of the Negro Race, 1956*, and several of his 'Public Letters', especially 'Press Dispatch on the Emmett Till Case, September 9, 1955' in *Essays, Speeches, and Public Letters*, (ed.) J. B. Meriwether pp. 92–112, 222–3.

27. Howe, *Faulkner: A Critical Study*, p. 117.

28. While Faulkner's characters do not always recognise the emotional deprivation implied by their nostalgia, Faulkner clearly does; for example, Quentin's memories of Roskus, Dilsey and Louis Hatcher, in *The Sound and the Fury*, pp. 81–3, 105–7, 154; the relationship of Roth Edmonds and Henry Beauchamp, in *Go Down, Moses*, pp. 91–2.

29. Cf. *Tess*, pp. 158–9: 'he seemed to discern something in [Tess] that was familiar, something which carried him back into a joyous and unforeseeing past, before the necessity of taking thought had made the heavens gray'; and *The Hand of Ethelberta*, p. 225: 'I wish I could

get a living by some simple humble occupation...and be Berta Chickerel again, and live in a green cottage as we used to do when I was small'.

30. For example, *The Hand of Ethelberta*, p. 219: 'The town gentleman was not half so far removed from Sol and Dan, and the hard-handed order in general, in his passions as in his philosophy. He still continued to be the male of the species, and when the heart was hot with a dream Pall Mall had much the same aspect as Wessex'; and *The Woodlanders*, p. 41: 'Nothing but a cast of the die of destiny had decided that the girl should handle the tool; and the fingers which clasped the heavy ash haft might have skilfully guided the pencil or swept the string, had they only been set to do it in good time.'

31. 'Crumby', according to the New Wessex Edition's notes, means 'appetising' (p. 454). Though, of course, Angel's insistence upon the literal nature of his 'virginal' assumption will bring them both to grief.

32. Cash, *The Mind of the South*, p. 69. See pp. 60–70 for a description of this process.

33. Ibid., pp. 30, 46–51, 56.

34. Ibid., Book 1, chs 1–3.

35. Ibid., pp. 63–5.

36. The contrast of Bayard and Horace was most highly developed in *Flags in the Dust*, the original version of *Sartoris*. See a useful critical discussion of *Sartoris* and *Flags in the Dust*, in Michael Millgate, *The Achievement of William Faulkner* (London, 1966) pp. 81–5. Cleanth Brooks remarks that 'Young Bayard and Horace constitute a neatly opposed pair of romanticists' (see his *William Faulkner: The Yoknapatawpha Country* (London, 1963) p. 103), but he denies that either is especially *Southern* in his deracination, identifying Bayard's as First World War anomie, and Horace's as Prufrockian despair. It seems to me that, taken together, the very different romantic excesses of Bayard and Horace do meaningfully relate to the Southern penchants for both violence and rhetorical daydreaming, which W. J. Cash sees as crucial to the Southern mind (e.g. see Cash, *The Mind of the South*, pp. 44, 52–3). They may also be seen as two young Southerners struggling to adjust to the modern world with unwieldy traditional ideals: Horace as romantic South aesthete, Bayard with a Southern code of machismo. Yet each strategy proves inadequate, and each man is overwhelmed by modernistic chaos.

37. Cash, *The Mind of the South*, pp. 93–4.

38. Between 1882 and 1927, there are records of 4951 deaths by illegal lynching in the USA, though the real figure is doubtless higher. The majority of these lynchings took place in the Deep South, and the majority of the victims were black. It is significant that Mississippi, which in 1920 had the smallest population of the states in the Deep South, claimed a higher number of lynchings during these years than any other state, i.e. 561. See Walter White, *Rope and Faggot: A Biography of Judge Lynch* (New York, 1929) pp. 19–20, 234, 237, 268, 231.

39. Fittingly, Jason's narrative is filled with even more sound and fury than those of the subnormal Benjy or neurotic Quentin, its language emotionally barren and full of significant reiterations ('I says', 'Like I say'), and its style heavily dependent upon stereotypes, generalisations and repetitions. His opening words are 'Once a bitch, always a bitch, what I say' (p. 163), and he goes on to coin a formidable variety of the stale clichés which form the small change of bigots in any society, managing to abuse 'trifling niggers', 'jews', women, and even men who wear red ties.

40. See Elizabeth Kerr, *Yoknapatawpha* (New York, 1969; 2nd edn, revised, 1976) p. 212. Examples of the actual horrors Faulkner could have presented, had he wished, are found in Walter White's study, e.g. pp. 35–6; or in James Silver, *Mississippi: The Closed Society* (New York, 1964) pp. 85–6.

41. In later years Faulkner liked to point out that he created Grimm 'before I'd ever heard of Hitler's Storm Troopers' (see *Faulkner in the University*, ed. F. L. Gwynn and J. L. Blotner (Charlottesville, Va., 1959) p. 41).

42. Robert A. Jelliffe (ed.), *Faulkner at Nagano* (Tokyo, 1958), pp. 23–4.

43. Skates, pp. 13–14.

44. Ibid., p. 165; and see J. Seyppel, *William Faulkner* (New York, 1971) p. 20: 'around 1940, the population of the Deep South consisted of approximately one Negro to every two whites … Mississippi, however, had 1,074,578 Negroes and 1,106,327 whites – nearly one-to-one ratio'.

45. Mississippi was, for example, the first Southern state to implement the unconstitutional disenfranchisement of blacks, in 1890. See Woodward, *The Strange Career of Jim Crow*, p. 66; Simkins, p. 349.

46. See Woodward, *Origins of the New South*, p. 159.

47. Ibid., p. 159.

48. Blotner, *Faulkner: A Biography*, pp. 54–5.

49. Ibid., p. 70.

50. For example, the lynching of Nelse Patton in 1908; ibid., pp. 113–14. Millgate discusses this horrific incident and its probable relationship to the death of Joe Christmas in *Light in August* (see Millgate, *Achievement*, pp. 282–3).

51. 'The immediate causes were often trivial. Of the quarrels resulting in the shooting of five men in one day in a Mississippi county, two arose over the opening of doors and two over petty debts' (in Woodward, *Origins of the New South*, p. 160).

52. See Richard Gray, *Literature of Memory*, for a detailed study of these two ideals and their influence upon Southern literature; see especially pp. 9–13.

53. Robert Beverley, quoted by John Pilkington, in his essay 'Nature's Legacy to William Faulkner', in Harrington and Abadie (eds), *The South and Faulkner's Yoknapatawpha*, p. 109. Cf. Faulkner's remark that 'The beauty – spiritual and physical – of the South lies in the fact that God has done so much for it and man so little' (see 'Verse Old and Nascent' (April 1925), in *Salmagundi* (Milwaukee, 1932) p. 37; quoted

in Brooks, *Yoknapatawpha Country*, p. 32).

54. Elizabeth Kerr's useful chapter entitled 'Caste and Class in Rural Society' notes that 'Varner is an example of the supply merchants that Cash describes as the real ruling class by the early 1900s, and like them was of the yeoman farmer stock which made up the ruling class in "primitive local communities". From Varner, with his two-storey house and his servants, down to the landless and destitute tenant farmer, is a gradation of economic levels, from comfort down through subsistence to privation' (see Kerr, *Yoknapatawpha*, pp. 136–7).

55. See John Faulkner, *My Brother Bill* (New York, 1963) pp. 158–9 (in 1964 Cardinal edn); Blotner, *Faulkner: A Biography*, pp. 986–8.

56. Cf. Hardy's comment in the *Life* that 'He has read well, who has learnt that there is more to read outside books than in them' (p. 107).

57. For example, Hardy, *Life*, p. 443; Gwynn and Blotner (eds), *Faulkner in the University*, pp. 3, 49–50, 68, 84.

58. John Faulkner, *My Brother Bill*, pp. 179, 217.

59. For example, see Bruce Catton, *The Penguin Book of the American Civil War* (London, 1966) p. 10; Kenneth M. Stampp, *The Peculiar Institution: Negro Slavery in the American South* (London, 1964) pp. 36–7; Simkins, pp. 111–12, 192–9.

60. Skates, pp. 80–1.

61. Ibid., pp. 79–80, 82. Cf. Faulkner's comments on the injustice of this 'ravishment' in Gwynn and Blotner (eds), *Faulkner in the University*, p. 43.

62. 'In the ten years between 1830 and 1840, Mississippi's population increased 175 percent. Slave population increased 197 percent; and by 1840 ... blacks outnumbered whites in the state' (Skates, p. 83).

63. See Skates, pp. 87–9, 104.

64. For example, *Go Down, Moses*, pp. 195–7, 263, 275; see also a more comic treatment in the story 'Lo!', in *Doctor Martino, and Other Stories*. Faulkner's depiction of man's self-undoing in 'The Bear' also includes more implicit, imagistic examples such as the description of the log-train (pp. 244–5), and of the crazy, avaricious Boon guarding 'his' squirrels (p. 252).

65. See *The Hamlet*, p. 273; 'Mule in the Yard', in *Uncle Willy and Other Stories*, pp. 143–58; and *The Town*, pp. 201–22.

66. Sutpen explains to General Compson that 'now he would take the boy in where he would never again need to stand on the outside of a white door and knock at it; and not at all for mere shelter but so that the boy, that whatever nameless stranger, could shut that door himself forever behind him on all that he had ever known, and look ahead along the still undivulged light rays in which his descendants who might not even hear his [the boy's] name, waited to be born without ever having to know that they had once been riven free from brutehood just as his own [Sutpen's] children were' (*AA*, p. 261).

   This is the only insight which Faulkner gives us into the ultimate purpose of Sutpen's 'design'; and it is clear that his idealistic egalitarian impulses are dominated by equally idealistic dynastic

ambitions. Needless to say, a 'nameless boy' does appear at Sutpen's
door, Charles Bon, but he is not welcomed in as an heir.

67. For example, the violent deaths of Henry Sutpen and Clytie in the
burning Sutpen house, in 1919; and the subsequent deaths of Rosa
Coldfield and (implicitly, by adding to his suicidal despair) Quentin
Compson in the same year. It is significant that Faulkner adds the date
of Quentin's death to the 'Genealogy' at the end of *Absalom, Absalom!*
(p. 384).

68. Lyall H. Powers, *Faulkner's Yoknapatawpha Comedy* (Ann Arbor, Mich.,
1980) p. 146.

69. Henchard seems a more bullying and intolerant employer, for
example in his treatment of Abel Whittle, but then we learn that
'Henchard had kept Abel's old mother in coals and snuff all the
previous winter' (*TMOC*, pp. 128–9). Similarly, Farfrae may treat his
men with more equanimity, but he also reduces their wages by a
shilling when he takes over (p. 245).

70. Brooks, *Yoknapatawpha Country*, p. 43.

71. See note 1 to this chapter; and cf. Skates, p. 140.

72. The railway reached Dorchester in 1847, and as a child Hardy
observed the novelty of this development along with the consequent
rapid decline of old coaching roads and inns. Railways are constantly
seen spreading further into the countryside throughout his novels.
In a similar way, Faulkner and his brothers witnessed the coming of
the first automobile to Oxford, in 1908, which eventually led to the
eclipse of the railroad in its turn. Two years later, the twelve-year-old
Faulkner watched a primitive aeroplane land on the race-track at
Memphis. See John Faulkner, *My Brother Bill*, p. 33; *Mississippi*, p. 38;
Blotner, *Faulkner: A Biography*, p. 139.

73. For example, the 'forsaken' coach-road at the opening of *The
Woodlanders*, p. 35; Farmer Springrove's coaching inn in *Desperate
Remedies*, pp. 153–4; and the 'fading weed-grown branch line' leading
to Jefferson in the 1940s setting of *The Mansion*, p. 372. Passenger
service at the Oxford depot was discontinued in 1941 (see Calvin S.
Brown, 'Faulkner's Localism', in *The Maker and the Myth: Faulkner and
Yoknapatawpha, 1977*, Evans Harrington and Ann J. Abadie (Jackson,
Miss., 1978) p. 23).

74. As regards Faulkner having read Hardy, see Blotner, *Faulkner: A
Biography*, pp. 299–300; and Gwynn and Blotner (eds), *Faulkner in the
University*, p. 142. Faulkner's library at Rowan Oak contains copies of
The Mayor of Casterbridge, Jude and Hardy's poetry.

75. Tess and Angel arrive at 'a spot where, by day, a fitful white streak of
steam at intervals upon the dark green background denoted intermittent moments of contact between their secluded world and modern
life. Modern life stretched out its steam feeler to this point three or four
times a day, touched the native existences, and quickly withdrew its
feeler again, as if what it touched had been uncongenial ... there was
the hissing of a train, which drew up almost silently upon the wet
rails, and the milk was rapidly swung can by can into the truck. The
light of the engine flashed for a second upon Tess Durbeyfield's

226 *Notes*

figure, motionless under the great holly tree. No object could have looked more foreign to the gleaming cranks and wheels than this unsophisticated girl, with the round bare arms, the rainy face and hair, the suspended attitude of a friendly leopard at pause.... [Later] the few minutes of contact with the whirl of material progress lingered in her thought. "Londoners will drink it at their breakfasts tomorrow, won't they?" she asked. "Strange people that we have never seen.... Noble men and noble women, ambassadors and centurions, ladies and tradeswomen.... Who don't know anything of us, and where it comes from"' (*Tess*, pp. 227–8).

    Cf. how Mink watches trains from inside Parchman prison farm: 'the trains themselves were looked at, seen, alien in freedom, fleeing, existing in liberty and hence unreal, chimaeras, apparitions, without past or future, not even going anywhere since their destinations could not exist for him: just in motion a second, an instant, then nowhere; they had not been.... [He now remembers how thirty-eight years before] he had gone down to the depot to see the New Orleans-bound passenger train come in – the hissing engine, the lighted cars each with an uppity impudent nigger porter, one car in which people were eating supper while more niggers waited on them, before going back to the sleeping cars that had actual beds in them; the train pausing for a moment then gone: a long airtight chunk of another world dragged along the dark earth for the poor folks in overalls like him to gape at free for a moment without the train itself, let alone the folks in it, even knowing he was there' (*TM*, p. 371).

76. Cash, *The Mind of the South*, pp. 42–3.
77. See *Sartoris*, pp. 252–9, 228–50; and the story 'Mountain Victory' in *Doctor Martino, and Other Stories*.
78. Other interesting examples of this paradigm are the confrontations between Rosa Coldfield and Clytie (*AA*, pp. 138–9); Gavin Stevens and Aunt Mollie Beauchamp (*GDM*, pp. 285–6); and Chick Mallison and Lucas (*IITD*, pp. 16–19, 26–7).
79. Gwynn and Blotner (eds), *Faulkner in the University*, p. 10.
80. See, for example, Blotner, *Faulkner: A Biography*, pp. 686–7.
81. George Marion O'Donnell's 1939 essay 'Faulkner's Mythology', in *Faulkner: A Collection of Critical Essays*, ed. Robert Penn Warren (Englewood Cliffs, NJ, 1966) pp. 23–34, makes the original (and sympathetic) case for a 'traditional' interpretation of Faulkner's Yoknapatawpha, while Maxwell Geismar's *Writers in Crisis* (Boston, Mass. 1942) exemplifies the frequent tendency of critics in the 1930s and 1940s to dismiss Faulkner as a sort of neurotic crypto-fascist (see Geismar, *Writers in Crisis*, pp. 141–83).
82. Quoted in Warren's 'Introduction: Faulkner: Past and Future', in Warren (ed.), *Faulkner: Critical Essays*, p. 9.
83. Wyndham Lewis, *Men without Art* (London, 1934) p. 54.
84. Hyatt H. Waggoner, *William Faulkner: From Jefferson to the World* (Lexington, Ky., 1966) p. 84.
85. Waggoner's study offers some illuminating insights into Faulkner's aesthetic purposes, seeing his work as a 'synthesis' of naturalism and

symbolism, which combines the lyrical freedom of the stream of consciousness mode with an ultimate objectivity of 'philosophic' purpose akin to that of Hawthorne or Melville: 'Faulkner's way was superficially more personal and subjective [than Hemingway's naturalism], but in a deeper sense it was objective: springing from a hunger for truth and reality, it explored and exploited the baffles and barriers between us and Truth.... Faulkner's fiction is characterized by its openness to experience, to all experience, even that which resists interpretation' (Waggoner, *From Jefferson to the World*, p. 260, and see pp. 258–66).

One is perhaps reminded of Woolf's claim that Hardy was 'at once poet and realist', whose novels have 'always about [them] a little blur of unconsciousness, that halo of freshness and margin of the unexpressed' (see 'The Novels of Thomas Hardy', in *Collected Essays*, vol. I (London, 1967) pp. 257–8).

86. Gwynn and Blotner (eds), *Faulkner in the University*, p. 3.
87. Michael Millgate, *Thomas Hardy: A Biography* (Oxford, 1982) p. 35.
88. Ibid., pp. 35–6.
89. Ibid., p. 136.
90. John Faulkner, *My Brother Bill*, p. 65.
91. Louis D. Rubin, *The Faraway Country: Writers of the Modern South* (Seattle, Wash., 1963) p. 65.
92. For example, Sam Fathers' father's casual disposal of three white men, *These Thirteen*, pp. 115–16; or the poisonings by which Doom usurps the chieftainship, pp. 111–14.
93. Hardy, *Life*, pp. 15–16.
94. Cf. *Jude*, pp. 37–8.
95. See 'That Evening Sun', also in *These Thirteen*.

NOTES TO CHAPTER 3. 'A FULL LOOK AT THE WORST'

1. *The Well-Beloved*, p. 36.
2. *Life*, p. 120.
3. Ibid., p. 176.
4. Ibid., p. 274.
5. Ibid., pp. 410–11.
6. A. O. J. Cockshutt, 'Hardy's Philosophy', in *The Genius of Thomas Hardy*, ed. M. Drabble (London, 1976) p. 141.
7. *Life*, p. 32.
8. *Tess*, p. 117. Michael Millgate's biography, published after I had written chapter 1, also emphasises the unusual synthesis of modern and traditional outlooks which the young Hardy made: 'Long experience of having to find his own intellectual way had made him an habitual eclectic, and he thus found little difficulty in ranging ideas newly derived from Darwin and Huxley alongside the necessitarian views already instilled in him by both the peasant fatalism of his

upbringing and the tragic patterns of the Greek dramatists. He spoke again and again in later years of his essentially emotional and non-intellectual approach to life and his lack of any systematic philosophy, and in his early adult years his most persistent search seems to have been for philosophical formulations which answered to his own perceptions of the world, to his instinctive sense of the way things were' (see Michael Millgate, *Thomas Hardy: A Biography* (Oxford, 1982) p. 132).

9. Owen Chadwick, *The Victorian Church*, 2 vols (London, 1966) vol. II, p. 34.

10. [The] inclination to restore meaning to the world by moralising evolution as a progressive and in some sense purposive force ... was frequently irresistible.... Indeed, once the Christian had accepted evolution as a fact, there could be much in common between his and the agnostic's attitudes to it. Both, after all, tended to be in favour of striving upward and onward' (see J. W. Burrow, 'Faith, Doubt and Unbelief', in *The Context of English Literature: The Victorians*, ed. L. Lerner (London, 1978) p. 170).

11. 'As early as 1850 Herbert Spencer was happy to point out that the "purifying process" by which animals kill off the sickly, the malformed and the aged, was equally at work in human society: "The poverty of the incapable, the distresses that come upon the imprudent, the starvation of the idle, and those shoulderings aside of the weak by the strong, which leave so many 'in shallows and in miseries', are the decrees of a large, far-seeing benevolence"' (see Walter E. Houghton, *The Victorian Frame of Mind* (New Haven, Conn., 1957) p. 209). Houghton is quoting from Spencer's *Social Statics; or, the Conditions Essential to Human Happiness* (London, 1851) p. 323.

12. Walter Allen, *The English Novel* (London, 1954 p. 246. Another useful description of Hardy's special dual vision is that provided by Douglas Brown: 'The bitterness of life with which Hardy's novels deal is not limited to what the agricultural society itself may have to endure. Hardy had, in Lawrence's phrase, looked out into the wilderness. He was lost, and there could be for him no return; he could not become a simple countryman, and he did not try to. But there has been, the novels say, a facing of despair, of chaos, of purposelessness – of all that profound and serious study, and experience of the larger world, revealed. And Hardy's art records as plainly a movement of acceptance, one made valid by the agricultural condition, where a kind of humility and stoicism grows, whose passiveness provides for a contrary persistence in purposeful activity'. See Douglas Brown, *Thomas Hardy* (London, 1954) pp. 133–4.

13. *Life*, pp. 224, 346.

14. *Life*, pp. 177, 185.

15. Brown, *Thomas Hardy*, p. 30.

16. As more recent critics have argued, e.g. Raymond Williams: 'It is common to reduce Hardy's fiction to the impact of an urban alien on the 'timeless pattern' of English rural life. Yet though this is sometimes

there the more common pattern is the relation between the changing
nature of country living, determined as much by its own pressures as
by pressures from 'outside', and one or more characters who have
become in some degree separated from it yet who remain by some tie
of family inescapably involved. It is here that the social values are
dramatised in a very complex way and it is here that most of the
problems of Hardy's actual writing seem to arise' (see Raymond
Williams, *The Country and the City* (London, 1973) p. 243).
17. For example, Brown sees in Clym's 'return' to the heath as a
furze-cutter, an example of Hardy's approval of 'the rejection of urban
life': 'There is no immediate answer to Clym's final question, "Mother,
what *is* doing well?" ... But fundamentally, the novel at large takes up
that kind of question, and the possibility of an answer.... When
near-blindness overtakes Clym, his return home seems absolute.
Deflected from "study", the source ... of "despair from without", he
becomes perforce a furze-cutter. By the end of the story his desire to
educate has been substantially modified. Clym wants only to preach
and teach the traditional morality of Egdon' (see Brown, *Thomas
Hardy*, pp. 59–60).
      I find this reading of Clym's actions highly dubious, not least in
attributing to Hardy an implied simplistic disapproval of education,
which hardly squares with the scrupulously balanced assessments of
The Dorsetshire Labourer. Is the reader *really* meant to *admire* Clym's
vacillating actions once he has 'returned'? I shall consider this a little
later in the chapter. Meanwhile, let me set beside Brown's interpretation Raymond Williams's comment upon Hardy's description of
Clym's idealism: 'The subtlety and intelligence of this argument from
the late 1870s comes from a mind accustomed to relative and historical
thinking, not merely in the abstract but in the process of observing a
personal experience of mobility. This is not country against town, or
even in any simple way custom against conscious intelligence. It is the
more complicated and more urgent historical process in which
education is tied to social advancement within a class society, so that it
is difficult, except by a bizarre personal demonstration, to hold both to
education and to social solidarity ('he wished to raise the class'). It is
the process also in which culture and affluence come to be regarded as
alternative aims, at whatever cost to both, and the wry recognition
that the latter will always be the first choice' (Williams, *The Country and
the City*, p. 245).
18. The sole important exception to this classification (in a novel which is
in many other ways isolated among Hardy's work) is Donald Farfrae.
19. For example, consider Troy's outlook upon the past: 'He was a man to
whom memories were an incumbrance, and anticipations a super-
fluity. Simply feeling, considering, and caring for what was before his
eyes, he was vulnerable only in the present' (*FFTMC*, p. 197); and
Hardy's comparison between Troy and Oak: 'In juxtaposition with
Troy, Oak had a melancholy tendency to look like a candle beside gas'
(p. 271).
20. Merryn Williams, *A Preface to Hardy* (London, 1976) p. 120.

21. For example, *A Pair of Blue Eyes*, pp. 364–5: 'The moral rightness of this man's life was worthy of all praise, but in spite of some intellectual acumen, Knight had in him a modicum of that wrongheadedness which is mostly found in scrupulously honest people. With him, truth seemed too clean and pure an abstraction to be so hopelessly churned in with error as practical persons find it. Having now seen himself mistaken in supposing Elfride to be peerless, nothing on earth could make him believe she was not so very bad after all.'

   And cf. Clym, whose mother tells Eustacia, 'though he is as gentle as a child with you now, he can be as hard as steel' (*TROTN*, p. 267); who demands of Thomasin, 'Can a man be too cruel to his mother's enemy?' (p. 363).

   And cf. Angel Clare: 'Within the remote depths of his constitution, so gentle and affectionate as he was in general, there lay hidden a hard logical deposit, like a vein of metal in a soft loam, which turned the edge of everything that attempted to traverse it' (*Tess*, p. 284).

22. Another germane example is the way in which so many of Hardy's characters are found to have some guilty sexual skeleton in the closet, which when dramatically revealed caused widespread havoc: cf. the hidden relationships between Manston/Miss Aldclyffe, Troy/Fanny Robin, Wildeve/Eustacia, Alec/Tess, Lucetta/Henchard, Fitzpiers/Mrs Charmond, Fitzpiers/Suke Damson. This circumstance therefore applies to all of Hardy's 'lady-killers' and all his '*femmes fatales*' – a device avidly discussed by some biographers, but curiously little by critics.

23. At one point Ethelberta confides to her father that, 'I wish I could get a living by some simple humble occupation, and drop the name of Petherwin, and be Berta Chickerel again, and live in a green cottage as we used to do when I was small. I am miserable to a pitiable degree sometimes, and sink into regrets that I ever fell into such a groove as this' (*THOE*, p. 225).

24. In the short stories 'Fellow Townsmen' and 'The Son's Veto', and in *The Well-Beloved*, respectively.

25. In the short stories 'A Few Crusted Characters', 'The Waiting Supper' and 'Fellow Townsmen', respectively.

26. The story is dated 1891. We are told that 'It is now a dozen or fifteen years since his visit was paid' (i.e. about 1879); that Lackland has been absent for 35 years (i.e. since *c.* 1844), and that he was 11 when he left (i.e. he was born *c.* 1833).

27. Michael Millgate, *Thomas Hardy: His Career as a Novelist* (London, 1971) p. 71.

28. For example: 'Isolation on a heath renders vulgarity well-nigh impossible. It would have been as easy for the heath-ponies, bats, and snakes to be vulgar as for her. A narrow life in Budmouth might have completely demeaned her. The only way to look queenly without realms or hearts to queen it over is to look as if you had lost them; and Eustacia did that to a triumph. In the captain's cottage she could suggest mansions she had never seen. Perhaps that was

because she frequented a vaster mansion than any of them, the open hills. Like the summer condition of the place around her, she was an embodiment of the phrase "a populous solitude" – apparently so listless, void, and quiet, she was really busy and full' (*TROTN*, p. 96).

29. Hence the wry comedy of *The Return of the Native*, Book Third, ch. 1: Clym tries to understand the reasons for his return to the uncomprehending heath folk:

> 'When I first got away from home I thought this place was not worth troubling about. I thought our life here was contemptible. To oil your boots instead of blacking them, to dust your coat with a switch instead of a brush; was there ever anything more ridiculous?' I said.
> 'So 'tis; so 'tis!'
> 'No, no – you are wrong; it isn't.'
> 'Beg your pardon, we thought that was your meaning?'
> 'Well, as my views changed my course became very depressing. I found that I was trying to be like people who had hardly anything in common with myself. I was endeavouring to put off one sort of life for another sort of life, which was not better than the life I had known before. It was simply different.'
> 'True, a sight different,' said Fairway.
> 'Yes, Paris must be a taking place,' said Humphrey.
> 'Grand shop-winders, trumpets, and drums; and here be we out of doors in all winds and weathers – '
> 'But you mistake me,' pleaded Clym. 'All this was very depressing' (*TROTN*, pp. 194–5)

30. Hardy seems to be unsure exactly how to present Diggory Venn, whether as realistic heath-man or supernatural symbolic figure, as his footnote regarding the novel's alternate endings shows (footnote to Book Sixth, ch. 3, p. 413).

31. Presumably it is Arabella and Sue to whom Hardy refers in his '*Preface*' when he speaks of 'a deadly war waged between flesh and spirit' (*Jude*, p. 23).

32. See Kellow Chesney, *The Victorian Underworld* (London, 1972) p. 363 *et seq.*

33. See, for example, Phillotson's early idealism about Jude and Sue (pp. 267–8), Jude's views on the collective responsibility for children (p. 293), and his views on the social origins of sexism (p. 306).

34. Terry Eagleton, 'Introduction' to the New Wessex Edition, p. 11.

35. *Faulkner at Nagano*, ed. Robert A. Jelliffe (Tokyo, 1956) pp. 156–7; *Faulkner in the University*, ed. Frederick L. Gwynn and Joseph L. Blotner (Charlottesville, Va., 1959) p. 177.

36. Jean Stein, 'William Faulkner: an Interview', in *William Faulkner: Three Decades of Criticism*, ed. F. J. Hoffman and O. Vickery (East Lansing, Mich., 1951) pp. 79, 80–1.

37. *Faulkner at West Point*, ed. Joseph L. Fant and Robert Ashley (New York, 1964) p. 94.

38. '[T]here's not too fine a distinction between humor and tragedy … even tragedy is in a way walking a tightrope between the ridiculous – between the bizarre and the terrible … the writer uses humor as a tool … he's still trying to write about people … about the human heart in some moving way, and so he uses whatever tool that he thinks will do most to finish the picture … of man' (Gwynn and Blotner (eds), *Faulkner in the University*, p. 39).

39. Ibid., pp. 62, 51.

40. See Faulkner's remarks regarding ways of looking at 'truth' in Gwynn and Blotner (eds), *Faulkner in the University*, pp. 273–4.

41. Ibid., pp. 133–4; speech 'Upon Receiving the Nobel Prize for Literature, 1950', in *Essays, Speeches and Public Letters*, p. 120.

42. Malcolm Cowley, 'Introduction to *The Portable Faulkner*'; reprinted as *The Essential Faulkner* (London, 1967) p. xx.

43. Gwynn and Blotner (eds), *Faulkner in the University*, p. 19.

44. Cf. Thomasin in Book Sixth, ch. 3 of *The Return of the Native* (pp. 409–13), to the unnamed black McCaslin descendant in 'Delta Autumn' (pp. 269–75) in *Go Down, Moses*.

45. In the latter, Mink is called Ernest Cotton.

46. '[H]is head slipped down into the V of the stanchion … and the weight and momentum of his whole body came down on his viced neck. In a moment now he would hear the bone, the vertebrae, and he wrenched his body again, kicking backward now toward where he believed the moving wheel would be, thinking, If I can just hook my foot in them spokes, something will have to give' (*TH*, p. 230).

47. Jean Stein, 'Interview', p. 80. And cf. Gwynn and Blotner (eds), *Faulkner in the University*, p. 9: 'my idea is that no person is wholly good or wholly bad'.

48. For example, Jason, Lena, Charles Bon, Bayard II and Ringo, Isaac and Mink are all portrayed in pursuit of other characters in some important way; while Bayard III, Horace, Joe Christmas, Quentin, Charles and Henry, all the characters in *Pylon*, or Harry and Charlotte, are oppressed by a sense of exile and estrangement from their environment, which fuels their search for some alternative form of fulfilment.

49. Hyatt H. Waggoner's study, centring as it does upon the moral and religious perspectives of Faulkner's work, is especially helpful in its commentary upon the use of these flashes of insight in the short stories. See Hyatt H. Waggoner, *William Faulkner: From Jefferson to the World*, ch. 9, pp. 194–211.

50. The Reporter is explicitly compared to Don Quixote with his 'air of worn and dreamy fury': *Pylon*, p. 49.

51. The editor complains that his readers want 'news', not the Reporter's subjective and portentous attempts at 'fiction' (pp. 49–51).

52. There are some interesting similarities between *Pylon* (1935) and Robert Penn Warren's *All the King's Men* (1946), which suggest that Warren may have unconsciously inherited some images from the earlier novel. I am thinking of the fetid Louisiana atmosphere (e.g. p. 268 in *Pylon*, p. 450 in *All the King's Men*, and the recurrence of the image of the 'clipped lawns'), as well as the tough-guy surface and

the romantic inner selves of the two protagonists; *All the King's Men* (London, 1974).

53. 'On Thursday Roger Schumann flew a race against four competitors, and won. On Saturday he flew against but one competitor. But that competitor was Death and Roger Schumann lost' (p. 314).

54. 'Mrs. Schumann departed with her husband and children for Ohio... where any and all finders of Roger Schumann are kindly requested to forward any and all of same' (p. 315).

55. Several critics allude to the relationship between *Pylon* and *Absalom, Absalom!*, for the two novels were written simultaneously: e.g. Michael Millgate, *The Achievement of William Faulkner* (London, 1966) p. 149; David Minter, *William Faulkner: His Life and Work* (Baltimore, Md., 1980) pp. 147–50; Judith Bryant Wittenberg, *Faulkner: The Transfiguration of Biography* (Lincoln, Nebr., 1979) pp. 130–40.

56. Letter to Malcolm Cowley (24 December 1945), *The Faulkner–Cowley File*, ed. Malcolm Cowley (New York, 1966) p. 74.

57. Millgate, for example, suggests that *Under the Greenwood Tree* originates in 'the evolution of a particular setting and a particular community, not a story', its narrative patterns following the seasons and the round of rural activities (see his *Thomas Hardy: His Career*, pp. 43, 46, 51). He makes much the same points regarding *Sartoris*, though without explicitly drawing any comparison (cf. *Achievement*, pp. 76–9). And cf. the two novelists' comments upon the genesis of their rural novels, which clearly show the instinctive and nostalgic impulses behind their creation. Hardy remarks that, 'I suppose the impressions which all unconsciously I had been gathering of rural life during my youth in Dorsetshire recurred to me, and the theme – in fiction – seemed to have absolute freshness. So... I began to write *Under the Greenwood Tree*' (*Cassell's Saturday Journal* (25 June 1892) p. 944). Faulkner said of *Sartoris* that while 'speculating idly upon time and death' the thought occurred to him that the day would come when he would no longer 'react to the simple bread-and-salt of the world' as he had done during his growing years, and so he began casting about: 'nothing served but that I try by main strength to recreate between the covers of a book the world as I was already preparing to lose and regret... desiring, if not the capture of that world and the feeling of it as you'd preserve a kernel or a leaf to indicate the lost forest, at least to keep the evocative skeleton of the desiccated leaf. So I began to write, without much purpose, until I realised that to make it truly evocative it must be personal... to preserve my belief in the savor of the bread and salt' (Joseph L. Blotner, *Faulkner: A Biography* (New York, 1974) pp. 531–2).

58. Gwynn and Blotner (eds), *Faulkner in the University*, p. 268.

59. Hardy's habitual shyness is immortalised in a wonderful anecdote recorded by Florence Hardy: see Robert Gittings, *The Older Hardy* (London, 1978) p. 205.

60. Cf. the description given by a visitor to Hardy's study in 1921: 'bare, simple, workmanlike and pleasantly shabby' (Millgate, *Hardy: A Biography*, p. 532).

61. James B. Meriwether and Michael Millgate (eds), *Lion in the Garden: Interviews with William Faulkner, 1926–62* (New York, 1968) p. 26.
62. Jean Stein 'Interview', p. 68; and cf. Gwynn and Blotner (eds), *Faulkner in the University*, pp. 159–60.
63. Blotner, *Faulkner: A Biography*, pp. 1453–4.
64. 'An Introduction to *The Sound and the Fury*', ed. James B. Meriwether, *Southern Review*, vol. 26 (Summer 1973) p. 412.
65. Letter from Faulkner to Cowley, in Cowley (ed.), *Faulkner–Cowley File*, p. 14. Cf. a remark attributed to Nietzsche, the source of which I have been unable to find: 'I have gradually come to understand what every great philosophy until now has been: the confession of its author and a kind of involuntary, unconscious memoir.'
66. Faulkner recognised that his literary creativity was inspirational in its origin, though requiring later selection and revision: 'I listen to the voices and when I put down what the voices say, it's right' (see Cowley (ed.) *Faulkner–Cowley File*, p. 114).
67. Judith Bryant Wittenberg's critical biography calls these personae 'linked characters ... who represent closely interrelated ego fragments rather than fully discrete individuals'. Of course, figures like Quentin and Shreve, Charles Bon and Henry Sutpen, Quentin and Benjy or the Bundren brothers clearly *are* credible individualised characters, but Wittenberg is undoubtedly right in identifying their simultaneous function as isolated parts of a larger totality, apparently inspired by the novelist's own ambivalent responses, which becomes a radical narrative method (see Wittenberg, *Faulkner: Transfiguration of Biography*, p. 75).
68. Cf. Varner's reflection that 'fatherblood hates with love and pride, but motherblood with hate loves and cohabits' (*LIA*, p. 22). The discords of the Faulkners' marriage are demonstrated by Maud Butler Faulkner's query to William on her death-bed, whether she would have to see his father in heaven. When he replied no, she said, 'That's good. I never did like him' (see Blotner, *Faulkner: A Biography*, p. 1762).
69. Millgate, *Hardy: A Biography*, pp. 21, 22–3.
70. Minter, *Faulkner: His Life and Work*, pp. 10, 17.
71. Ibid.
72. Millgate, *Hardy: A Biography*, pp. 21, 29–40, 176–7, 186; Minter, *Faulkner: His Life and Work*, pp. 10, 12, 17, 19–20, 117.
73. See Minter, *Faulkner: His Life and Work*, pp. 17–18; Wittenberg, *Faulkner: Transfiguration of Biography*, pp. 24–5.
74. Cf. Hardy's admiration for a courageous unmarried mother, and for Fielding's Molly, in *Life*, pp. 157, 298. For a useful commentary upon Faulkner's view of the differences between the sexes, see Cleanth Brooks, *William Faulkner: The Yoknapatawpha Country* (New Haven, Conn., 1963) pp. 68, 107; and also Linda Welshimer Wagner's essay 'Faulkner and (Southern) Women', *The South and Faulkner's Yoknapatawpha*, ed. Evans Harrington and Ann J. Abadie (Jackson, Miss., 1977) pp. 128–46.
75 John Faulkner, *My Brother Bill* (New York, 1963) p. 153.

76. See Minter, *Faulkner: His Life and Work*, pp. 9, 16; Wittenberg, *Faulkner: Transfiguration of Biography*, pp. 20, 21, 23, 25.
77. See Wittenberg, *Faulkner: Transfiguration of Biography*, p. 23. It seems likely that Faulkner regarded his father as a moral, and perhaps even a physical, coward, though the evidence is admittedly fictional. For example, see Charles Bon's feelings of 'despair and shame' in *Absalom, Absalom!* p. 321; and cf. the incident of Murry and the snake (John Faulkner, *My Brother Bill*, pp. 38–9).
78. Wittenberg, *Faulkner: Transfiguration of Biography*, p. 6.
79. See John B. Cullen, with Floyd C. Watkins, *Old Times in the Faulkner Country* (Chapel Hill, NC, 1961) pp. 3–4; Blotner, *Faulkner: A Biography*, pp. 120–40; Minter, *Faulkner: His Life and Work*, pp. 11–12. Faulkner's tendency to self-effacement and silence are reminiscent of the young Hardy's 'habits of quiet observation and physical withdrawal' (Millgate, *Hardy: A Biography*, p. 17).
80. Hardy, *Life*, pp. 31–2.
81. Minter, *Faulkner: His Life and Work*, p. 3. Such an awareness of the pressures of history and the sense of place was, of course, highly unusual in the United States. This peculiar attribute of Southern culture provides another link with Hardy's rural England, which he saw as a place of 'ancient lands, / Enchased and lettered as a tomb, / And scored with prints of perished hands, / And chronicled with dates of doom' ('On an Invitation to the United States', *CP*, p. 110).
82. Millgate, *Hardy: A Biography*, p. 37.
83. See Minter, *Faulkner: His Life and Work*, p. xi; Blotner, *Faulkner: A Biography*, pp. 179–80; Wittenberg, *Faulkner: Transfiguration of Biography*, pp. 27–8.
84. Blotner remarks that Jack Falkner 'always felt that his admired older brother "more or less unconsciously patterned his life after the old Colonel's"' (Blotner, *Faulkner: A Biography*, p. 105). Wittenberg points out some 'striking parallels' between the lives of Faulkner and his great-grandfather (*Faulkner: Transfiguration of Biography*, pp. 10–11); cf. Minter, *Faulkner: His Life and Work*, p. 23.
85. The term 'pioneer-ancestor' I have taken from Edmond Volpe, *A Reader's Guide to William Faulkner* (New York, 1964) p. 19; and cf. Wittenberg, *Faulkner: Transfiguration of Biography*, pp. 9–10.
86. Wittenberg, *Faulkner: Transfiguration of Biography*, p. 157.
87. Millgate remarks that 'Elfride, like Cytherea of *Desperate Remedies*, is a forerunner of all those Hardy heroines whose parents fail them through selfishness, insensitivity, or death. Bathsheba, Ethelberta, Eustacia, Anne, Paula, Elizabeth-Jane, Tess and Sue are all forced to fight their own battles without parental help or in the face of actual parental opposition' (*Hardy: His Career*, p. 71).
88. Minter explains: 'Burdened with families that are so large and inbred as to seem suffocating, the Compsons, Sartorises and McCaslins feel caught and held ... they find stillness and repetition easy, motion and innovation almost impossible.... Left without parental tenderness and love, Benjy, Quentin, and Caddy turn to Dilsey and to each other.... Resenting their parents, some of these characters avoid parenthood

altogether. Those who do not avoid it find repetition almost inevitable' (Minter, *Faulkner: His Life and Work*, pp. 17–18).

89. Millgate, *Achievement*, p. 105.

90. This scene makes its first appearance in *Sartoris*, on the first night of Bayard's visit to the MacCallums. Tormented and unable to sleep, he considers killing himself with Buddy's shotgun, looks outside into the 'chill corpse-light' of the stars, and then lies on his bed, 'hearing the winter rain whispering on the roof ... he lay presently in something like a tortured and fitful doze, surrounded by ceiling images and shapes of stubborn despair and the ceaseless striving for ... not vindication as much as comprehension' (*Sartoris*, pp. 238–9). It is repeated in the story 'Mountain Victory', when Saucier Weddel lies in the mountain family's loft: 'Overhead, through the cracks in the roof the sky showed the thick chill, black sky which would rain again tomorrow.... He lay rigid on his back in the cold darkness, thinking of home.... "It's nice to be whipped; quiet to be whipped. To be whipped and to lie under the broken roof, thinking of home"' (*DM*, pp. 340–1). It also seems to be reflected in the scene in 'Delta Autumn' when Isaac, rebuked by Roth's black mistress, lies in his tent brooding over the 'ruined woods' (*GDM*, p. 275).

91. Cf. Robert Gittings's comments upon Hardy's poems in the collection *Moments of Vision*: 'Often Nature provides symbols, which are connected with places and persons in his life.... A sunny stream represents happiness, though often happiness of an impermanent kind ... its opposite symbol for unhappiness [seems to be] a pond on a heath, often reflecting moonlight, always an image of coldness and parting. The flight of a heron from trees beside the pond always means some final loss' (Robert Gittings, *The Older Hardy*, p. 171).

92. See note 36 in this chapter.

93. Murry Falkner was continually frustrated in his career, largely through the domination of his father. During his son's formative years he ran a livery stable, later a hardware store, not very energetically. See Blotner, *Faulkner: A Biography*, pp. 79–81; Wittenberg, *Faulkner: Transfiguration of Biography*, pp. 15–16.

94. Faulkner exploits this hypocrisy to great tragi-comic effect in his characterisations of Isaac McCaslin's Uncle Hubert Beauchamp and of Jason's Uncle Maury, who was evidently instrumental in encouraging Mrs Compson to become an empty-headed hypochondriac and his nephew to become an unscrupulous profiteer. Uncle Maury's letter to Jason justifies yet another encroachment upon his sister's bank balance in pursuit of his hare-brained speculations: 'This is in confidence, you will understand, from one business man to another; we will harvest our own vineyards, eh? And knowing your mother's delicate health and that timorousness which such delicately nurtured Southern ladies would naturally feel regarding matters of business, and their charming proneness to divulge such matters in conversation, I would suggest that you do not mention it to her at all.... It is our duty to shield her from the crass material world as much as possible' (*TSATF*, pp. 200–1).

95. See the 'Appendix' to *The Sound and the Fury* (New York, 1946, Modern Library edn) pp. 16–18; hereafter referred to as 'Appendix'.
96. Gwynn and Blotner (eds), *Faulkner in the University*, p. 77.
97. See 'Appendix', p. 13.
98. 'Introduction' to *The Sound and the Fury*, pp. 413–14.
99. See Blotner, *Faulkner: A Biography*, pp. 142, 154–5.
100. Gwynn and Blotner (eds), *Faulkner in the University*, p. 14.
101. *Soldier's Pay*, p. 126.
102. Gwynn and Blotner (eds), *Faulkner in the University*, p. 84; Robert A. Jelliffe (ed.), *Faulkner At Nagano*, p. 105.
103. Gray, *Literature of Memory*, p. 256.
104. Ilse Dusoir Lind, 'Faulkner's Women', in *The Maker and the Myth: Faulkner and Yoknapatawpha, 1977*, ed. Evans Harrington and Ann J. Abadie (Jackson, Miss., 1978) p. 103.
105. '[T]he dusk was peopled with ghosts of glamorous and old disastrous things. And if they were just glamorous enough, there was sure to be a Sartoris in them, and then they were sure to be disastrous. Pawns. But the Player, and the game He plays ... He must have a name for His pawns, though. But perhaps Sartoris is the game itself – a game outmoded and played with the pawns shaped too late and to an old dead pattern.... For there is death in the sound of it, and a glamorous fatality, like silver pennons downrushing at sunset, or a dying fall of horns along the road to Roncevaux' (*Sartoris*, p. 281). For valuable analyses of Faulkner's use of ambivalent attitudes in this passage, see Millgate, *Achievement*, pp. 25–6; Gray, *Literature of Memory*, pp. 231–3.
106. *Mosquitoes*, p. 280.
107. Michael Millgate, 'Faulkner and the South: some Reflections', in Harrington and Abadie (eds), *The South and Faulkner's Yoknapatawpha*, pp. 201–2: Millgate continues by suggesting that the pastoral writer 'is, in effect, inviting the members of his predominantly urban audience to contemplate themselves and their values in terms of the implicit comparison with a society whose modes of life, conduct, and belief have a simplicity, directness and coherence with which they in their sophistication are no longer in touch ... this is not necessarily a matter of celebrating rural values at the expense of the urban.... It is rather a matter of seeing life in its essentials.... It is, in short, the Wordsworthian stance' (p. 202).
108. John Barrell, *The Idea of Landscape and the Sense of Place: An Approach to the Poetry of John Clare* (Cambridge, 1972) pp. 184–7.
109. James Dickey, *Deliverance* (New York, 1970).
110. Robert Penn Warren, 'William Faulkner', from Robert Penn Warren, *Selected Essays* (New York, 1958) pp. 59–79.
111. Ibid., pp. 64–7.
112. For example, cf. the conclusions of Elizabeth Kerr, *Yoknapatawpha* 2nd edn, revised (New York, 1969) pp. 237–8, and John Pilkington, *The Heart of Yoknapatawpha* (Jackson, Miss., 1981) pp. 296–7.
113. I will give brief references to the source of each character's date of birth. Horace Benbow was born in 1886 (Brooks, *Yoknapatawpha Country*, p. 450); Joe Gilligan is 32 (*SP*, p. 35); the novel is set in 1919 (p. 86), so he

was born *c.* 1888; Eula Varner in 1889 (Brooks, *Yoknapatawpha Country*, p. 452). Then in rapid chronological succession come Quentin Compson (ibid., p. 447); Gavin Stevens (ibid., p. 449) and presumably Ratliff, since they are of the same age (Faulkner says in *The Mansion* that they are 'approaching their sixties' (p. 397) and the setting is then 1946); Byron Bunch and Joe Christmas, who are both past 30 in *Light in August* (p. 37) a novel which seems to be set in the mid-1920s (see also Brooks, *Yoknapatawpha Country*, p. 380); Caddy Compson (ibid., p. 447); Bayard and Narcissa Benbow (ibid., p. 450); Jason Compson (ibid., p. 447); Lucius Priest, who is 11 in 1905 (*TR*, pp. 8, 20); and Cash and Darl Bundren (Darl was old enough to be 'in France at the war' (*AILD*, 202) and the novel is set in the mid-1920s, by the evidence of the 'graphaphone'). Faulkner himself was born in 1897, and would appear to be roughly coeval with Margaret Powers – aged between 19 and 25 in 1919 (*SP*, pp. 28, 86); Roth Edmonds (Brooks, *Yoknapatawpha Country*, p. 448); Percy Grimm, who is about 25 and was too young to fight in the war (*LIA*, p. 338); Gowan Stevens (Brooks, *Yoknapatawpha Country*, p. 449); and Julian Lowe (*SP*, pp. 42, 86). The tall convict was born about 1902 (*TWP*, p. 19), Lena Grove about 1905 (she is about 20 when she gets pregnant: *LIA*, pp. 6–7); Linda Snopes in 1908 (Brooks, *Yoknapatawpha Country*, p. 452); Harry Wilbourne in 1910 (*TWP*, p. 25: Charlotte is probably a little older); and Temple Drake in 1910/11 (Brooks, *Yoknapatawpha Country*, pp. 394–5).

It is true that the Snopes family generally antedate this period –Mink is born in 1883 (ibid., p. 452), and Flem is presumably his contemporary (he is described as 'of no establishable age between twenty and thirty' (*TH*, p. 48) in about 1906): but the New South's Snopesism is necessarily one of the bewildering influences and pressures under which the young protagonists grew up.

114. Volpe, *Reader's Guide*, p. 17. And cf. Lyall H. Powers's *Faulkner's Yoknapatawpha Comedy* (Ann Arbor, Mich., 1980), which argues that all of Faulkner's novels can be read as a single 'Saga', chronicling the development of several Yoknapatawphan protagonists in a variety of guises, and marked by 'a singleness of purpose' and a consistency of expression in the development of…themes' (p. 254; and see particularly pp. 253–61).

115. The childhood sections of *The Sound and the Fury* are set in 1905–10; plus 'That Evening Sun' (1899 or 1900) and 'A Justice' (1902 or 1903). Time present in *Absalom, Absalom!* is 1909–10. *The Reivers* is set in 1905. *The Hamlet* covers the first decade of the twentieth century, with a few flashbacks into the 1890s, though confused children are not very prominent in its story. 'Barn Burning' is set about 1895 (see p. 11), while 'That Will be Fine' seems to be about 1900.

116. W. J. Cash, *The Mind of the South* (New York, 1941) p. 338. *Soldier's Pay* is set in 1919; *Sartoris* in 1919–20; *Mosquitoes, As I Lay Dying, Light in August* and much of *The Town* some time in the 1920s; Jason's and Dilsey's sections of *The Sound and the Fury* in 1928; *Sanctuary* in 1929 (according to Brooks, *Yoknapatawpha Country*, p. 394–5; in 1930, according to Volpe, *Reader's Guide*, p. 383); 'Old Man' is set in 1927.

117. *Pylon* is set in the early 1930s; *The Wild Palms* in 1937–8; and *Requiem for a Nun* in about 1938.
118. For example, Ike's confrontation with Roth and his mistress; Mink's return to Memphis and the world.
119. Faulkner remarks in a note of about 1931 that 'So far I have not bothered much about chronology, which, if I am ever collected, I shall have to do' (James B. Meriwether, *The Literary Career of William Faulkner: A Bibliographical Study* (Princeton, NJ, 1961) p. 41.

   Similarly, Millgate suggests that Hardy's Wessex is 'evocative rather of a sense of pastness than of identifiable moments in time' (*Hardy: His Career*, p. 247).
120. Cf. *Sartoris*, pp. 121–2, 126–7.
121. Though one wonders how much Horace's quest, like the Reporter's desire to help Laverne, is related to a romantic infatuation with Ruby as well as with an impersonal desire for justice. To this extent, the odious Narcissa's instincts may be correct.
122. For example, Horace and Ruby: 'But he knew he was just talking. He knew that she knew it too, out of that feminine reserve of unflagging suspicion of all people's actions which seems at first to be mere affinity for evil but which is in reality practical wisdom' (p. 160). This quotation serves as a useful authorial antidote to those who interpret *Sanctuary* as unrelievedly misogynistic: Faulkner's approval of Ruby's enduring strength is evident throughout *Sanctuary*, though often underestimated.

   Again, there are close correspondences with Hardy's admiration of women's stoicism; cf. *Two on a Tower*, p. 247; *Life*, p. 157.
123. Cf. *The Sound and The Fury*, pp. 76, 154; *As I Lay Dying*, p. 65; *Absalom, Absalom!*, pp. 290–1.
124. See, respectively, Millgate, *Achievement*, p. 120; Brooks, *Yoknapatawpha Country*, p. 136.
125. For example, Bayard's farming and hunting; Cash's pride in his carpentry, or Jewel's in his horse.
126. That is, the joy of sex, procreation of children, fertility of harvest.
127. For example, Temple goes towards the barn, 'the torn leaves [of a mail-order catalogue] in her hand, splotched over with small cuts of clothes-pins and patent wringers and washing-powder.... Then she began to run, snatching her feet up almost before they touched the earth, the weeds slashing at her with huge, moist, malodorous blossoms' (p. 74). Or cf. the description of the 'bright, soft ... wanton morning' on which Popeye abducts Temple, 'rife with a promise of noon and heat, with high fat clouds like gobs of whipped cream.... The bougainvillaea against the veranda would be large as basket-balls and lightly poised as balloons and looking vacantly and stupidly at the rushing roadside Temple began to scream' (p. 110).
128. Horace's aversion to his wife's liking for shrimp clearly has sexual connotations (pp. 16–17).
129. For example, 'When he touched her she sprang like a bow, hurling herself upon him, her mouth gaped and ugly like that of a dying fish' (p. 190).

130. The best that can be said for Temple in *Sanctuary* is that she may make a modest claim to be seen as one of Faulkner's 'betrayed children', if one can base psychological theories upon the evidence of her father's ritualised behaviour, and Temple's repetitive obsession with his status ('my father's a judge'). Her reference to Popeye as 'Daddy' (1920s slang) in a sexual context (p. 188) may also help to explain her highly ambiguous relationship with the gangster.

131. David Oberbey, 'In the Shadows', in *Movies of the Forties*, ed. Ann Lloyd (London, 1982) pp. 141–3.

132. *Sanctuary*'s reiterated motif of the black people's songs outside the jail seems especially significant, firstly in view of the traditional role of black American music as an agent of racial solidarity, resistance and catharsis in the face of suffering, especially gospel music (see Frederick Douglass, *Narrative of the Life of Frederick Douglass: An American Slave* (Boston, Mass. 1845; reprinted Cambridge, Mass., 1900) pp. 36–8; Paul Oliver, *The Story of the Blues* (London, 1969) pp. 6–10; *Conversation with the Blues* (London, 1965) pp. 1–2.

133. Cf. *Sanctuary*, pp. 47–9; *The Woodlanders*, p. 393. Ruby's invective is also clearly related to Addie's scorn for Cora in *As I Lay Dying*, pp. 137–8.

134. 'Little shirt-tail boys that think because Lee breaks the law, they can come out there and treat our house like a … it's the ones like him, the ones that are too young to realise that people don't break the law just for a holiday' (pp. 128–9).

135. Minter remarks that 'As a rule to which Ruby Lamar is the only significant exception, the novel's women tend toward one of two extremes: if they are not advocates of repression and enforcers of control, they are seducers of men and proponents of license' (*Faulkner: His Life and Work*, p. 126). Part of the motivation behind my extended discussion of *Sanctuary* has been a feeling that Ruby's importance, both within *Sanctuary* and as a member of a distinctive type of Faulknerian protagonist, has been too often overlooked in critical discussion.

NOTES TO CHAPTER 4. 'NOVELS OF CHARACTER AND ENVIRONMENT'

1. Douglas Brown, *Thomas Hardy* (London, 1954) p. 84.

2. See the poem 'The Coquette, and After', *Collected Poems*, p. 139. Angel Clare's double standard regarding pre-marital sex provides the most obvious example of Hardy's remarkably modern outlook upon sexual inequality.

3. 'General Preface' to the Wessex edition of 1912.

4. Hardy's 'Preface' to *Far from the Madding Crowd* (1895–1902) p. 38.

5. A resemblance first noted by Michael Millgate, *Thomas Hardy: His Career as a Novelist* (London, 1971) p. 346.

6. Hardy's 'General Preface' to the Wessex edition of *Far from the Madding Crowd* (1912) p. 444.
7. From an interview with Jean Stein, quoted in *Lion in the Garden: Interviews with William Faulkner, 1926–62*, ed. James B. Meriwether and Michael Millgate (New York, 1968), p. 255.
8. From an interview in *Cassell's Saturday Journal*, 25 June 1892.
9. In the manuscript of ch. 50 – 'Greenhill was the Nijnii [*sic*] Novgorod of Wessex' (quoted by Millgate, *Hardy: His Career*, p. 95). Here, as in subsequent acknowledged notes, I am indebted to the scholarship of Millgate, who is noteworthy for being apparently the sole critic to have (briefly) remarked the astonishing unity of Hardy's and Faulkner's literary microcosms (see especially *Hardy: His Career*, pp. 345–50). He points out that other occurrences of the word 'Wessex' in *Far from the Madding Crowd* result from later revisions.
10. *The Mayor of Casterbridge*, pp. 243–4.
11. Ibid., p. 144.
12. Ibid., pp. 91–2. As W. J. Keith and Millgate have pointed out, Hardy's cataloguing of these village names seems a deliberate reference to the related worlds of other Hardy novels; see Millgate, *Hardy: His Career*, p. 236; and W. J. Keith, 'Critical Approaches to Hardy's Wessex', *Association of Canadian University Teachers of English: Report* (1963) pp. 22–3.
13. See *The Collected Letters of Thomas Hardy*, ed. R. L. Purdy and M. Millgate, vol. ı (Oxford, 1978) p. 171.
14. In 1895–6 for Osgood, McIlvaine & Co.; in 1902, when the plates for this edition were taken over by Macmillan; most extensive revisions for the Macmillan Wessex Edition of 1912, and yet more for reprintings in 1920; and for the Mellstock edn in 1919–20. See Millgate, *Hardy: His Career*, p. 352, for a fuller account of this process.
15. 'Preface' to *Far from the Madding Crowd* (1895) pp. 37–8.
16. 'General Preface' to *Far from the Madding Crowd*, Wessex edition (1912) pp. 444–5.
17. In 'The Science of Fiction', reproduced in *Thomas Hardy's Personal Writings*, ed. Harold Orel (London, 1967) p. 317.
18. Interview in *Cassell's Saturday Journal*, 25 June 1892.
19. Donald Morrison (compiler), *Exhibition of Hardy's Drawings and Paintings* (Dorchester, 1968) p. 6. The map, 'Cruchley's Railway & Telegraphic Map of Dorset', is in the Dorset County Museum, along with Hardy's sketch map of the setting of *The Return of the Native*.
20. See the map which Faulkner drew for the frontispiece of *The Portable Faulkner*, ed. Malcolm Cowley (New York, 1946).
21. Andrew Enstice, *Thomas Hardy: Landscapes of the Mind* (London, 1979) p. 18; and see pp. 5–30. Hardy's aim, argues Enstice, is to make Casterbridge more ancient, unchanged and complementary to its rural surroundings than the Dorchester of the 1840s really was: as Hardy himself admitted: 'when I consider the liberties I have taken with its ancient walls, streets, and precincts through the medium of the printing-press, I feel that I have treated its external features with the hand of freedom indeed. True, it might be argued that my

Casterbridge ... is not Dorchester – not even the Dorchester as it existed sixty years ago, but a dream-place that never was outside an irresponsible book. Nevertheless, when somebody said to me that "Casterbridge" is a sort of essence of the town as it used to be, "a place more Dorchester than Dorchester itself", I could not absolutely contradict him.... At any rate, it is not a photograph in words, that inartistic species of literary produce' (*Life*, p. 351).

22. '[T]hough the people in most of the novels ... are dwellers in a province bounded on the north by the Thames, on the south by the English Channel, on the east by a line running from Hayling Island to Windsor Forest, and on the west by the Cornish coast, they were meant to be typically and essentially those of any and every place ... beings in whose hearts and minds that which is local should be really universal' ('General Preface' to *Far from the Madding Crowd*, Wessex Edition (1912) p. 444).

23. See Samuel Hynes, 'Hardy and Barnes: Notes on Literary Influence', *South Atlantic Quarterly*, vol. 58 (1959) p. 48; also Millgate, *Hardy: His Career*, pp. 125–9, who is able to show that Barnes had fleetingly used the term 'Wessex' in print in 1868, before Hardy, as the latter must have been aware.

24. For example, William Barnes's poems, 'The Hwomestead A-Vell Into Hand', 'The Common A-Took In', and 'Eclogue: Two Farms in Woone', in *Poems of Rural Life in the Dorset Dialect* (London, 1879); and Thomas Nelson Page's stories, 'Marse Chan: A Tale of Old Virginia', '"Unc' Edinburg'"': A Plantation Echo', and 'Meh Lady: a Story of the War', in *In Ole Virginia* (London, 1889).

25. See Hardy's description of the novel in *Life*, p. 56.

26. Millgate comments upon the 'symbolic' nature of each man's house-moving (*Hardy: His Career*, pp. 200–1; *The Achievement of William Faulkner* (London, 1966) p. 29), without drawing a comparison between them.

27. 'She had a singular insight into life, considering that she had never mixed with it.... We call it intuition. What was the great world to Mrs. Yeobright? A multitude whose tendencies could be perceived, though not its essences. Communities were seen by her as from a distance ... her life was very complete on its reflective side' (*TROTN*, p. 212).

28. 'General Preface' to *Far from the Madding Crowd*, Wessex Edition (1912) p. 444.

29. *Life*, p. 177.

30. Ibid., p. 285.

31. Cf. Hardy's own comment: 'It was not as if he had been a writer of novels proper, and as more specifically understood, that is, stories of modern artificial life and manners showing a certain smartness of treatment. He had mostly aimed at keeping his narratives close to natural life and as near to poetry in their subject as the conditions would allow' (*Life*, p. 291).

Regarding Hardy's anthropomorphism, it is interesting to note that his habit, in his novels, of ascribing feelings and atmosphere to *things*, becomes quite overt in his poems of a few years later. For example, in 'Voices from Things Growing in a Churchyard', people have *become* things, and speak to us, directly, as flowers, berries or ivy (*CP*, pp. 623–5).

32. See T. S. Eliot, *After Strange Gods* (London, 1934) pp. 54–5.
33. *Life*, p. 185.
34. Again, for an authoritative study of Hardy's stylistic fluctuations I must refer the reader to John Bayley's *An Essay on Hardy* (Cambridge, 1978); and must also acknowledge Virginia Woolf, whose essay 'The Novels of Thomas Hardy' (in *Collected Essays*, ed. L. Woolf, vol. I (London, 1967) p. 258) seems to have been the first critical analysis to have described this characteristic in Hardy's writing.
35. 'The only way of expressing emotion in the form of art is by finding an "objective correlative"; in other words, a set of objects, a situation, a chain of events which shall be the formula of that particular emotion; such that when the external facts, which must terminate in sensory experience, are given, the emotion is immediately evoked. If you examine any of Shakespeare's more successful tragedies, you will find this exact equivalence: you will find that the state of mind of Lady Macbeth walking in her sleep has been communicated to you by a skilful accumulation of imagined sensory perceptions' (see 'Hamlet', in *Selected Essays* (London, 1932) p. 145).
36. Namely, *The Return of the Native*, Book Fourth, chs 5 and 6: 'The Journey Across the Heath' and 'A Conjuncture, and its Result upon the Pedestrian'.
37. *Life*, p. 230.
38. Virginia Woolf, 'Novels of Thomas Hardy', p. 258.
39. Walter Allen, *The English Novel* (London, 1954) p. 98.
40. *Life*, p. 443.
41. *As I I Lay Dying*, pp. 137–8. Cf. also Henry Knight's suggestion that 'it is only those who half know a thing that write about it. Those who know it thoroughly don't take the trouble' (*APOBE*, p. 162).
42. '[W]here dissolution itself was a seething turmoil of ejaculation, tumescence, conception, and birth, and death did not even exist … because there was no death, not Lion and not Sam: not held fast in earth but free in earth and not in earth but of earth, myriad yet undiffused of every myriad part, leaf and twig and particle, air and sun and rain and dew and night, acorn oak and leaf and acorn again, dark and dawn and dark and dawn again in their immutable progression and, being myriad, one' (*GDM*, pp. 250–1).
43. Herman Melville, *Moby Dick*, ch. 35, 'The Mast-Head'; *Go Down, Moses*, p. 251. The irony regarding Isaac's greeting the snake is, of course, that though able to accept the evil innate in nature, Isaac cannot reconcile himself to the evil committed by his actual grandfather, Carothers McCaslin.
44. See 'Red Leaves', *These Thirteen*, pp. 104–5.
45. R. W. B. Lewis, *The American Adam* (New York, 1955), pp. 103–5.
46. For example, cf. *The Woodlanders* (p. 326): 'The leaves overhead were now in their latter green – so opaque, that it was darker at some of the

densest spots than in winter time, scarce a crevice existing by which a ray could get down to the ground'; and *Go Down, Moses* (p. 156): 'He ranged the summer woods now, green with gloom, if anything actually dimmer than they had been in November's grey dissolution, where even at noon the sun fell only in windless dappling upon the earth'.

47. *Life*, p. 116.
48. C. Vann Woodward, *The Burden of Southern History*, revised edn (Baton Rouge, La., 1968) p. 37.
49. For example, *Requiem for a Nun*, p. 208; and cf. *Faulkner in the University*, ed. Frederick L. Gwynn and Joseph L. Blotner (Charlottesville, Va., 1959) p. 277. *The Reivers* is perhaps the exception which proves the rule.
50. Cleanth Brooks, *William Faulkner: The Yoknapatawpha Country* (New Haven, Conn., 1963), p. 44.
51. Ibid., pp. 41, 43.
52. Hence a Victorian guide-book remarks that, 'Dorsetshire has been justly described as "perhaps in a small compass the most representative of southern English counties." Its classical division is into Felix, Petraea, and Deserta – the happy vales, the stony heights, and the deserted heaths … the three Latin epithets may be geologically translated into the clays, the chalks, and the sands' (*A Handbook for Residents and Travellers in Wilts and Dorset*, Murray's English Handbook series, 5th edn (London, 1899)). Hardy's Dorset enjoyed a corresponding variety of occupations, with sheep-farming on the high chalk ridges, arable farming in the valleys below, dairy farming in the rich river valleys, forestry and cider-making in the central and northern hills, and stone quarrying in the Isles of Portland and Purbeck. All these activities are reflected in the Wessex novels.
53. Skates, p. 6.
54. Herman Lea, *Thomas Hardy's Wessex* (London, 1913) pp. xxii–xxiii.
55. Cleanth Brooks, *William Faulkner: Yoknapatawpha Country*, p. 30.
56. W. J. Cash, *The Mind of the South* (New York, 1941) pp. 46–8.
57. Brooks, *William Faulkner: Yoknapatawpha Country*, p. 30.
58. Millgate, *Achievement*, p. 190.
59. The 'First Cause' is a term used by Hardy frequently – e.g. *Tess*, p. 195; *Life*, p. 410. The 'Immanent Will' is envisaged as the guiding force of *The Dynasts*, evoked in that work's opening line, 'Shade of the Earth: "What of the Immanent Will and Its designs?"'
60. A. O. J. Cockshutt, 'Hardy's Philosophy', in *The Genius of Thomas Hardy*, ed. M. Drabble (London, 1976) p. 144.
61. Cf. *Life*, p. 165.
62. *The Woodlanders*, p. 326. This chapter (40) is the first of three consecutive chapters in which Hardy concentrates upon the way by which Giles 'dissolves into the wood by imperceptible degrees'. The phrase is that of Jean Brooks, whose essay on *The Woodlanders* contains a subtle and illuminating commentary upon Giles's 'gentle slide towards death [which] mirrors the absorption of all human, animal and vegetable purposes in the whitey-brown of the earth, that

is the obverse side of Autumn fertility' (see Jean R. Brooks, *Thomas Hardy: The Poetic Structure* (London, 1971) pp. 227–9).

63. For example, Giles's skill in planting (pp. 93–4); the eerie and mysterious relationship between South and his elm; or Melbury's 'neighbourly kindliness' to other woodlanders, such as the hollow-turner (p. 240).

64. *Life*, p. 177.

65. *The Woodlanders*, p. 52. Many critics have remarked upon the novel's use of this principle, e.g.: 'there are so many such interlocking circumstances that we cannot pick on any one, or two, or three, as being crucial. Collectively, they operate as a kind of metaphor for the deeper, more inclusive, less tangible Necessity that drives the action towards its inevitable, but humanly unpredictable conclusion.... The coincidences and mishaps that stud the pages of Hardy's novels are therefore more often symptoms than causes' (David Lodge, 'Introduction' to New Wessex Edition, pp. 18–19). Or: 'The poetic underpattern of *The Woodlanders* is appropriately a close network of interrelated images which make it the despair and delight of the critic. Every scene and every character triggers off a wealth of thematic reflection and cross-reflection that develop under the human action the stylized ritual of nature's larger purposes working themselves out through character and event' (Jean R. Brooks, *Hardy: Poetic Structure*, p. 219).

66. *The Woodlanders*, p. 119; and Faulkner, *Go Down, Moses*, p. 252.

67. John Holloway, *The Charted Mirror* (London, 1960) pp. 95–6.

68. See Holloway, *Charted Mirror*, pp. 98–105.

69. And as Millgate points out, 'Winterborne' is also a Dorset place-name, with more symbolic reference here (see Millgate, *Hardy: His Career*, p. 258).

70. See pp. 128, 138 for Giles's lack of tact towards Mrs Charmond; and we are earlier told that 'He was, in fact, not a very successful seller either of his trees or of his cider, his habit of speaking his mind when he spoke at all militating against this branch of his business' (p. 67).

71. 'One speciality of Fitzpiers was respected by Grace as much as ever: his professional skill. In this she was right. Had his persistence equalled his insight instead of being the spasmodic and fitful thing it was, fame and fortune need never have remained a wish with him. His freedom from conventional errors and crusted prejudices had indeed been such as to retard rather than accelerate his advance in Hintock and its neighbourhood, where people could not believe that Nature herself effected cures, and that the doctor's business was only to smooth the way' (p. 343). And cf. Reverend Maybold, his predecessor Parson Grinham, and the incidence of witchcraft in Mellstock in *Under the Greenwood Tree*, p. 169, for another example of modernising improvement.

72. One exception is Millgate, who remarks that 'Giles's self-sacrifice is absolutely of a piece with his sense of social inferiority, his remorse at having failed to reveal to Grace his knowledge that she cannot be divorced, and those fundamental inhibitions of character at which Hardy may deliberately have hinted in his surname' (Millgate, *Hardy: His Career*, p. 258).

73. For examples, cf. David Lodge, 'Introduction' to New Wessex Edition, pp. 10, 21; F. R. Southerington, *Hardy's Vision of Man* (London, 1971) p. 119; Desmond Hawkins, *Hardy: Novelist and Poet* (Newton Abbot, 1976): 'To modern readers this episode must seem grotesque and contrived.... But for all its implausibilities and its quaint air of Victorian prudery the scene develops a powerful climax' (Hawkins, *Hardy: Novelist and Poet*, p. 111).

74. Lodge, 'Introduction' to New Wessex Edition, p. 21.

75. A remarkable example of the latter is attested by a surviving photograph of Hardy's uncle John Antell, a bitter, drunken, self-educated shoemaker who may have contributed to Hardy's conception of Jude Fawley: 'When Antell was dying of a wasting disease – presumably cancer, or "lumbar abscess", as his death certificate called it – he was himself responsible for the posing of a remarkable photograph in which his emaciated figure leans upon a chair which bears, on a carefully lettered placard, the accusatory words "SIC PLACET", addressed presumably to God, Fate, or even the President of the Immortals' (Michael Millgate, *Thomas Hardy: A Biography* (Oxford, 1982) p. 108, and plate 11).

76. '"Concrete", I said. "God Amighty, why didn't Anse carry you to the nearest sawmill and stick your leg in the saw? That would have cured it. Then you could have stuck his head into the saw and cured a whole family.' *AILD*, p. 190).

77. It would be tedious to argue here about whether or not Faulkner could be called a conventional Christian believer. Of course, like Hardy, he respected and demonstrated Christian virtues through his own form of liberal humanism, while similarly despising the intolerance and dogma of the established churches of his time and place; and like Hardy he seems to have been sceptical about the *literal* authenticity of the Christian myth, hedging about his responses to questions on this point with politely ambiguous reservations; e.g. Gwynn and Blotner (eds), *Faulkner in the University*, pp. 86, 203; *Faulkner at Nagano*, ed. Robert A. Jelliffe (Tokyo, 1956) p. 23.

78. See Cleanth Brooks, *William Faulkner: Yoknapatawpha Country*, pp. 36, 43.

79. Ibid., p. 40.

80. Millgate compares the first chapter to the opening of *The Mayor of Casterbridge* or *The Return of the Native*, and relates the switching between different plots to *Bleak House* or *Our Mutual Friend* (*Achievement*, p. 124).

81. For example, the tensions between himself and Murry; the traumatic loss of his childhood sweetheart to another, and his eventual marriage to her after divorce; the fascination with his great-grandfather.

82. Joe certainly never sees Lena. The only possible knowledge he can have of her is through his conversation with his grandmother, moments before he is killed.

83. In linking Percy Grimm to the New South, what is significant is not his taste for violence (which, as I suggested in chapter 2, was an unremarkable feature of Southern life through its history) but the

mechanical and depersonalised way in which Grimm expresses this compulsion. That traditional Southern individualism, exemplified in the violent, excessively *personal* clashes between John Sartoris and Redmond, Bayard II and Grumby, or Lucas Beauchamp and Zack Edmonds, is succeeded by a cold 'humourless' logic and organisation. The Southerner's traditional disdain for uniformity and subservience, epitomised in the notoriously anarchic bearing of Confederate troops, has been replaced by Grimm's 'blind obedience' (p. 339), and (most significantly) by his contempt for the local. He ignores the sheriff's advice, he speaks of the civilians of Jefferson as 'these people', and his perceived allegiance is not to his town, state or the South, but to the abstract concept of the white 'American' race and 'Uncle Sam' (pp. 339, 341).

84. After staring greedily at the victim's body, 'some of them with pistols in their pockets began to canvas about for someone to crucify... she had supplied them at last with an emotional barbecue, a Roman holiday' (p. 217). In this state of mind the mob will believe only what it wants to believe, as the earlier persecution of Hightower's black cooks testifies)pp. 55–6). Ritual and mass conformity accompany this abdication of individual conscience – the faces of the mob are 'identical' (p. 218), their actions 'like a lot of people performing a play' (p. 56).

85. '[T]hat to me was the tragic, central idea of the story – that he didn't know what he was' (Gwynn and Blotner (eds), *Faulkner in the University*, p. 72).

86. '[S]he advanced in identical and anonymous and deliberate wagons as though through a succession of creak-wheeled and limpeared avatars, like something moving forever and without progress across an urn' (p. 8).

87. It is, of course, especially indicative of his epic status, representing a panoramic range of Southern experience, that Joe has lived as both a white and a black man.

88. '"This face alone is not clear. It is confused.... Then he can see that it is two faces which seem to strive.... in turn to free themselves one from the other, then fade and blend again. But he has seen now, the other face, the one that is not Christmas. "Why, it's ..." he thinks, "... it's that ... boy. With that black pistol, automatic they call them. The one who ... into the kitchen.... With all air, all heaven, filled with the lost and unheeded crying of all the living who ever lived, wailing still like lost children among the cold and terrible stars"' (pp. 369–70).

89. The phrase is that of Brooks, in *Hardy: Poetic Structure*, p. 228, whose fine discussion of Giles I have already acknowledged.

90. For example, the beginning of chapter 14, p. 240, where layers of 'telling' grow quite spontaneously out of the narrative almost faster than Faulkner can keep up with them.

91. For example, Joe and his detested foster-father are identical in their attitudes of stubbornness and non-compromise; Hines and the grandson whom he hates both violently interrupt black church services. The hysterically racist Hines and the philanthropic Joanna

Burden are equally isolated from the townsfolk by their different fanaticisms. The doomed and conflicting lovers Joe and Joanna are ironically well-suited in many ways, being both lonely, isolated spiritual orphans at war with their own divided selves. They both need someone to confide in, they cling destructively together like drowning swimmers, and after Joe had murdered Joanna he instinctively understands her reciprocal plans: 'he knew that she was not convinced and she knew that he was not. Yet neither surrendered; worse: they would not let one another alone; he would not even go away' (p. 210).

92. For example, Hightower boasts of 'that fine shape of eternal youth and virginal desire which makes heroes... they were not men after spoils and glory; they were boys riding the sheer tremendous tidal wave of desperate living. Boys' (p. 363).

But Faulkner's journey back into the Hightower family memories reveals that the grandfather was middle-aged with a full-grown son at the time of his death, not a pallid young Tennysonian hero but 'a hale, bluff rednosed man with the moustache of a brigand chief ...lusty and sacriligeous', with a 'direct, coarsely vivid humour' and 'swagger' (pp. 353–5). Clearly, Hightower's private vision, like Narcissa Benbow's virtue, is merely a confection without substance.

93. Gwynn and Blotner (eds), *Faulkner in the University*, pp. 25–6.
94. Stein, 'Interview', p. 80.
95. As is evident from his discomfiture in *Go Down, Moses* and *The Town*; and cf. Faulkner's fairly stern critique of Stevens in Gwynn and Blotner (eds), *Faulkner in the University*, pp. 140–1.
96. See, for example, Faulkner's remarks to Malcolm Cowley regarding the composition of *Absalom, Absalom!* and Cowley's reflections upon them ('he tried to present characters rather than ideas'): *The Faulkner–Cowley File*, ed. Malcolm Cowley (New York, 1966) pp. 14–18. And cf. Gwynn and Blotner (eds), *Faulkner in the University*, p. 10.
97. See Faulkner's detailed explanation of the image of Caddy in his 'Introduction' to *The Sound and the Fury*, pp. 413–14; Stein 'Interview', p. 73.
98. See, for example, Faulkner's habit of quoting his characters: 'A character of mine once said' (Meta Carpenter Wilde and Orin Borsten, *A Loving Gentleman* (New York, 1976) pp. 84–5).
99. See Gwynn and Blotner (eds), *Faulkner in the University*, p. 267: 'To me, all human behaviour is unpredictable.... If [the writer] began to preach or proselytise or pass judgment... the fire might go out.... He's interested in all men's behavior with no judgment whatever. That it's motion, it's life, the only alternative is nothingness, death.'
100. Judith Bryant Wittenberg, *Faulkner: The Transfiguration of Biography* (Lincoln, Nebr., 1979) p. 191.
101. Bayley, *Essay on Hardy*, p. 198.
102. For example, *Intruder in the Dust*, pp. 148–51.
103. Lyall H. Powers, *Faulkner's Yoknapatawpha Comedy* (Ann Arbor, Mich., 1980) pp. 3–4.

104. '[T]he one that is least troubled by change was … Ratliff … he had
accepted a change in culture, a change in environment, and he has
suffered no anguish, no grief from it … he's in favor of change,
because it's motion and it's the world as he knows it' (Gwynn and
Blotner (eds), *Faulkner in the University*, p. 253).

NOTES TO CHAPTER 5. 'A SERIES OF SEEMINGS'

1. See, for example, his reduction of the men's wages, on taking over
Henchard's business (p. 245); his worry that having to stay
somewhere overnight while searching for Henchard 'will make a hole
in a sovereign' (p. 351); and his chillingly pragmatic decision to
propose to Elizabeth-Jane – 'an exceptionally fortunate business
transaction put him on good terms with everybody, and revealed to
him that he could undeniably marry if he chose. Then who so
pleasing, thrifty, and satisfactory in every way as Elizabeth-Jane?' (pp.
184–5).
2. For example, p. 119: 'Meanwhile the great corn and hay traffic
conducted by Henchard throve under the management of Donald
Farfrae as it had never thriven before. It had formerly moved in jolts;
now it went on oiled castors. The old crude viva voce system of
Henchard, in which everything depended upon his memory, and
bargains were made by the tongue alone, was swept away. Letters
and ledgers took the place of "I'll do't", and "you shall hae't"; and, as
in all such cases of advance, the rugged picturesqueness of the old
method disappeared with its inconveniences.'
3. Cf. the convention that Jody's customers help themselves and leave
the money in a cigar-box; Jody's habitual errors at the till; his
willingness to give credit; and Flem's contrasting accuracy with
money, and refusal to give credit (*TH*, pp. 24, 53).
4. H. J. Massingham, *Men of Earth* (London, 1943) pp. 155–6.
5. *Life*, pp. 177, 185.
6. Ian Gregor, 'Introduction' to *The Mayor of Casterbridge*, New Wessex
Edition, p. 18.
7. 'Preface' to *Jude*, New Wessex Edition, p. 23.
8. *Faulkner in the University*, ed. Frederick L. Gwynn and Joseph L.
Blotner (Charlottesville, Va., 1959) pp. 273–4.
9. His library at Rowan Oak contains a copy of *The Mayor of Casterbridge*.
10. Henchard's rise and fall suggests analogies with mythical rituals of the
elected god-king who must be sacrificed and replaced. Hardy's novel
also compares Henchard, with varying degrees of explicitness, to
Achilles (p. 106); Prometheus (in his love of fire, p. 107); Faust (p. 143);
Bellerophon (p. 144); and Prester John (p. 154). The title of Faulkner's
novel points more directly to its mythical overtones. 'In the Old
Testament (2 Sam. 13), Absalom, one of David's sons, kills his brother
Amron for raping their sister Tamar' (see John T. Irwin, *Doubling and*

Incest/Repetition and Revenge: A Speculative Reading of Faulkner (Baltimore, Md., 1975) p. 25.

Critical descriptions of each novel help to show the two novels' common high literary ambitions and ancestry: e.g. Millgate remarks that 'Hardy establishes Henchard in all his particularity of time, place, and class, and then surrounds him with patterns of classical, biblical, and Shakespearian imagery ... susceptible to analogies with Oedipus, Samuel, and Lear ... he emerges as a figure on the grand scale of a Heathcliff or Captain Ahab' (Michael Millgate *Thomas Hardy: A Biography* (Oxford, 1982) p. 253). Cf. Minter's comments upon *Absalom*'s 'allusional density: its evocations of stories from the Old Testament; from Greek drama and myth; from Cervantes, Shakespeare, Melville, and Conrad' (David Minter, *William Faulkner: His Life and Work* (Baltimore, Md., 1980) p. 153).

11. Millgate suggests that one important 'source' for Henchard's qualities of ambition, authority, vigour, violence, and sexual aggressiveness which Hardy knew to be most lacking in himself' was 'his maternal grandfather George Hand' (*Hardy: A Biography*, p. 253, and cf. pp. 12–13). Wittenberg similarly suggests that 'Sutpen also had vital personal meaning for Faulkner as a portrait of his own great-grandfather, the Old Colonel, and as one of his last statements about the dashing figure who had psychologically dominated his formative years' (Judith Bryant Wittenberg, *Faulkner: The Transfiguration of Biography* (Lincoln, Nebr., 1979) p. 151).

12. Gregor, 'Introduction', p. 17.

13. Henchard's succession of different homes, and the imagery associated with them, reflect aspects of his character, e.g. his ancient elephantine furniture and folios (p. 97) reflect the traditional nature of his regime as mayor, while Farfrae and Lucetta acquire new furniture; or, as his career disintegrates, he moves into Jopp's cottage, 'built of old stones from the long dismantled Priory, scraps of tracery, moulded window-jambs, and arch-labels, being mixed in with the rubble of the walls' (p. 245). Sutpen's decline is similarly associated with his ruined plantation, '*a part of him encompassing each ruined field and fallen fence and crumbling wall of cabin or cotton house or crib*' (p. 160), while the superb evocations of his mansion convey much of its flawed and sinister grandeur: 'It loomed, bulked, square and enormous, with jagged half-toppled chimneys, its roofline sagging a little; for an instant as they moved, hurried, toward it Quentin saw completely through it a ragged segment of sky with three hot stars in it as if the house were of one dimension, painted on a canvas curtain in which there was a tear ... the dead furnace-breath of air in which they moved seemed to reek in slow and protracted violence with a smell of desolation and decay as if the wood of which it was built were flesh' (*AA*, p. 366).

14. Faulkner makes the repetition of Sutpen's traumatic rejection quite explicit: 'and sure enough and after fifty years the forlorn nameless and homeless lost child came to knock at it and no monkey-dressed

nigger anywhere under the sun to come to the door and order the child away; and Father said that even then ... he must have felt and heard the design – house, position, posterity and all – come down like it had been built out of smoke' (p. 267). 'Fifty years' is not literally correct, of course.

15. It is, for instance, interesting to compare the role of the jeering mob at Sutpen's wedding (*AA*, pp. 56–7) to the episode of the skimmity ride (*TMOC*, pp. 301–2).

16. Here I follow John T. Irwin's suggestion that Quentin is the 'central narrator ... the other three only function as narrators in relation to Quentin' (*Doubling and Incest*, p. 26). One curious result of the 'framing' device of Faulkner's novel, and its consequent narrative dissimilarity to Hardy's novel, is that when we compare their ambivalence of tone, the closest equivalent in *Absalom, Absalom!* to Hardy's authorial consciousness is provided by the dialectic between Quentin and Shreve; Faulkner has drawn back a stage further, hidden behind his narrative structure. Consequently, critical descriptions of Hardy's ambivalence are often curiously relevant to Quentin's situation. For example, Millgate's description of the tension between 'intellectual progressivism and emotional conservatism' echoes Quentin's blend of Harvard-endorsed perceptiveness and emotional regression (Michael Millgate, *Thomas Hardy: His Career as a Novelist* (London, 1971) p. 210); and Raymond Williams comments that, 'To see tradition both ways is indeed Hardy's special gift.... He sees as a participant who is also an observer; this is the source of the strain ... [causing] spurts of bitterness and nostalgia', which evokes Quentin's position exactly (see Raymond Williams, *The Country and the City* (London, 1973) pp. 249–50).

17. Faulkner remarked in a letter to Malcolm Cowley that Quentin 'grieved the fact ... that a man like Sutpen, who to Quentin was trash, originless, could not only have dreamed so high but have had the force and strength to have failed so grandly' (*The Faulkner–Cowley File*, ed. Malcolm Cowley (New York, 1966) p. 15).

18. To Joseph Conrad's *Heart of Darkness*. Charles travels upriver to confront Mississippi's, and his own father's, 'heart of darkness' – in Faulkner's terms here, racism; though part of Thomas Sutpen's tragedy, and by extension that of the South, is that, unlike Kurtz, he will not recognise 'the horror' which has undermined his family and his society. But Quentin will. Faulkner was a reader of Conrad from an early age (see Joseph L. Blotner, *Faulkner: A Biography* (New York, 1974) pp. 110, 160).

19. 'his very body was an empty hall echoing with sonorous defeated names; he was not a being, an entity, he was a commonwealth. He was a barracks filled with stubborn backward-looking ghosts' (*AA*, p. 12).

20. It is interesting, in this respect, to consider the similarity of Eustacia Vye and Eula Varner, both evoked as careless goddesses of sensuality isolated in obscure rural backwaters where it is difficult for

them to find lovers worthy of their charms. One wonders if the equally striking similarity of name is a mere coincidence! See David Jarrett, 'Eustacia Vye and Eula Varner, Olympians: The Worlds of Thomas Hardy and William Faulkner', in *Novel: A Forum on Fiction*, vol. 6 (Winter 1973).

21. I must acknowledge that my attention was drawn to this memorable image by John Bayley's discussion of Hardy's style: see *An Essay on Hardy* (Cambridge, 1978) p. 18.

22. Alfred Kazin, 'Faulkner's Vision of Human Integrity', *The Harvard Advocate*, vol. 155 (November 1951) pp. 8–9, 28–33.

23. Michael Millgate, *The Achievement of William Faulkner* (London, 1966) p. 189.

24. 'He was still alive when he left the saddle … then he was on the ground … and remembering what he had seen of stomach-wounds he thought: If I don't get the hurting started quick, I am going to die. He willed to start it, and for an instant he could not understand why it did not start. Then he saw the blank gap, the chasm somewhere between vision and where his feet should have been, and he lay on his back watching the ravelled and shattered ends of sentience and will projecting into the gap, hair-light and worm-blind and groping to meet and fuse again…. Then he saw the pain blast like lightning across the gap … looking up out of the red roar, into the face which with his own was wedded and twinned forever now by the explosion of that ten-gauge shell … then, as the slanted barrel did not move: "God damn it, couldn't you even borrow two shells, you fumbling ragged … " and put the world away. His eyes, still open to the lost sun, glazed over with a sudden well and run of moisture which flowed down the alien and unremembered cheeks too, already drying, with a newness as of actual tears' (*TH*, pp. 194–5).

25. A remark to a correspondent in a letter of October 1891, quoted in Millgate, *Hardy: His Career*, pp. 266–7.

26. Gwynn and Blotner (eds), *Faulkner in the University*, p. 197.

27. Ibid., p. 96.

HARDY: SECONDARY SOURCES

Allen, Walter, *The English Novel* (London, 1954).
Anon., 'Representative Men at Home: Mr Thomas Hardy at Max Gate, Dorchester', *Cassell's Saturday Journal*, 25 June 1892.
Barber, D. F. (ed.), *Concerning Thomas Hardy* (London, 1963).
Barnes, William, *Poems of Rural Life in the Dorset Dialect*, 3 vols (London, 1879).
Barrell, John, *The Idea of Landscape and the Sense of Place: An Approach to the Poetry of John Clare* (Cambridge, 1972).
Barrie, J. M., 'Thomas Hardy: the Historian of Wessex', *The Contemporary Review*, vol. 56 (July 1889) pp. 57–66.
Bayley, John, *An Essay on Hardy* (Cambridge, 1978).
Beatty, C. J. P. (ed.), *The Architectural Notebook of Thomas Hardy* (Dorchester, 1966).
Bettey, J. H., *Rural Life in Wessex, 1500–1900* (Bradford-on-Avon, 1977).
Bourne, George, *Change in the Village* (London, 1912).
Brooks, Jean R., *Thomas Hardy: The Poetic Structure* (London, 1971).
Brown, Douglas, *Thomas Hardy* (London, 1954).
Butler, Lance St John, *Thomas Hardy* (Cambridge, 1978).
Caird, Sir James, *English Agriculture in 1850–51* (London, 1852; new edn, London, 1968).
Chadwick, Owen, *The Victorian Church*, 2 vols (London, 1966).
Chesney, Kellow, *The Victorian Underworld* (London, 1972).
Clark, G. and Thompson, W. H., *The Dorset Landscape* (London, 1935).
Cox, J. Stevens (ed.), *Thomas Hardy: Materials for a Study of his Life, Times and Works*, 72 monographs (St Peter Port, Guernsey, 1962–).
Davidson, Donald, 'The Traditional Basis of Thomas Hardy's Fiction', *Southern Review*, vol. vi (1940), pp. 162–92.
Deacon, Lois and Coleman, Terry, *Providence and Mr. Hardy* (London, 1976).
Drabble, M. (ed.), *The Genius of Thomas Hardy* (London, 1976).
Eliot, T. S., *After Strange Gods* (London, 1934).
Enstice, Andrew, *Thomas Hardy: Landscapes of the Mind* (London, 1979).
Firor, Ruth, *Folkways in Thomas Hardy* (New York, 1932).
Gittings, Robert, *Young Thomas Hardy* (London, 1975).
——, *The Older Hardy* (London, 1978).
Gregor, Ian, *The Great Web: The Form of Hardy's Major Fiction* (London, 1974).
Hagan, John, 'A Note on the Significance of Diggory Venn', *Nineteenth-Century Fiction*, vol. 17 (1961) pp. 147–55.
Haggard, Rider, *Rural England* (London, 1902).
Hardy, Florence Emily, *The Early Life of Thomas Hardy* (London, 1928).
——, *The Later Years of Thomas Hardy* (London, 1930); reprinted as *The Life of Thomas Hardy* (London, 1962; reprinted with corrections, 1972).
Hawkins, Desmond, *Hardy: Novelist and Poet* (Newton Abbot, 1976).
Holloway, John, *The Charted Mirror* (London, 1960).
Horn, Pamela, *The Rural World 1780–1850* (London, 1980).

Houghton, Walter E., *The Victorian Frame of Mind, 1830–70* (New Haven, Conn., 1957).

Howe, Irving, *Thomas Hardy* (New York, 1967).

Huss, Roy, 'Social Change and Moral Decay in the Novels of Thomas Hardy', *Dalhousie Review* (1967) pp. 28–44.

Hynes, Samuel, 'Hardy and Barnes: Notes on Literary Influence', *South Atlantic Quarterly*, vol. 58 (1959) pp. 44–54.

Jefferies, Richard, *The Toilers of the Field* (London, 1892).

——, *Hodge and His Masters* (London, 1880).

Kay-Robinson, D., *Hardy's Wessex Re-Appraised* (Newton Abbot, 1972).

Kerr, Barbara, *Bound to the Soil: A Social History of Dorset, 1750–1918* (London, 1968).

Klingopoulous, G. D., 'Hardy's Tales Ancient and Modern', in *From Dickens to Hardy: Pelican Guide to English Literature*, vol. 6, ed. Boris Ford (London, 1958).

Lea, Herman, *Thomas Hardy's Wessex* (London, 1913).

Lucas, John, *The Literature of Change: Studies in the Nineteenth-Century Provincial Novel* (Sussex, 1977).

Marlow, Joyce, *The Tolpuddle Martyrs* (London, 1971).

Massingham, H. J., *Men of Earth* (London, 1943).

——, *The Small Farmer* (London, 1947)

——, *The English Countryman* (London, 1942).

——, *The Wisdom of the Fields* (London, 1945).

Meynell, Viola (ed.), *Friends of a Lifetime: Letters to Sydney Carlyle Cockerell* (London, 1940).

Millgate, Michael, *Thomas Hardy, A Biography* (Oxford, 1982).

——, *Thomas Hardy: His Career as a Novelist* (London, 1971).

Mingay, G. E., *Rural Life in Victorian England* (London, 1976).

O'Sullivan, T., *Thomas Hardy: An Illustrated Biography* (London, 1975).

Page, N. (ed.), *Thomas Hardy: The Writer and his Background* (London, 1980).

Paulin, Tom, *Thomas Hardy: The Poetry of Perception* (London, 1975).

Pinion, F. B., *A Hardy Companion: A Guide to the Works of Thomas Hardy and their Background* (London, 1968).

Purdy, R. L., *Thomas Hardy: A Bibliographical Study* (Oxford, 1954).

Samuel, Raphael (ed.), *Village Life and Labour* (London, 1975).

Saville, John, *Rural Depopulation in England and Wales, 1851–1951* (London, 1957).

Sherren, W., *The Wessex of Romance* (London, 1908).

Skilling, J. P. and M. R., *Thomas Hardy and his Birthplace* (London, 1977).

Somerville, Alexander, *The Whistler at the Plough* (Manchester, 1852).

Southerington, F. R., *Hardy's Vision of Man* (London, 1971).

Sutherland, Douglas, *The Landowners* (London, 1968).

Tate, W. E., *The English Village Community and the Enclosure Movements* (London, 1967).

Toucan Press, The, *The Thomas Hardy Year Book* (1970–). An annual publication of essays and articles on Hardy (St Peter Port, Guernsey).

Treves, Sir Frederick, *Highways and Byways in Dorset* (London, 1906).

Unwin, Bayer, *The Rural Muse: Studies in the Peasant Poetry of England* (London, 1954).

Weber, Carl J., 'Chronology in Hardy's Novels', *PMLA*, vol. 53 (1938).
——, *Hardy of Wessex. His Life and Literary Career* (London, 1940).
White, R. J., *Thomas Hardy and History* (London, 1974).
Williams, Merryn, *A Preface to Hardy* (London, 1976).
——, *Thomas Hardy and Rural England* (London, 1972).
Williams, Raymond, *The Country and the City* (London, 1973).
Woolf, Virginia, *Collected Essays*, ed. L. Woolf, 4 vols (London, 1967).

FAULKNER: SECONDARY SOURCES

Baldwin, Joseph Glover, *The Flush Times of Alabama and Mississippi* (New York, 1853).
Beck, Warren, *Man in Motion: Faulkner's Trilogy* (Madison, Wisc., 1961).
Blotner, Joseph, L., *Faulkner: A Biography*, 2 vols (New York, 1974).
Brooks, Cleanth, *William Faulkner: The Yoknapatawpha Country* (New Haven, Conn., 1963).
——, *William Faulkner: Towards Yoknapatawpha and Beyond* (New Haven, Conn., 1978).
Cash, W. J., *The Mind of the South* (New York, 1941).
Catton, Bruce, *The Penguin Book of the American Civil War* (London, 1966).
Core, G. (ed.), *Southern Fiction Today: Renascence and Beyond* (Athens, Ga., 1967).
Cowley, Malcolm, 'Introduction' to *The Portable Faulkner* (New York, 1946); reprinted as *The Essential Faulkner* (London, 1967).
—— (ed.), *The Faulkner–Cowley File: Letters and Memories, 1944–62* (New York, 1966).
Cullen, John, *Old Times in the Faulkner Country* (Chapel Hill, N.C: 1961).
Dauner, Louise, 'Myth and Humor in the Uncle Remus Fables', *American Literature*, vol. 20 (1948–9) pp. 129–43.
Davidson, Donald, *Still Rebels, Still Yankees* (Baton Rouge, La., 1957).
Douglass, Frederick, *Narrative of the Life of Frederick Douglass: An American Slave*, ed. Benjamin Quarles (Cambridge, Mass., 1960).
Faulkner, John, *My Brother Bill* (New York, 1963).
Friedman, Lawrence J., *The White Savage: Racial Fantasies in the Postbellum South* (Englewood Cliffs, N.J., 1970).
Gray, Richard, *The Literature of Memory: Modern Writers of the American South* (London, 1977).
Grayson, William John, *The Hireling and the Slave, Chicora, and Other Poems* (Charleston, S.C., 1856).
Harrington, Evans and Abadie, Ann J. (eds), *The Maker and the Myth: Faulkner and Yoknapatawpha, 1977* (Jackson, Miss., 1978).
——, *The South and Faulkner's Yoknapatawpha: The Actual and the Apocryphal* (Jackson, Miss., 1977).
Harris, Joel Chandler, *Nights with Uncle Remus: Myths and Legends of the Old Plantation* (Boston, Mass. 1883).
Hoffman, F. J. and Vickery, O. W. (eds), *William Faulkner: Three Decades of*

Criticism (East Lansing, Mich., 1960).

Howe, Irving, *William Faulkner: A Critical Study*, 2nd edn, revised (New York, 1951).

Irvine, Peter L., 'Faulkner and Hardy', *Arizona Quarterly*, vol. 26 (1970) pp. 357–65.

Irwin, John T., *Doubling and Incest/Repetition and Revenge: A Speculative Reading of Faulkner* (Baltimore, Md., and London, 1975).

Jarrett, David, 'Eustacia Vye and Eula Varner, Olympians: the Worlds of Thomas Hardy and William Faulkner', *Novel: A Forum on Fiction*, vol. 6 (Winter 1973).

Jehlen, Myra, *Class and Character in Faulkner's South* (New York, 1976).

Kennedy, John Pendleton, *Swallow Barn: Or, a Sojourn in the Old Dominion* (1832; reprinted New York, 1872).

Kerr, Elizabeth, *Yoknapatawpha* (New York, 1969).

Lewis, R. W. B., *The American Adam: Innocence, Tragedy and Tradition in the Nineteenth Century* (New York, 1955).

Lewis, Wyndham, *Men Without Art* (London, 1934).

Longley, John Lewis, *The Tragic Mask: A Study of Faulkner's Heroes* (Chapel Hill, N. C., 1957).

Meriwether, James B., 'Faulkner's "Mississippi"', *Mississippi Quarterly*, vol. 25 (Spring 1972) pp. 15–23.

Meriwether, James B., *The Literary Career of William Faulkner: A Bibliographical Study* (Princeton, N.J., 1961).

Millgate, Michael, *The Achievement of William Faulkner* (London, 1966)

——, *William Faulkner* (Edinburgh and London, 1961).

Miner, Ward, L., *The World of William Faulkner* (Durham, N.C., 1952).

Minter, David, *William Faulkner: His Life and Work* (Baltimore, Md., 1980).

Moody, Anne, *Coming of Age in Mississippi* (New York, 1968).

O'Connor, William Van, *The Tangled Fire of William Faulkner* (Minneapolis, Minn., 1954).

Oliver, Paul, *Blues Fell this Morning* (London, 1960).

——, *The Story of the Blues* (London, 1969).

——, *Conversations with the Blues* (London, 1964).

Osofsky, Gilbert (ed.), *Puttin' On Ole Massa: The Slave Narratives of Henry Bibb, William Wells Brown, and Solomon Northup* (New York, 1969).

Page, Thomas Nelson, *In Ole Virginia* (London, 1889).

Paterson, John, 'Hardy, Faulkner, and the Prosaics of Tragedy', *Centennial Review of Arts and Sciences* (1962) pp. 156–75.

Pilkington, John, *The Heart of Yoknapatawpha* (Jackson, Miss., 1981).

Powers, Lyall H., *Faulkner's Yoknapatawpha Comedy* (Ann Arbor, Mich., 1980).

Rubin, Louis D., *The Faraway Country* (Seattle, 1963).

——, and Jacobs, Robert D. (eds), *Southern Renascence: The Literature of the Modern South* (Baltimore, Md., 1953).

—— (ed.), *South: Modern Southern Literature in its Cultural Setting* (New York, 1961).

Seyppel, J., *William Faulkner* (New York, 1971).

Silver, James, *Mississippi: The Closed Society* (New York, 1964).

Simkins, Francis Butler and Roland, Charles Pierce, *A History of the South*

(New York, 1972).

Skates, John Ray, *Mississippi* (New York, 1979).

Slatoff, Walter J., *Quest for Failure: A Study of William Faulkner* (Ithaca, N.Y., 1960).

Stafford, John, 'Patterns of Meaning in *Nights with Uncle Remus*', *American Literature*, vol. 18 (1946–7) pp. 89–108.

Stampp, Kenneth, M., *The Era of Reconstruction, 1865–1877* (London, 1965).

———, *The Peculiar Institution: Negro Slavery in the American South* (London, 1964).

Stein, Jean, 'William Faulkner: an Interview', *Paris Review* (Spring 1956); reprinted in *William Faulkner: Three Decades of Criticism*, ed. F. J. Hoffman and O. Vickery (East Lansing, Mich., 1960).

Stephenson, Wendell Holmes and Coulter, E. M. (eds), *A History of the South*, 10 vols (Baton Rouge, La., 1947–67).

Tate, Allen, *Collected Essays* (New York, 1959).

———, 'The New Provincialism', in *The Man of Letters in the Modern World* (New York, 1965).

Taylor, W. R., *Cavalier and Yankee: The Old South and the American National Character* (Cambridge, Mass., 1961).

Thompson, Lawrance, *William Faulkner* (New York, 1963).

Tuck, Dorothy, *A Handbook of Faulkner* (New York, 1965).

USA, Bureau of the Census, *Bureau of the Census, Historical Statistics of the US, Colonial Times to 1957* (Washington, D.C., 1960).

Vickery, Olga, W., *The Novels of William Faulkner* (Baton Rouge, La., 1959).

Volpe, E. L., *A Reader's Guide to William Faulkner* (New York, 1964).

Waggoner, Hyatt, H., *William Faulkner: From Jefferson to the World* (Lexington, Ky., 1966).

Warren, Robert Penn (ed.), *Faulkner: A Collection of Critical Essays* (Englewood Cliffs, N.J., 1966).

———, *Segregation: The Inner Conflict in the South* (New York, 1956; London, 1957).

———, *Selected Essays* (New York, 1958).

Webb, James W. and Green, A. Wigfall, *William Faulkner of Oxford* (Baton Rouge, La., 1965).

White, Walter, *Rope and Faggot: A Biography of Judge Lynch* (New York, 1929).

Wilde, Meta Carpenter and Borsten, Orin, *A Loving Gentleman: The Love Story of William Faulkner and Meta Carpenter* (New York, 1976).

Wittenberg, Judith Bryant, *Faulkner: The Transfiguration of Biography* (Lincoln, Nebr., 1979).

Woodward, C. Vann, *The Origins of the New South, 1877–1913* (Baton Rouge, La., 1951).

———, *The Burden of Southern History* (Baton Rouge, La., 1968).

———, *The Strange Career of Jim Crow* (New York, 1955).

Index

Minter, David, *William Faulkner: His Life and Work*, 32, 108, 110, 111, 181, 219, 233, 234, 235–6, 240, 250
Mississippi (the state of), ix, x, 29–36, 38–9, 41, 44–6, 48–51, 55–6, 59, 61–7 *passim*, 100, 106, 110, 158, 160–3 *passim*, 165–6; *see also* Yoknapatawpha, Faulkner's conception of
Mississippi (Skates), 35, 44, 45–6, 48–9, 165, 219, 220, 223, 224, 225, 244
Mississippi: The Closed Society, 223
Mitchell, Margaret, 30
Moby Dick, 159, 243
Morrison, Donald, *Exhibition of Hardy's Paintings and Drawings*, 241
Movies of the Forties, 240
My Brother Bill, 48, 63, 224, 225, 227, 234, 235
'Myth and Humor in the Uncle Remus Fables', 221

Narrative of Arthur Gordon Pym, The, 220–1
Narrative of the Life of Frederick Douglass, an American Slave, 240
'Nature's Legacy to William Faulkner', 223
Negro, the: *see* black characters, Faulkner's portrayal of; *see also* racism; slavery
'New Provincialism, The', 55, 218
Nietzsche, Friedrich Wilhelm, 234
Nights with Uncle Remus: Myths and Legends of the Old Plantation, 221
Novalis (Baron Friedrich Leopold von Hardenburg), 193
'Novels of Thomas Hardy, The', 153–4, 227, 243

Oberbey, David, 'In the Shadows', 240
O'Donnell, George Marion, 'Faulkner's Mythology', 226
Older Hardy, The, 233, 236
Old Times in the Faulkner Country, 235

Oliver, Paul
Conversations with the Blues, 240
Story of the Blues, The, 240
Orel, H. (ed.), *Thomas Hardy's Personal Writings*, 241
Origins of the New South, 1877–1913, The, 45, 220, 223
Our Mutual Friend, 246

Page, N. (ed.), *Thomas Hardy: The Writer and his Background*, 215
Page, Thomas Nelson, 30, 141, 221
In Ole Virginia, 242
'Marse Chan: a Tale of Old Virginia', 242
'Meh Lady: a Story of the War', 242
'Unc' Edinburg': a Plantation Echo', 242
Patriotic Gore, 37, 220
'Patterns of Meaning in *Nights with Uncle Remus*', 221
Paulding, James Kirke, *Westward Ho! A Tale*, 220
Peculiar Institution: Negro Slavery in the American South, The, 224
Penguin Book of the American Civil War, The, 224
Pilkington, John
Hearth of Yoknapatawpha, The, 237
'Nature's Legacy to William Faulkner', 223
Pinion, F. B., *Hardy Companion: A Guide to the Works of Thomas Hardy and their Background, A*, 215
Poe, Edgar Allan, *Narrative of Arthur Gordon Pym, The*, 220–1
Poems of Rural Life in the Dorset Dialect, 217, 242
poor-whites, Faulkner's portrayal of: *see* farmers
Porteus, Crichton: *see* Looker, Samuel J.
Powers, Lyall, H., *Faulkner's Yoknapatawpha Comedy*, 53, 193, 225, 238, 248
Preface to Hardy, A, 82, 229